TODO
IN TUSCANY

THE DOG AT THE VILLA

LOUISE BADGER AND LAWRENCE KERSHAW

TODO
IN TUSCANY

THE DOG AT THE VILLA

HODDER

First published in Great Britain in 2012 by Hodder & Stoughton
An imprint of Hodder & Stoughton
An Hachette UK company

First published in paperback in 2012

1

A CIP catalogue record for this title is available from the British Library

Hardback ISBN 978 1 444 70827 1
Paperback ISBN 978 1 444 70830 1
Ebook ISBN 978 1 444 70829 5

Printed and bound by Clays Ltd, St Ives plc

Hodder & Stoughton policy is to use papers that are natural, renewable
and recyclable products and made from wood grown in sustainable forests.
The logging and manufacturing processes are expected to conform to the
environmental regulations of the country of origin.

Hodder & Stoughton Ltd
338 Euston Road
London NW1 3BH

www.hodder.co.uk

This book is dedicated with all our love to Teresa and Silvano, Maurizio, Barbara and Diego, who together with Carol and Todo gave us Poggiolino

Contents

Contents

Authors' Note

We have changed many of the place names and those of some individuals in our story in order to protect the privacy, way of life and livelihood of our neighbours and ourselves.

PREFACE

'We're not in South London anymore'

Lawrence heard it before me. First a series of low staccato barks then a loud, mournful howl.

I was still mostly asleep. Groaning, I pulled the duvet over my head.

'What the heck is that?' he exclaimed.

I tried my best to ignore him until his getting out of bed made me sit up. 'It's two-thirty in the morning,' I protested, but by now he was opening the wooden shutters of the bedroom window.

For the twenty years of our married life in London, the view that would have greeted us at such a moment was that of the row of terraced houses on the opposite side of the street, illuminated by bright orange streetlights. Now I could see Lawrence struggling to adjust to the moonlit darkness. That picture-book Tuscan landscape, which had seemed so welcoming during the day, had merged into an ominous black with just a few dots of lights from the distant hills and villages.

'It's Todo,' Lawrence half-whispered before calling down to the baying beast beneath our window. 'What's wrong, boy? Be quiet!'

The noise continued, the only sound in an otherwise still night. We definitely weren't in South London any more.

It seemed clear that Todo wasn't going to stop howling without some encouragement; Lawrence looked at me wearily. 'No, don't worry, I'll go; Lawrence'll fix it . . .'

As I listened to him trudge downstairs, I switched on the bedside light – in fact, the only light in our bedroom. Bare wires protruded from the centre of the ceiling where once would have hung an elegant chandelier. It looked remarkably like all the other rooms of our new Italian dream house, named Poggiolino. Three full days of work had made little impression on the chaos which lay everywhere: unopened packing cases, ripped-up carpet, piles of the previous owner's clutter. This was miles away from moving house in London; to be precise, a thousand miles away. The excitement of achieving something we'd been talking about for eight years had kept us going through the stresses of buying the house, selling ours and the move across the Continent, but now reality was intruding into the fantasy.

The low rumble of Lawrence's voice made its way upstairs, and I heard him trying to calm and reassure the dog. Todo – the other gift from Poggiolino's previous incumbent. *Who buys a house with a dog?* I asked myself, lying there in an only half-made-up bed. Then another thought entered my head, one of those middle-of-the-night thoughts that seem to stop the heart and chill the bone: *Just what have we taken on here?*

I

Who Buys a House with a Dog?

After three days spent moving all our worldly goods, three cats and a business across Europe, we'd fallen into bed, exhausted. This was it: our life-changing decision, our bold, brave, crazy new start. But lying awake listening to Todo's howls, it just felt lonely and overwhelming.

Here we were in a strange and quirky house that had most certainly seen better days, perched halfway up a Tuscan hillside, our entire possessions stacked downstairs in cardboard boxes, our family and friends all hundreds of miles away and our bridges well and truly burned.

Aside from bricks and mortar, the only thing that had come with the house was Todo. The estate agent had been very specific: 'If you buy the house, you have to have the dog.'

Could this be some kind of quaint Italian custom? Did dogs get passed on with houses? No, he said, this was an unusual case. Todo's owner had died two years earlier, the place had stood empty since then, and despite attempts to move him, Todo had refused to leave.

When the estate agent brought us to view the property, an excited mass of ragged brown and black fur pressed its long nose through the gaps in the gate. Knee-high, with a shaggy coat and large, floppy ears, it was his face that caught our attention. Bright chestnut eyes stood out above a long snout, framed by much paler fur.

'He's grinning,' laughed Lawrence. And it seemed true – a lighter line of fur curving around his muzzle, almost up to his ears, gave him a huge, enchanting smile.

As we stooped to say hello and stroke him, I could see that his fur was matted and tangled and his feather-brush tail knotted with grass seeds. In that single moment my heart was captured.

Apart from Signora Teresa, housekeeper to Todo's former owner who came in twice a day to feed him, he had been on his own for all that time, and yet it appeared that this lonely vigil hadn't crushed or cowed him. He was thrilled to see us.

Todo wasn't the only reason we decided to buy Poggiolino but, if we were both honest, certainly the chief one. When we came back to see the house again, a couple of days after our first visit, he gave us an even more enthusiastic greeting. It felt as though he had been waiting for us. How could we not love him?

Our affection for the house took a little longer to develop. It was in our price range – just – which was encouraging, since we'd feared our budget wouldn't run to more than a tumble-down barn, given that this had become one of the most popular destinations in Europe. Yes, the setting was idyllic, tucked into a hillside above a pretty valley, but the abandoned property appeared to offer very little else. Dilapidated and dirty, the entire ground floor tiled in a lurid shade of avocado with faded brown shutters at the windows, it looked like a rather unfortunate cross between a Swiss chalet and a Californian bungalow.

Unlike our London home, it hadn't grabbed us immediately. Yet, as we talked about it over dinner that night, we both felt there was something special there – a hidden beauty waiting to be revealed, secrets to unfold, faded glamour that might be restored.

We learned from the agent that the former owner had been an American, Carol MacAndrew, who built the house thirty years earlier and lived there until her death at the age of ninety-six. Elegant, charming and by all accounts formidable, she had left an indelible mark on the house and on the lives of those who knew her. Despite falling into a sad state of disrepair, her home still bore the traces of a life that belonged to a more glamorous age. As I lay in bed that night I could feel it: the house had a past.

And of course there was Todo, who had been her dog. Nothing we had learned about him so far – admittedly not very much – explained this anguished 2 a.m. wake-up call. On our subsequent visits during the house-buying process, he'd always seemed just as calm and well behaved as on our first encounter. So what, I wondered as I waited for Lawrence to come back to bed, had transformed him from friendly mutt into this howling apparition?

By the time Lawrence reappeared, almost an hour had passed. 'I think he's calmed down,' he said, climbing back into bed. 'God knows what that was all about, but I suppose it must be the first night anyone's slept here since Carol died. It'll be a one-off thing.'

'I hope so. What if he does this every night?'

It didn't bear thinking about. I turned off the light but sleep didn't come easily to either of us. Earlier in the day we'd said goodbye to our good friends Bruce and Hugh, who had made the journey with us from England with a van-load of plants and cats. For three days we'd stayed with them in a hotel in Lucca, just ten minutes away, and during that time they'd been invaluable. I cried when they left, partly because I was sad to see them go but also because, as I watched the trail of dust behind their van, it dawned on me that this was now for real. An Italian home had been our dream for many years but our new house wasn't yet functional, was set deep in the countryside – we'd both lived all of our lives in big cities – and far from everything we knew. There was no one to help us, we weren't fluent in the language and a call to the concierge wouldn't fix things. We'd taken on a huge challenge – were we going to be up to it?

Eventually I drifted off to sleep, and when we woke the sun was streaming through the cracks in the shutters. I got up and made my way downstairs to let Todo in. Lawrence's soothing had worked; the rest of the night had been quiet and the dog's beaming face greeted me as I opened the back door.

I spent some time stroking and patting him, assuring him that all was fine and that of course we didn't mind that he'd disturbed our first night's sleep in Poggiolino.

Lawrence ignored him.

And so to the first breakfast in our new house. Only problem, we didn't actually have a kitchen. We'd hated the plastic and Formica monstrosity that had been in place when we first saw the house, but its absence was still a blow. We arrived to find that it had been removed at the behest of a local priest to be given to the poor, but right now it was difficult to shake the view that charity ought to begin at home – our home. All that remained was a tap from which only cold water ran, but not into a sink – that had gone too, and in its place sat our red washing-up bowl.

Scavenging what food we could, we headed outside. The garden was, in fact, an olive grove with ancient, gnarled trees dotted across five steps of land – called *poggios*, hence the house's name – falling steeply away. From the bottom of the garden the land continued to slope down towards a stream, and then rose on the other side in a mixture of warm, earthy colours. After more silvery green olive groves, manicured vineyards and tall cypresses, one's eye met the little church of San Martino di Compito at the top of the hill opposite. A faded cream building with traditional red roof-tiles and a stone tower, it blended perfectly with the backdrop of wooded hills and painted houses. Inside the tower perched a set of heavy bells which chimed out on the quarter-hour.

'This is why we came,' said Lawrence, stretching out his legs and throwing back his head, eyes shut, to soak up the sun. Todo basked at his feet.

'It's gorgeous,' I agreed. 'But we've got an awful lot to do. Five more minutes and then we'd better make a start.' I hated to sound like a nag but I couldn't completely shake the fretful feeling that had gripped me in the middle of the night, and I knew that the best cure would be to make some progress.

But where to begin? How on earth would we sort out the mass of furniture, boxes, rugs, bags and assorted paraphernalia? As I stood surveying the mountain of chaos, I had a glorious thought. 'I know what we should do first – let's give Todo a bath.'

'Great idea.'

Lawrence's enthusiasm might have owed more to the deferral of the unpacking than to a desire to wash a couple of years' worth of dirt from our new best friend, but it hardly mattered.

The sink in the utility room was too small, so we opted for the downstairs bathroom. This was attached to the bedroom which had once been Carol's. A generous-sized room at the back of the house, when we first saw it we were astonished to find that it had been papered entirely in chintzy dark blue and silver wallpaper. And when I say entirely, I mean *entirely*; the backs of the shutters, the doors, even the light sockets were covered in it, in the bathroom as well as the bedroom. No doubt it had seemed luxurious back in the seventies, but now it created an effect which might have been more suited to a backstreet bordello.

Apart from anything else, it made the room appear so dark. Even on this spring day with the shutters flung wide to let in the clear, bright sunshine, we had to turn on the lights.

As Lawrence went to and fro with the kettle and I sorted out an old towel, Todo watched with evident fascination. He followed first me and then Lawrence, uncertain whether to be pleased or not, but giving his tail a kind of half-wag now and then because, whatever was happening, he was with us and that was good.

'Do you think he's ever had a bath before?' I said. 'Let's take it very slowly, just in case he hates it.'

'Bath time, Todo,' Lawrence said, stroking the back of his head as Todo looked up with enquiring eyes. Gently he lifted him – encountering no resistance – and put him into the tub.

The moment Todo's feet entered the water his smile broadened and his tail wagged with conviction. This was clearly not a new experience for him. As we were beginning to learn, he loved attention and affection and even the application of some smelly human shampoo didn't diminish his pleasure at being fussed over.

As I lathered him from head to tail and his fur clung to him, he seemed so much smaller and his eyes grew enormous. His tail, which never ceased to wag, sprayed me with water continuously, but it was impossible to mind. The water turned brown with the years of accumulated dirt from his coat and Lawrence peered at the murky suds. 'Judging by the colour of that, he'll turn out to be white when it's all over.'

Two rinses later it was time to release him, at which point mayhem erupted. He ignored my attempt to towel-dry him and bounded out of the bathroom, heading to the terrace, where he stopped and shook himself vigorously, sending water arcing into the air in a perfect spiral. It was like turning on a sprinkler, and most of it landed on us as we arrived behind him.

'Thanks Todo.' I wiped water from my face as he threw himself to the ground and began to roll on the grass.

I had bought a brush for him before we left London, and when he'd finished his post-bath ritual he came and sat happily beside me as I knelt to brush his fur. Cautious at first, I tried to untangle some of the many knots and pick through the matted hair before snipping off clumps that wouldn't budge. Todo was clearly enjoying it and was happy to stay put, which made it so much easier. His grunts of pleasure, especially when I tackled those floppy ears, made us laugh, and it was a joy to see his coat gleaming in the sun.

All three of us knew that this was something more than just a bath; it was a cleansing of all the sorrow he'd had to endure over the past two years. We weren't just getting rid of the dirt and grime but of the neglect and loneliness and sadness which had followed the loss of his beloved Carol.

The process of buying Poggiolino hadn't always been easy but the thought of rescuing Todo from his hopeful wait had kept us going, and the look on his face now as he nuzzled my hand told me it had all been worthwhile. So what if we only had a microwave to cook with, if our bed was propped up at one corner by books and we had no telephone connection? We had Todo.

For half an hour we all sat on the terrace as, now sweet-smelling and clean, he rested his head on my lap, as if to show his appreciation. The bathing had put us all in a great mood and a delicious feeling of excitement had replaced my worry about the scale of the task at hand. Lawrence and I looked at each other and smiled, hardly daring to believe that we were here, that we had done it. But lovely as it was sitting outside, we had work to do.

Lawrence decided to go and start putting our office together in Carol's bedroom. Once he was on his hands and knees with an assortment of screwdrivers, Allen keys and half-assembled shelving, I decided to leave him to it and start organising the furniture in the sitting-room. Judging by the swearing coming from his direction shortly afterwards, things weren't going well.

As I moved the sofa, chairs, tables and rugs around, Todo decided to help by sitting in exactly the place where I was about to put each item, stopping me in my tracks.

'Come on Todo, budge,' I said for the fourth or fifth time, trying to keep the exasperation out of my voice. He stood up, wagged his tail, and then sat straight down again. Eventually he took the hint and wandered over to the corner, where he lay, watching closely as I arranged everything.

The sitting-room was the nicest room in the house – large and square with a high ceiling and two sets of graceful French windows which opened onto the terrace, allowing the light to flood in. Between them was a simple fireplace with a mantel-piece made from a large piece of hand-carved olive wood and in the corner an archway led to a dining-room.

When we first saw the house, the room held an assortment of battered chairs, there were torn and faded curtains at the windows, and the mantelpiece was crowded with jars, old ornaments, photos and postcards, and a bunch of luggage keys with leather tags. Curious I had picked them up and read the inscriptions: 'Carol's large Pullman', 'Carol's plaid case', 'Carol's large valise' . . . they conjured up images of a time of elegant, luxurious travel and attentive porters – a world away from the budget flights we used to jet back and forth between Italy and London. Now we had finally removed the dilapidated furniture and minutiae of another life, I looked at this well-proportioned room and could picture Carol hosting parties for the great and good of Lucca.

I glanced over at Todo, so curious and attentive to my every move. Was he remembering how it had been during her time? Was the armchair always in the other corner? Did the sofa use to face the windows? Or did it all feel a world away from what he had known?

An hour later Lawrence appeared, announcing with a self-congratulatory flourish, '*È finito*, it's finished,' in his best *Godfather* accent.

All that was left was for me to offer him the obligatory, 'Oh wonderful, darling, haven't you done well?'

Later in the afternoon we had a lovely excuse to down tools, as Teresa had invited us for coffee. Brushing ourselves down, we called Todo, who happily followed us up the steps beside the house to the back gate.

We didn't have far to go. Teresa lived opposite Poggiolino, just a little further up the road. We had met her on our first visit to the house, when she arrived with the keys, and a handful of times since, and each time I had grown to like her more.

When we showed off the newly bathed Todo she nodded and smiled approvingly before ushering us into her front room, where we sat on a large sofa covered in knitted throws, waiting for her to appear from the kitchen with coffee and a plate of homemade almond cakes.

I asked her about Todo's howling but she could offer no explanation. 'I don't remember him doing it with La Signora,' she replied. Teresa always called Carol 'La Signora' and we were touched by this mark of respect, long after their working relationship had come to an end. Carol's husband, on the other hand, was generally 'Jim', though occasionally 'Signor Jim' and once or twice, with affection, '*il bevuto*' – the drinker.

It was clear from the snippets both the estate agent and Teresa had told us that the story of our predecessor had much more to unfold. Besides Todo, one of the things that had appealed to us about the house was that it had its own history – one that echoed ours, as Carol and Jim had also come to Italy in their forties, and had been music lovers, just like us.

I glanced outside. Todo, sitting on the patio, was becoming restless. And though Teresa was politeness personified, I didn't want to appear pushy. I was very aware that my Italian wasn't really up to subtle enquiries. There were a great many questions I wanted to ask but they, and Teresa's stories, would have to wait for another day.

As we stood to leave, she wrapped some of her cakes in a napkin before handing them to me, and I saw Lawrence's face light up at the thought of real food. As our resident chef, the absence of a working kitchen was worrying him.

Back in the house we began unpacking our office files and computers. We had no idea how long it might take to get the Internet installed, but – with what was to prove a ridiculous degree of optimism – we aimed to be up and running within a few days. We needed to be. This wasn't a holiday; we had a business to run. As agents to a small catalogue of classical

singers, musicians and entertainers, we were totally dependent on a phone line and a good Internet connection.

We worked for the next few hours while Todo stuck his nose
helpfully into every box as we opened it. He'd barely left our
sides all day. Clearly a dog who loved company, he continued
to wag his tail enthusiastically, getting under our feet every
five minutes. I could hardly bear to think of him wandering
around outside the locked house, alone for two long years.
Every now and then one of us would stop work to stroke him.
We still had no idea what had upset him in the night but we
were keen to avoid a repeat performance and hoped that lots
of reassurance might settle him.

Eventually, with the light outside fading, we called it a day.

'I can't face a microwave meal tonight; let's try that place
around the corner,' Lawrence suggested.

'Good idea. But what do we do with Todo?'

'Well, we can't take him with us. He'll be OK for an hour,
won't he?'

'We've seen dogs in restaurants before.' Somehow, even
though I knew Lawrence was right, it pained me to leave Todo
on only our second night.

'Let's ask when we get there. I don't think we should assume
it's the done thing.'

Promising Todo we'd be back soon, we set off down the hill
to the nearby village. Before long we were tucking into excellent pizza and cold beer, though I was aware that Lawrence
was eating very quickly, even for someone who enjoys his
food. Was he thinking the same as me – that Todo might
assume we were just visitors passing through and that he'd
been left alone again?

We were home within the hour and he greeted us as though
we'd been gone for a month, dashing out of the front door as

soon as it was unlocked then rushing between us, dispensing contented grunts in both our directions.

As I had done the night before, I took Todo through the utility room to the outside boiler-room, before patting his bed where he lay down obligingly. I was pleased that he seemed more settled than he had the previous evening. Perhaps tonight we'd all get some much-needed rest.

'I don't believe it.' Lawrence's tone was even more agitated than the previous night as he got out of bed and opened the shutters.

'Todo, this is ridiculous,' he shouted. 'Go back to bed!'

Had he done this every night? Surely it couldn't have been tolerated. But then again, perhaps it had been, and no one really noticed. Maybe he was a yard dog and he thought it his duty to make a racket to scare off predators and burglars?

Poor Lawrence made another weary exit downstairs. In my exhausted state, reason – and the positivity of the daylight hours – went out of the window. I was right back in the grip of the same worries as the previous night. All I could think was: *Have we done the wrong thing?* There was so much that we needed to learn, so many difficult tasks to manage in order to live successfully in our new house and new country. Telephones, Internet, heating, hot water, building work, a new kitchen, making friends, travelling back and forth to London, not to mention a new language, for goodness sake! All this and we couldn't even get the dog to sleep properly. I was still in a fever of anxiety an hour later as the same thought kept going round and round in my head.

Will we get this right or are we kidding ourselves that we can cope?

2

Cucina di Cane

Weary after another broken night, I contemplated hiding under the covers for the morning, but, leaving Lawrence to a well-deserved lie-in, reluctantly got up and went down to open the back door. Todo shot inside, tail wagging nineteen to the dozen.

'Look at you, all innocence and big eyes. No one would think you'd had us awake for half the night.' Tired as I was, I couldn't be angry with him. His delight at seeing us each time we reappeared was enough to melt the hardest heart.

Throwing open the French windows to greet another sparkling day, I made two coffees and took them back upstairs, leaving Todo with his breakfast.

Half an hour later he began to howl.

'Surely not during the day too!' grumbled Lawrence.

We rushed downstairs to find him standing in the middle of the terrace, facing the hills, his head thrown back and in full voice. But this was no anguished howl; this was a sweet pure sound, high-pitched and almost joyful.

Not daring to move, I stood completely entranced. Lawrence pointed into the distance. 'It's the bells of San Martino. He's singing along with them!'

For almost three minutes as the church bells pealed forth, entreating the villagers of San Martino and San Francesco di Compito to come to Sunday morning prayer, Todo accompanied them in a high falsetto. Ears cocked, tail waving from side to side, he'd occasionally shoot us a shy glance, which made us feel we shouldn't really be intruding on this personal moment.

We are both lifelong music lovers, so to discover that Todo was similarly passionate felt like a fateful coincidence. Lawrence was deeply moved. When the bells – and the dog – finally subsided, he hugged Todo. 'Who's my little Smokey Robinson?'

Todo, thoroughly pleased with himself, lapped up the praise, even if he probably didn't know who the King of Motown was.

We had no idea what had prompted his extraordinary performance, but the following Sunday, nine-thirty on the dot, he was waiting on the terrace and as the bells began to ring out, he once again sang along. We mused over whether he was singing for Carol, whose funeral had been held in the church, or whether he simply loved the sound of the bells. Whatever it was, we were to discover that this ritual took place every Sunday, and it became one of the great pleasures of our week.

After lunch we decided it was time to release our three cats and introduce them to Todo. The house had two very large attic spaces, or *sottotetti*, and for the first few days we had kept the cats in the largest of these, allowing them time to adjust to their new environment.

Bob, the youngest, was an even-tempered ginger tom with a friendly nature, so we weren't too worried about him. But the two older cats, Woody and Cyd, were a brother and sister we'd found at a London rescue centre, and we often referred to them, not always in jest, as 'the ferals'. They'd been discovered at sixteen weeks under a shed, completely wild and unused to being around people.

Woody, named after Woody Allen, was a glorious all-ginger cat with a worried air; quiet, slow and very, very cautious. Cyd, named for Cyd Charisse, was a graceful, elegant cat, tabby and white with hints of her brother's ginger. She remained the more distant of the pair and could rarely be touched or held. It had taken us, and them, six months with the help of a wonderful animal behaviourist to be able to co-exist in the same house. We almost gave up and returned them to the rescue centre after they refused to come out from behind a cupboard in our office for two days. But they finally settled into a routine and, in Woody's case, even joined us on the sofa for the evening.

Now, seven years later, we were afraid we might have completely destroyed any sense of security they had achieved by uprooting them. What they made of being caged up for two days and transported a thousand miles, we couldn't imagine. And they would have to get used to not just a new home, but a new companion who might or might not be feline-friendly.

Lawrence held Todo on the lead as I opened the doors of the cages and all three cats scooted down the stairs. Spotting the open doors and the huge expanse of green beyond, they were out like a shot and it appeared that Todo had barely noticed them.

Cautiously confident, we waited a few minutes before releasing him. Unfortunately Bob chose that moment to pop his head around the door. Galvanised into action, Todo leapt after him, barking loudly. Thankfully, while his speed was impressive his accuracy was less so. Bob shot up the nearest olive tree while Todo continued his trajectory all the way down to the bottom of the garden and then looked around, baffled, for his prey.

This scene was to be repeated a few times over the coming days, but with over a hundred mature olive trees in the garden and the grove beyond, the cats were never short of a refuge and, much sooner than we could have hoped, a friendship of sorts struck up between Bob and Todo. Being an affectionate cat, Bob wasn't about to let Todo stop him claiming his share of our attention, and Todo, who was naturally friendly and couldn't be bothered to keep up the façade of ferocious beast for long, soon learned to accept him as just another addition to the household. As for the ferals, in time even they adjusted and would come cautiously into the house, though they were never quite as much at ease with Todo as Bob.

On that first Sunday afternoon we decided to leave the cats to explore and take Todo for a walk. I reached for the lead. When we'd first put it on him that morning, he'd seemed puzzled to be suddenly attached to Lawrence. Now, as I clipped it onto his new collar again, he stood patiently with the air of one who is humouring a rather foolish whim.

We set off past the lean-to where the car was parked and along the short dirt drive to the road. From there we headed up the hill, past Teresa's house. Or, at least, that was the idea. After a couple of minutes Todo stopped and stood stock-still, rooted firmly to the ground.

'He's obviously not used to the lead. I'll take it off,' I said. I did, calling to him as I started to jog towards Lawrence, who had gone on ahead. Lawrence started laughing and I turned to see Todo still standing in the same spot, looking at me in sheer bewilderment.

'C'mon, Todo!' I yelled.

He didn't budge.

Undaunted, I produced a ball on a rope and waved it around before throwing it behind me into the olive grove. Todo started to walk off in the opposite direction. I was getting a little cross and my mood wasn't helped when Todo began to run after Lawrence who had started towards the olive grove.

'Why won't he do it for me?'

'Because you haven't got a piece of smoked ham in your hand!'

'What! You . . . cheat!'

'Carol was very old when she got him so she couldn't have taken him for walks. I doubt he has a clue what we're on about. I brought the ham along in case we needed bait.' Lawrence gave me a grin along with this, admittedly sensible, justification.

Todo had taken the bait alright, but that didn't mean he had changed his mind about coming for a walk. I looked over to see him hurtling towards the nearest field and the vineyard beyond.

For twenty minutes we chased him around the vines, the olive trees and the blackberries which grew wild throughout the fields. He would slow down then turn to face us, his bright eyes darting around as we ran to catch up, before racing off again in the other direction. The sight of those golden ears flopping up and down was magical. After two years of neglect and confinement, this was his celebration of new companionship and freedom.

In the early evening, the sun still warm and the fabled Tuscan light working its magic as the hills around us changed from hazy blue to pink, then purple, the clouds like candyfloss, we stopped and hugged each other. Todo, puzzled that the game had finished, pawed at our legs.

Tired but exhilarated, I could only utter breathlessly, 'This is the best feeling I've had in years.'

Lawrence had to agree, and as the three of us headed back through the long grass towards Poggiolino, it looked like home.

'How old do you think Todo is?' Lawrence remarked. 'He was running like a puppy out there.'

'I don't know. Eight perhaps, or nine? I wish we had a better idea.'

We had asked Teresa to tell us Todo's story on one of our visits to the house, while still in the process of trying to buy it. She told us that he was a lupetto cross, a breed popular with hunters. He'd been abandoned as a puppy and left by the side of a road, where a young neighbour, Paolo, from across the valley, found him. Unable to keep him, Paolo took him to the local priest who, knowing of her kindness to animals, suggested he take the puppy to Teresa.

She decided immediately that this comic little rascal would be La Signora's. Carol had always kept dogs. ('Pekinese! So yappy.' Teresa clearly wasn't a fan.) However it had been some time since the last Peke had died and she wanted Carol to have a new companion.

She brought the puppy to La Signora who took one look and shouted, '*Porta via, porta via!*' Take him away. '*Che muso, come un grugno.*' What a snout, just like a pig. But Teresa kept Todo in the kitchen with her, knowing that Carol would relent in time and would not turn him away.

She smiled at us. 'It took only two weeks. And then – she loved him.'

I wanted to cheer. But when we asked how long ago all this had happened, Teresa could only guess. Her grandson Diego was eight, and she thought it had been just before he was born.

So far we hadn't been able to find any other clues to

Todo's age. 'Perhaps a vet could work it out?' Lawrence suggested that night, as he put together a makeshift supper of salad and cheese.

I had a thought. 'What about all those old notebooks we found?' Why don't we look through them and see if we can find any clues to his age?'

We had arrived to find, among all the broken furniture and rubbish, a vast number of papers, notebooks and ledgers scattered around the house. Some had been in a large, old-fashioned cupboard of dark, heavy rosewood – a very Tuscan piece of furniture, which dominated the hallway. The first time we opened its doors, I couldn't quite dispel the vision of stumbling across a gateway to Narnia. Todo sniffed around with evident interest and we wondered if the smell of the cupboard reminded him of Carol, a theory that was reinforced when we found a faded lavender bag inside.

This cupboard was the only piece of Carol's furniture that we decided to keep. It was too big to be easily moved and provided useful storage space, but it was also a beautiful object that connected us and the house to its past. We gathered up all the papers and notebooks and put them in it, planning to look at them later.

Now we settled in the sitting-room, armed with an espresso (Lawrence had rushed out and bought a machine on our second day), and took a pile of documents each. Among them were journals and financial and household accounts, all filled out in Carol's small, neat, spidery hand. She had clearly been a meticulous record keeper and her carefully reported investments, household spending and diary entries, along with a small bundle of newspaper and magazine cuttings, allowed us a glimpse into a world which was so different to our own that it might have existed a century before.

'Wells Fargo, AT&T communications, General Motors . . . she must have been worth a fortune.' Lawrence was poring over dusty sheets detailing Carol's many investments. 'And look at these invitations, to all the big music festivals: Verona, Pesaro, Florence. She clearly knew everyone.'

While Lawrence went through financial ledgers and piles of cuttings, I looked at Carol's diary entries. From the early 1960s right up to the year she died she had carefully recorded her social activities and the daily events in her life. She wrote of the lunch she had with two friends from San Francisco; ordering vinegar and glass jars so that her olive harvest could be cured and stored; attending the opening of the new Ferragamo collection in Florence; a Music Society meeting and a seating plan for a dinner for twelve at Villa Carola – the much grander villa she and Jim had owned before they built Poggiolino.

On 10 January 1983 she wrote: '*The saddest day of my life, my dear Jim is gone.*'

That simple, restrained sentence conveyed all the heartbreak of losing her husband and companion of many years and finding herself alone.

'There's glamour for you.' Lawrence pressed a faded sheet of newspaper into my hand. It was a page of the *San Francisco Examiner*: the 'In Society' section dated April 1963. An interview with Carol MacAndrew by society editor Frances Moffat titled '*Capers in her Garden*'. The article described her '*Italian knit suit*' and '*heavy Yugoslavian bracelets*' and said that in California she had been manager of special events for a major airline and her husband had been a successful commercial artist.

It went on to describe the couple's new life in Italy. They had settled in a large villa with five acres, where Carol specialised in growing capers (she '*thought they came in bottles before she went to Italy'*) and employed a man of all work, Salvatore, *'a treasure fast disappearing in Italy'*.

Lawrence was reading over my shoulder. Now he turned to me. 'She built Poggiolino in the grounds of the original villa, so it must be nearby. We should go and see it.'

We were both thoroughly caught up in Carol and Jim's story.

'Why do you think they moved to Italy?' I said. 'It sounds as though they had a good life in the States.'

'I don't know,' Lawrence mused. 'Perhaps we'll find an answer in her diaries.' He was leafing through another of the journals. 'Look at this. 15 October 1996: Todo to the vet.'

He stopped suddenly. He'd seen the shocked look on my face and the realisation had dawned on him too. 'If Todo was with Carol by then, it means he's already about eleven.'

I looked across at Todo. He'd been dozing, but hearing his name he looked up, tail thumping cheerfully on the floor.

Lawrence paused. 'How long would you expect a dog of his size to live?'

Unlike him, I'd had dogs throughout my childhood, so I was the unofficial expert on all matters canine. 'Twelve, thirteen . . . but they can sometimes live longer.'

We sat silent for a moment, sad that our time with him would, inevitably, be shorter than we had hoped. I felt close to tears.

Lawrence was cradling Todo's snout in his hand. 'Well make sure *you* do. We've moved a thousand miles to be with you; we're not going to let you leave us for a while yet.'

Standing up he wandered over to the newly installed CD player to put on *Turandot*, one of his favourite operas. Our first trip to this area had been in 2004 when one of his clients had conducted the piece at the nearby Puccini Festival.

'Do you know, when we drove to the festival we came within

five or six miles of Poggiolino? Todo was here then; it wasn't long before Carol died. I can't think how hard it must have been for him.'

Todo came padding towards me. Perhaps it was just my imagination, but at that moment he did look his age. Slower, a little droopy, tail down, he knew it was the end of the day.

'C'mon Todo, time for bed. You've had a good day, haven't you?' I set off towards the back door, but he wouldn't budge.

I went back and led him gently into the utility room, towards the open back door, where he stopped again. I reached for a bag of his treats on the top of the fridge and handed him one which disappeared in a second. Kneeling down beside him, I whispered that it was late and he needed to go to sleep.

He buried his head in my lap and as I stroked him under his chin and at the tips of his long ears he gave a little moan of distress and lifted his head to look at me, his eyes willing me to understand. In that moment I knew.

'Oh Todo, you don't sleep out there, do you? *That's* why Teresa called this the *cucina di cane,* the dog kitchen. *This* is where you sleep!'

Lawrence, who'd heard the excitement in my voice, came in to find me hugging Todo. I went out to the boiler-room, collected his basket and bedding and put it in the corner. 'This was your room, wasn't it? Well, now it is again.' Todo jumped in and settled within seconds. Lawrence and I shook our heads at one another, relieved that we'd figured out the cause of Todo's night-time distress.

'I suppose Teresa had to put him out there while the house was empty,' Lawrence said. 'We just didn't realise.'

That night all three of us slept soundly.

3

Poggiolino

The enchantment of Italy had seeped into our souls from our very first visit. In those sun-filled weeks we'd travelled two thousand kilometres from the almost Alpine north of Verbania to the picture-postcard perfect vistas of the countryside around Siena. And without exception each newly discovered location presented us with extraordinary natural beauty, sumptuous food, marvellous wine and warm, generous, outgoing people. Coming from London, the ease of enjoying oneself came as a shock. One morning at the cavernous Santa Maria Novella Railway Station in Florence, Lawrence spotted a poster for the Arena Opera in Verona. Two nights later we sat among a crowd of 5,000 on the stone steps of the ancient Roman amphitheatre drinking in the Egyptian splendours of the famous Zeffirelli production of *Aida*.

In the eight years since, we had returned as often as we could, daydreaming about one day owning a holiday home, until

Lawrence said, 'We'll probably never be able to afford a second home in Italy; why don't we just sell the one we've got in England and move there?' The idea seemed outrageous and impossible, but it nagged away at us until we finally decided to do something about it. We still weren't sure of the idea of definitely moving to Italy, the obstacles remained daunting, but we arrived in Tuscany in early December 2006 for a four-day recce to see what house prices were like, put our names on a few agents' lists and look around at possible locations. It was like giving ourselves permission to play at making our dream a reality.

Falling in love with something beyond our very modest price limit was not an option. We had done that once before, overstretching ourselves to buy and renovate the terraced South London house that came to be known as 'the Money Pit'. It had got to the point where we both lay awake at night sick with worry about how to keep up with our enormous mortgage and the loans we'd taken out for repairs. If we were actually to make this move there would be plenty of things to worry about, continuing to run our own business being top of the list, without giving ourselves unnecessary burdens.

We were lucky with our timing; at the point when the front railings of our house collapsed and we realised we just couldn't pour in any more money, property prices were soaring and the pound–euro exchange rate was in our favour. Having called in estate agents, we realised that if we achieved our asking price, we could pay off all our debts and be left with enough to buy a home outright. In London what we had would probably have bought us a decent two-bedroom flat. But in Italy, where prices were not quite so stratospheric, we hoped we just might manage a house.

We were both forty-five that year – me in February, Lawrence in November – and we felt that if we were going to take the plunge and do something really different, it had to be sooner rather than later. We didn't want a retirement plan; we wanted a new way of living and working and a chance to experience everyday life in Italy. What we longed for was an adventure. We had chosen not to have children which meant that we had a lot of freedom, and while we didn't want to climb mountains or sail around the world, neither of us wanted to pass the years in a dull blur of work, trips to the supermarket, evenings in front of the TV and waiting to retire.

There was a lot about our life in London that we would miss. We had a lovely house and garden, satisfying work, good friends and plenty of access to music and culture. But we wanted something more.

We'd received a good offer for our house very quickly, and it was this that prompted our mission to Tuscany. Suddenly our dream began to seem achievable. In a whirl of excitement, we discussed where we wanted to live. We knew we wanted to be close to Lucca, where the gently undulating terrain is thick with olive groves, rather than in the dark chestnut and oak forests of the Garfagnana foothills beyond the city. But the days when you could take your pick of restored farmhouses or picturesque villas in that area were long gone, and 'bargains' had become few and far between.

In the first week of December we went to see Roy Santi, an estate agent who had moved to Italy from England twenty years earlier. Roy hummed and stroked his beard when we told him what we wanted, before suggesting we go to see a house that he thought we might, just possibly, find interesting. He knew it was a long shot, the house wasn't a traditional Tuscan one, but it was worth a look.

'The woman who lived there was passionate about music,' Roy said. 'She co-founded the Music Society of Lucca, to encourage local composers and musicians. They put on an annual season of concerts which became very well known. When she died, some years after her husband, she left the house to the Society. And with you two being in the music business, well, there's a connection.'

Half an hour later we arrived at Poggiolino. Lawrence and I waited outside the gate, laughing in amazement at the over-excited bundle of matted fur that had dashed to greet us, while Roy went to find Signora Teresa, who kept the keys. Once inside she stood watching intently as we fussed over the dog. Lawrence asked his name.

'*Questo è Todo*,' she had replied. '*Lui è il cane della casa. Sta aspettando da molto tempo.*' This is Todo. He is the dog of the house. He has been waiting a long time.

We wondered what she meant by 'waiting'.

We looked around the house quickly that first time. We had no intention of buying anything yet. I'd been studying my *Sunday Times Buying a Property in Italy* guide, which warned: 'beware of buying the first house you view'.

Looking back at the house from the garden you could see that it had been thoughtfully built, nestling into the gentle slope of the hillside. Tucked in behind it we found a small empty pool, no more than three metres along each side, while in front lay the garden, sloping steeply down to a fence and dotted with olive trees, underneath which three men stretched into the branches. They had covered the ground with orange and green nets already full of the newly harvested olives. Looking up, they paused, wishing us *salve*, and watched with evident interest as we wandered around, Todo at our heels.

To our surprise we noticed a fully grown mandarin tree at the side of the terrace, exotic and unexpected in the winter landscape. One of the men picked a handful of the ripe fruit, offering them to us.

The location was lovely but the house – cold, dark, very dirty and full of cobwebs – seriously lacked appeal. It would need a lot of work to bring it up to date and make it habitable and we had no intention of taking on that kind of burden all over again.

We said goodbye to the olive-pickers and Teresa and headed back up the steps to the car with Roy. Todo came with us and stood by the gate as we drove away. Through the window I could see him turn and walk slowly down the steps, his tail hanging limply, his head drooping.

'Do think about it,' Roy said. 'The Music Society is keen to sell because they've already turned down a couple of offers. It's out of your price bracket, but now it's been on the market for some time I think they'd agree to the kind of price you can afford. And of course they'd like the musical connection, I think that would help.'

We'd gone away convinced that the house wasn't for us. But somehow neither of us could shake it – or the shaggy little dog with the huge grin – from our thoughts.

Two days later we went back for another visit. This time, after another wildly enthusiastic greeting from Todo, we looked for potential while waiting for Teresa with the keys. 'We could lighten this room by adding another window or two,' Lawrence said as he stood in the small, dark dining-room. 'And what about knocking down the top half of the wall into the kitchen? That way they'd both seem less poky.' He was getting into his stride. 'Then we could take out the second downstairs bathroom – no house needs three for goodness sake – and knock it through to the little bedroom; the space would be perfect for an office.'

'Hang on a minute,' I said, my eyebrows raised. 'I thought we weren't going to do any more renovating.'

Lawrence grinned. 'I'm not really talking about renovation, just a few cosmetic improvements. Most of the house just needs clearing out and re-decorating.'

The kitchen needs more than that, I thought, running my fingers over the worktops and leaving a trail in the greasy dust which betrayed the long time since it had been used. On one wall hung a picture-calendar and, peering closer, I saw it still lay open at June 2005.

Turning around I looked at Teresa staring intently at me then towards the calendar. She said nothing but I could tell her thoughts. Poggiolino had stood frozen in time since Carol MacAndrew's death.

We had learned with the Money Pit that houses need to be loved and nurtured to reveal their secrets and beauty. And we had both begun to realise that when we looked beyond the cobwebs and the clutter there was a subtle elegance and scale to this house. It was abandoned but not derelict, waiting for someone to come along and give it back a life. I had already felt it in the charming but somewhat dilapidated summer house, where I noticed a large reclining deck chair, still draped in a faded plaid blanket. I didn't have to ask the question of Teresa. 'La Signora, before it got too cold she would sit in here in the afternoon sun, Todo by her side, reading, listening to music; maybe just thinking.' On its left, hanging from a hook in the wall, was a large-brimmed straw hat decked with white ribbon. Turning back to the chair I felt the urge to press my hand along the top of the seat, just to see if it might still be warm. It could have been that Carol had popped out for coffee with friends . . .

That afternoon we headed for Pistoia, a beautiful medieval city close to Lucca. After wandering around the central piazza and the cathedral, we settled into a small restaurant and ordered *ribollita*, Tuscan bean soup. Over steaming bowls and hunks of crusty bread, we talked about Poggiolino.

'I can see that the house could become special again,' I said. 'But if I'm honest, it's Todo I want just as much as Poggiolino. Maybe more.'

I wondered if Lawrence might think me a sentimental fool but he just smiled. 'Todo's been waiting for someone to come and live in the house and love him, and I think it should be us. Let's make an offer.'

Just like that.

Slightly giddy at our decision, we phoned Roy who patiently explained that factors that might help to reduce a price in the UK – such as the state of the house – wouldn't work with the Italians. On his advice we offered the maximum we could afford. Roy said he would talk to the President of the Music Society and get back to us. We headed for Pisa and the airport filled with disbelief at our own audacity and chattering non-stop about heady plans for the future.

Sitting on the plane we went through the photos of the house that we'd taken on Lawrence's camera. It was only then that we realised Todo had managed to get himself into every single one; the steps, the kitchen, the terrace, the bedroom, Todo was there.

One picture in particular was heartbreaking; Todo's smile as wide as could be, his tail wagging so fast it appeared just a blur, while he gazed up at us. I saw a loving dog, begging us to come, to give him back his life.

On the drive back from Stansted Airport to South London, we stopped at a giant Tesco to buy something for supper. The concept of a quick visit to a supermarket is alien to Lawrence and he'd already wandered off in the direction of shelves selling things we didn't need, when I heard his phone ring.

'Bloody clients, phoning on a Sunday,' I thought, wondering which of our artists had forgotten where they were supposed to be, and when.

'Hi Roy, we landed an hour ago. Yes, I can talk now.'

I sidled as close as I could but it was impossible to hear what Roy was saying.

'Fine; thanks.' Lawrence put the phone back in his pocket. I looked for a clue in his expression but the Valium he'd taken for his flying nerves was clearly still at work. He looked blank.

'That was Roy . . . The Music Society said yes . . . We've got Poggiolino.'

And so, standing in front of the 'Reduced to Clear' sausages and pies, we became the owners of a house – and dog – in Tuscany.

Our friends looked somewhat incredulous when we announced breezily that we'd offered on the first and only house we'd seen, and they began to question whether we were slightly unhinged when we mentioned that the primary attraction of the house was a scruffy little dog. But then again, we had form when it came to making instinctive decisions about life-changing matters. Our whole relationship was founded on precisely that philosophy.

We met in 1986, when Lawrence was working for a classical musicians' agency in London and I was running events for an arts organisation in Leeds. We kept in touch after a business meeting, and that friendship led before too long to a weekend jaunt to York. With the same impulsiveness that twenty years later pushed us to buy Poggiolino, after just four weeks we made the decision to get married. The rest is history, or rather twenty happy years of travelling the world with famous musicians, plucking up the courage to leave our secure jobs to start our own agency, and pouring seemingly endless reserves of cash and energy into the Money Pit. We both loved London, and would be forever grateful for the opportunities it had given us and the people we had been lucky enough to get to know. But those friends, despite their initial scepticism, backed us completely when we told them we were going in search of the next adventure. It wasn't a struggle for them to see the appeal. Many people fall in love with Italy, after all, and the reason that the dream became a reality for us, in the end, was that we were in the fortunate position of being able to make it happen.

In the days after Roy's phone call we were utterly elated. We pored over everything we could lay our hands on that would tell us about house-buying in Italy. The process is in two stages, not unlike the English exchange and completion. The first stage, the commitment to buy, is the *compromesso*, while the second and final stage is the *rogito*. But there, as we would discover, the similarity ends. Both systems have dozens of potential complications and we had certainly encountered a few of the English ones during our three previous purchases. But while in England we had been on hand, in Italy, with both language and distance against us, we could only hope and trust that all would be well.

The first hint of trouble came when Roy told us that he was having to do some careful negotiating with the Music Society, as the sixteen-strong committee was divided over whether they should have accepted such a low offer. If just one were to vote against, the house wouldn't be ours, but luckily the Society's President was determined to sell the house and he managed to persuade the dissenters to fall into line.

Roy asked us to be in Lucca to sign the *compromesso* on 8 January. We spent the build-up to Christmas in a fervour of finger-crossing and planning for our new life. What would we take with us? How would we get it all there? And when would we tell our clients what we were doing?

Two days before Christmas we celebrated our nineteenth wedding anniversary over lunch in Borough Market. Sitting in a busy restaurant we both loved, we felt very lucky. I shy away from the term soul mate, but Lawrence and I had been the best of friends for nearly two decades, sharing everything. Now we were embarking on a new phase, where we would be even more dependent on our team of two. We were both excited and a little nervous as we raised our glasses in a toast to the future. By our twentieth anniversary, we hoped, we would be living in Italy.

The next day Roy rang to say that there was a major hitch.

'The lawyer on the committee has been having a closer look at Carol's will. Apparently it says the house must only be used for the good of the Society and he thinks that might mean it can't be sold.'

Lawrence went pale. 'What! Surely they should have realised this before now?'

'You'd think so, wouldn't you?' Roy's jokey tone fell flat. 'They've discovered that Carol made a new will in 2002 as she began to suffer from dementia. Apparently she had talked with some friends about the idea of turning the house into a music school or a place where artists could stay while studying. I'm sure there's no big drama here; you know what Italy's like for bureaucracy. Leave things with me and hopefully we'll get this sorted.'

We travelled out to Lucca on 7 January heavy with anxiety. The next day we went with Roy to see the Notaio. More senior than a lawyer, these officials oversee legal transactions and contracts and we were desperately hoping he would help us out of the legal tangle that threatened to lose us the house.

The Notaio, a man with the film-star looks of Mastroianni and the presence of a minor royal, swept into the room and, on being told that there was a problem, demanded to read the will.

'It says the house should be used to assist and be for the good of the Society. What more good can they have than being given half a million euros?'

I wanted to kiss him. Instead I beamed, Lawrence beamed and the Notaio beamed back.

'Look,' he continued, 'you want to buy this house?'

We nodded.

'You have the money?'

'Yes.'

'Then let us draw up a *Proposta d'Acquisto* and we'll go from there.'

I racked my brain, trawling through the information I'd read in my property-buying guides, but I was pretty sure this wasn't in any of the books.

We looked at Roy.

'A *Proposta d'Acquisto* is where you write a letter confirming you want to buy the house and stating the price you'll pay and some other legal bits. It's a sign, in good faith, of your intent, and the Society has thirty days to reply that they wish to take you up on the offer.'

It sounded rather vague to us, but at least it was a step forward. The *Proposta* was drawn up, we signed, and the Notaio looked pleased.

As we headed back to London we decided to put our doubts firmly to the back of our minds. We took to regularly watching *Under the Tuscan Sun* and reassuring each other that if it could happen to Frances Mayes, it could happen to us.

A month later, after endless negotiations with the Music

Society, Roy rang to tell us that all obstacles had been removed in time for us to sign the *compromesso* on 22 February.

Once again we were back at the Notaio's office, this time with a great deal of smiling and shaking of hands. As we signed the document we couldn't stop grinning at one another. This was it; there was no turning back. Todo and Poggiolino were ours at last.

4

La Signora's Todo

That glorious moment in the Notaio's office was followed by a spectacularly delicious meal and one too many bottles of our soon-to-be-local wine. But then we were plunged into sorting the minutiae of packing up our lives. The good thing was that we were too busy to worry much about anything.

Anything apart from Todo. We returned twice more before the big move and each time we felt more and more worried. He was visibly declining and I had an awful fear that he could die before we made it. During the last weeks he was in our thoughts every waking moment, but we could do nothing, apart from pray that he would hang on for us.

In March we took my mother, Angela, who was visiting from Australia. She fell immediately under the spell of Poggiolino and Todo, who brightened visibly while we were there, especially when he saw the treats we had brought for him.

We spent a day at the house, making plans and exploring

the land beyond the garden. When we'd signed the *compromesso* we learned that we wouldn't just be acquiring the garden of Poggiolino, as we had thought, but an acre and a half of olive grove and field beyond it. The field turned out to be waist-high in blackberry brambles and weeds.

Todo stayed close by us the whole time. Spending a second winter alone had clearly taken a heavy toll on him. His huge smile and constantly wagging tail were less in evidence, and when we left he stood forlornly at the gate.

We didn't see him again until mid May, almost two months later, when we came for our final signing. Once the formalities at the Notaio's office were complete we had hardly enough time to rush to the house before our flight to London. We had treats with us and were longing to see Todo and tell him the exciting news that he was now ours.

He wasn't waiting by the gate, which filled us with alarm. We started down the steps to the front door, calling his name, and finally he appeared round the side of the house. He seemed very hesitant. His coat had become even more matted and while he accepted our strokes and pats, his tail barely wagged and we could see that he was struggling.

When the moment came to leave, I felt tears sting my eyes. It was almost two years since Carol had died and he had lost everything except for Teresa's kindness. Two years for a dog is the equivalent of twelve human years and although he had remained hopeful for so long, it looked as if his hope was running out. Even his beautiful grin seemed to have turned down at the corners, and he didn't come to the gate when we left. We felt truly dreadful leaving him again. He couldn't know that in just seven days we would be returning for good. We headed for the airport hoping that he would wait for us.

If Teresa was a life support for Todo, she was also a huge

comfort to us. She was clearly quietly devoted to him, and to her role as custodian of Poggiolino. Each time we visited, Teresa was there to let us into the house. In her mid sixties, her solid bearing, short grey hair, sensible skirt and black shoes were typical of the local women. We could barely follow her Compitese dialect, which was very different from the Italian we were painstakingly learning in London, but we usually managed to get the gist, and her expressive gestures helped fill in the gaps.

She invited us to her home for coffee for the first time, a month before the *compromesso* was signed at a time when negotiations were still difficult and we had real fears we might not win the committee's vote. We felt it an honour laden with significance. Over cups of thick dark coffee, she told us stories, often very funny ones, about Carol, for whom she had worked for thirty years. Apparently La Signora had built Poggiolino 'in only six months'. We agreed that in rural Italy, with its plethora of planning regulations and permissions, this was something quite extraordinary. Carol was clearly a woman who got things done and I wondered whether we would ever match up.

Before we left, Teresa went to a sideboard, took out an envelope and handed it to me. Inside I found a handful of photographs. The first few were of Poggiolino in the process of construction. I was fascinated to see the house when it was just a shell without windows, doors or even plaster. In one, a small, bare-chested elderly man, portly and with greying hair, stood at what would be the front door. Teresa laughed, raising an imaginary glass to her mouth, 'Signor Jim . . . *tutti amavano Jim!*' Everyone loved Jim.

Smiling back at me from the next photo was a smartly dressed woman in her mid sixties with short, neat, silver hair and bright red lipstick. 'La Signora,' Teresa said, her voice resonant with pride and affection. Carol was sitting on the terrace of what looked like a grand and very beautiful villa.

Teresa explained that Carol and Jim had bought it when it was the rather dilapidated Villa Vannini which, after a number of years and much expensive restoration work, became Villa Carola. Lawrence and I looked at each other and smiled. Carol clearly hadn't held back when it came to leaving her imprint. Here was another thing we had in common: a passion for money pits.

Over time, Teresa went on, the big villa became too difficult for them to maintain, so they sold it to their friend Signor Martini, a fellow member of the Music Society, and built Poggiolino.

Carol's had been a charmed life among the *Lucca Bene*, the grand society of the city; lawyers, bankers and accountants, the great and the good. She threw parties and musical soirées, travelled back to America at least twice a year and went to all the great music festivals. She worked tirelessly for the Music Society, hosting events, entertaining visiting artists and fundraising.

In her early nineties, Carol began to notice signs of forgetfulness and eventually dementia was diagnosed. She battled the disease for over two years, in and out of hospital, her condition worsening. Most of those who'd enjoyed her hospitality and friendship disappeared from her life. When La Signora finally died the only people at the funeral in San Martino, the little church on the hill opposite Poggiolino, were Teresa and her husband Silvano, Maestro Herbert Handt, the conductor who had founded the Music Society with Carol, his wife Laura and Carol's old friend Albertina.

As for Todo, he and Carol had remained inseparable to the end.

'What happened after she died?' asked Lawrence.

Teresa told us she had decided that Todo would live with her, but every time she brought him over to her house he would find his way out of the garden and back to Poggiolino. Many times she and the rest of the family tried to stop him, but every night he trotted back down the hill. Unsure what to do, she had called Albertina who phoned the President of the Music Society and told him, 'This is Carol's dog; we must do what Carol would have wanted. He will stay at Poggiolino and we will pay Teresa to take care of him and the house until there's a new owner.' There was no dissent from the committee and the arrangement had been put in place.

Lawrence and I glanced at one another, silenced by this extraordinary tale of devotion and single-minded determination. Was it hope, or grief, that made Todo turn his back on the comfort and companionship of Teresa's home to return to his cold vigil beside the empty house below?

We thanked Teresa and rose to leave. I took one last look at the photos before putting them back into the envelope and handing it to her.

She held up her hand. '*Non, non; loro sono.*' No, they're yours.

I knew this simple act held great significance. It was as if she were handing over Poggiolino and Todo to us.

Teresa's unfailing generosity and willingness to welcome us, a pair of foreigners, was one of the things that helped me to feel more confident about buying Poggiolino. Despite the fact that I loved the country and part of me yearned for an adventure just as much as Lawrence, initially I had been uncertain about the move to Italy. After all, I had emigrated once before. My father had found Britain a depressing country in the late sixties and, like many middle-class professionals, he was tempted by the scope and freedom of Australia. So in 1970, when I was nine, my sister eleven and my brother thirteen, we left the close-knit community of Chorleywood in rural Buckinghamshire and moved to the other side of the world, leaving behind aged aunts, a grandmother, our friends and the English way of life. My father found the freedom he was seeking in Australia and my mother made the best of a migrant life, but I never settled. I was twenty-three when I returned to Britain, determined that I would never leave again. It was only after Lawrence and I had everything in place for the move that I realised I was doing what my father had done, at the same age. I was struck by the irony, but of course I knew that this was a totally different moment in my life. I was no longer the child who had to go along with her father's decision. And Italy was hardly the other side of the world. This time, leaving Britain felt like an adventure; it was daunting, our new life would undoubtedly be challenging, but it wasn't a leap into the total unknown.

For Lawrence, the decision was far more straightforward. The youngest of four children brought up by a single mother in a tough working-class area of Liverpool, he had been a bright child who thrived on learning and went on to win a place at Cambridge.

He had always relished new situations and felt ready for a different life. Other than our friends and family, there was little he would miss; his passion for watching football and all things sporting could be maintained via Sky Italia. In fact he would be joining a culture even more obsessive about football than the one we were leaving and would be able to enjoy fourteen more channels of *calcio* (football) and several daily sports newspapers. The general topic of conversation among Italian men we had met so far tended to focus on sport and Ilaria

D'Amico, a tall, dark-haired siren in the style of Sophia Loren who we were led to understand was possibly the most glamorous and beautiful sports presenter in the world.

Ironically, on the day we moved, his beloved Liverpool were playing AC Milan in the final of the European Champions League. The biggest match for two years since their last triumph in the competition and Lawrence could only follow it via his mobile, as we began the thousand-mile journey south to Poggiolino and Todo.

Our day began at the crack of dawn when we set off in convoy with our friends Bruce and Hugh, whose transit van contained most of our London garden, including nine camellias, each with its own passport and bill of good health, which we had been assured by the man from Defra (the Department for Environment, Food and Rural Affairs) was essential if we were to take them across international borders. Lawrence had kindly informed me that they do sell plants in Italy, but these were old friends and I couldn't bear to go without them.

We arrived in Folkestone on a perfect spring day and more or less maintained our good spirits, aside from the moment both of us wanted to scream when nobody at customs so much as glanced at the camellias, or bothered checking the cat passports that had cost us £750.

We reached the French city of Bourg-en-Bresse, the halfway point of our journey, by late evening. We'd hoped to toast a famous victory but those damned Italians had gained their revenge for the defeat two years earlier in Istanbul, winning the match 2–1. Lawrence's only consolation was being able to watch the goals on television in the hotel.

We were due to arrive at Poggiolino early the next evening and couldn't wait to see Todo. Every time Lawrence checked his mobile phone he would pause at the photo of Todo he'd put on the screen. Grubby and unkempt, that broad grin still firmly in place, we would tell him, 'We're coming!' until we finally turned into the little driveway – *our* driveway – with Bruce and Hugh close behind.

As we opened the gate, a chestnut blur raced up the steps from the house and threw itself at us.

I grinned at Lawrence, tears in my eyes. 'We needn't have worried.'

I could see that Lawrence was hugely relieved as he bent to stroke Todo. 'Apparently not. He's made of strong stuff, this boy.'

Todo looked better than he had for months. It was as if he had known that his long wait was coming to an end.

That night the four of us picnicked on the terrace of Poggiolino, feasting on sumptuous local cheese and wine. Todo darted from one to another, grinning from ear to ear and sniffing around for the crumbs of cheese we allowed to fall to the floor. Any doubts about our decision to come here fizzled out in the party atmosphere.

The removal truck was due at 7.30 a.m. the next day. At 8.45 a.m., Lawrence's mobile rang. The question from the other end of the line was not reassuring. 'Where exactly are you?'

Was there a glitch? I had something of a headache after the festivities of the night before, which didn't help. Lawrence, sounding very calm, said, 'Yes, I know the school in San Francesco, we're just a mile away from that. What's the problem?' He turned to me. 'The driver's confused. He's parked at the big *agraria*, the plant nursery in the village. I said we'd go and meet him.'

When we arrived the Polish driver, Krzysztof, was standing impatiently beside a huge double-wagon truck. 'I can't get up the road to your house, it's too narrow,' he said.

Lawrence led him to one side and an animated conversation took place. From the bit I could hear, I understood that Lawrence was pointing out, with admirable restraint, that the removal company had known our address for a month and had told us our stuff would be in a smaller van, so that it could get up the narrow roads.

However, as Krzysztof said, with irrefutable logic, the truck was here now, and it wasn't going anywhere. Not only that, but he had another delivery to make later that afternoon near Rome, so he needed to get going.

Lawrence walked into the office of the *agraria* to be met by a huge AC Milan flag and the broad smile of the owner. He took it well, congratulating the victor and explaining that he was born in Liverpool and had been a fan for forty years. The ice broken, Beppe assured us he was happy to have our possessions unloaded in his car park while we found another company to transport them to the house.

As our sofas, armchairs, beds, boxes and dining table were dumped one by one on the asphalt, Lawrence worked his way through the local phone book, trying to find a removal company that could help out at short notice.

'No joy so far,' he said gloomily, after the fifth call.

'What are we going to do?' Of all the problems I had anticipated, ending up stranded in a car park, surrounded by the contents of our old home, had not even featured. I sat down heavily in an armchair and wished devoutly that I had remembered to pack some painkillers for the headache that was getting worse by the minute.

It was at that point that a visitor to the *agraria* came over and introduced himself. We recognised him as one of the olive harvesters we had encountered on our first visit to the house, the man who had handed us the mandarins. He told us his name was Umberto and explained that he had worked for Carol MacAndrew for more than twenty years. We told him what the problem was and he turned to Beppe. 'How about Davide?'

'*Sì, sì, Davide,*' Beppe yelled, reaching for the phone.

Davide turned out to be a local man with a medium-sized truck and, thankfully, he was free to help. Triumphantly Beppe informed us that he would be there at four o'clock, after the lunch break.

'*Beppe, grazie mille,*' said Lawrence as we all shook hands. 'We're so grateful.'

'Well, you deserve it . . . after losing the final.' Beppe knew how to twist the knife.

We were a little unsure about abandoning all our worldly goods in a car park for a couple of hours, but as we left a woman came out of her house, which looked onto the *agraria* and, waving frantically at us, yelled, 'Have a good lunch. I'll make sure everything's fine here.' We waved back and grinned, relieved to have found a temporary caretaker. After a meal of ciabatta with pecorino and salami, washed down with cold Peroni beer, we all felt better. At four, with the temperature over 30°C, we arrived back at the *agraria*. Some minutes later Beppe arrived and threw open the gates, and thirty minutes after that a truck pulled in. The driver was dark-haired, handsome and grinning broadly. It wasn't a white steed and he wasn't wearing armour but this was definitely a knight.

'Right,' he announced. 'We've only time for one load now. Then I'll come back at 8 p.m. I have to go to dinner with my mama.'

Of course you do, I thought.

Having surveyed our collection of furniture and boxes he began barking orders, telling us which was to go on first and supervising exactly where and how it should be stacked as the rest of us worked up a substantial sweat. He didn't actually do any of the lifting himself, but never mind, we were just grateful for his help. Surprisingly quickly, the truck was full and we set off back to the house with Davide behind. Four hours later, with the sun just beginning to drop in the sky, the whole process was repeated and by ten that night everything we owned was finally stacked inside our new home. No matter that it had taken about twelve hours longer than anticipated: we were in. I was exhausted but euphoric.

Todo had been fascinated by the whole moving-in process, following us up and down the steps to the truck and in and out of the house as we heaved and grunted back and forth with the seemingly endless load. He must have realised that something big was happening, and we took it in turns to reassure him that yes, we were here and in a couple of days we would be living in the house with him.

We felt awful leaving him again that night, but we were going back to the hotel for the next couple of days, while we got the house cleaned, put furniture together and began sorting out the chaos. I stroked him and settled him in his bed for the night, explaining that we would be back in the morning. He seemed peaceful, and I told myself he understood.

Hot, tired and sticky, the four of us headed off for dinner in Lucca. It didn't seem fair that Todo, who had played so big a part in bringing us here, wouldn't be there for the toasting of our heroic labours. But we all deserved to celebrate in style so we promised ourselves that in the future he would more than make up for missing this one meal and we raised a glass, in fact more than one, to both him and Poggiolino.

5

Dopo Domani

The most urgent thing in those first few weeks was finding a way to work. We weren't retiring; we had a business to run and if we didn't run it we wouldn't be able to stay. It was as simple and as terrifying as that.

With a temporary office cobbled together in Carol's room, what we needed was a phone and Internet connection. We had to be available to our clients, and to the concert halls, the TV producers and opera houses we relied on for a living. We couldn't afford to be away from computers and phones for more than a few days, a good Internet connection was vital, but we didn't even have a telephone line to provide it.

Bigger companies have IT departments. We have Lawrence. Everything depends on him, because my IT know-how extends as far as: 'Does it work when I turn it on?' Before we arrived he had ordered a new phone line from Telecom Italia and found the one company that could give us a good ADSL service and Internet. The new line was due the following month, and meanwhile we wanted to reconnect the existing line that was in Carol's name. Simple enough, we hoped. But we were getting nowhere, the Catch 22 of Telecom Italia being that you can only talk to them on one of their lines . . .

In the meantime we were trying to manage our Internet connections using 3G data cards, all the rage a year or so earlier and very helpful to us when we'd been on holiday, but nowhere near up to the job now. Other than that, all we had was the Internet café in Lucca, and with the number of daily communications involved in running several careers, we would have had to virtually move in there – not an appealing prospect.

The highlights of our first week included Lawrence losing his cool after the ninth time a representative of Telecom Italia told him we would be connected '*dopo domani*'– after tomorrow, several hours spent (via a dodgy mobile connection) trying to soothe the ruffled feathers of our two most diva-like clients, and the discovery that our bank balance was now at zero in two countries.

At first we'd believed that Telecom Italia's cheery 'after tomorrow' literally meant the day after tomorrow. But after the third or fourth time we began to understand that it meant some time, maybe . . . or not.

'We'll have to go to the TIM shop,' Lawrence concluded gloomily. TIM was a help centre in Lucca's main street, where you could go and talk to someone in person. Lawrence joked that they'd set these places up because even *they* realised how rubbish the telephone service was.

As we headed out to the car, Todo followed. 'Why don't we take him along?' I suggested. 'You never know, he might help.'

We had no idea whether he would like going in the car or not, so we put a blanket on the back seat, expecting to have to encourage him inside. The second the door was open he jumped in, made himself at home and looked at us as if to say, 'Come on, let's get going.'

As we drove off he stared intently out of the windows, moving from one side to the other, as if to get the best view of the landscape as we passed. He seemed almost mesmerised, and completely ignored us if we spoke to him. He was in his own world.

Later we told Teresa about it and she roared with laughter. 'Oh yes,' she said. 'La Signora drove everywhere, very, very fast, even when she was very old. And she took Todo with her, always.'

The picture of ninety-something Carol traversing the winding local roads and *autostradas* at breakneck speeds, with Todo alongside her, ears flying behind him in the wind, was an enchanting one.

In Lucca I made for our usual car park, just outside the city walls. With Todo on the lead – he was beginning to get the hang of it by this time – we headed for the TIM shop.

Upon entering we were met by the dazzling smile of a voluptuous young girl looking up from behind the desk, 'Ah, *amore* . . .' Assuming she was referring to Todo and not Lawrence, I smiled as we approached.

Lawrence – taking, I thought, just a little too long to explain our predicament, during which time the assistant laughed, encouraged his Italian and flashed her eyes – finally asked, 'So can we just take over the line Mrs MacAndrew had?'

'No.'

'No, or maybe . . .'

'No, it's not done. You need a new line.'

'We already have one coming, next month. Here's the order.'

Manuela – her name was on a tag – looked over the paper Lawrence handed her.

I have discovered that in these situations Italians have a default setting of No. Ask a second time and you might just be presented with a Maybe. The third time very rarely fails to elicit a positive response.

'I can't promise anything but let me see what I can do. Can you come back in a few days?'

'It'll be a pleasure, Manuela. *Grazie*,' Lawrence replied. *Creep*.

Driving home, congratulating ourselves on a mission almost accomplished, I drank in the beauty of the landscape. We had never before been to Italy in May, and it is truly the most wonderful month. The Lucchese countryside is a riot of colour and scent. Every road, even the busy *autostrada*, is lined with brilliant red poppies, making the most mundane street look picturesque. The olive trees dotting the hills are covered with silvery green and the pale cream of new buds, while the grass is tall and soft, every patch threaded with wildflowers.

May is also the month of roses, lovingly cultivated in gardens and growing wild over the abandoned buildings scattered across the landscape. Alongside them are the last of the camellias, and the huge blowsy heads of peonies, the soft white and blue of wisteria and the brilliant purple blue of irises. All of this and more we revelled in every time we went out; a world of colour and fragrance that delighted the senses. Sometimes, when I stood and looked at the fields of poppies stretching away from our garden, I could hardly believe our luck. We had done it, we were here, living in Italy; this was our view. It was hard to worry about our difficulties with the phone line when I stood breathing in lungfuls of perfumed air, Todo at my side.

Todo was also plainly loving his new life. The first time the doorbell rang, he rushed to the front of the house, wild with excitement, barking madly. Attempts to restrain his enthusiasm made no difference. He went through the same performance every time the bell rang, leaping up to the gate and wagging his tail madly at the prospect of a visitor. The only one he didn't like was the postwoman and he would go crazy when he heard her motorbike pulling up outside the fence. One of us had to hold him while the other collected the post, because if he managed to get out he would bark wildly and jump up at the fence, hackles up and frothing at the mouth.

Our first visitors had been the cleaners, a couple of charming and cheerful local brothers, both short and tubby with large, gentle faces and even larger hands, whom we'd nicknamed Tweedledum and Tweedledee. They spoke only to tell us they took their lunch at midday and would return at 2 p.m. We were to hear this rule repeated on several occasions over the next months, by a succession of builders, plumbers, electricians and glaziers. And it was observed by all of them with an almost religious zeal.

With the exception of their lunch hours, Tweedledee and Tweedledum beavered away without a break, employing an assortment of mops and brushes as they moved from room to room, scrubbing at the years of grime, dust and neglect for two whole days, but when they'd finished, although it all smelled and felt cleaner, the house barely looked any different. What we needed was paint, and lots of it, but that would have to wait until the repairs and renovations had been finished.

The next visitor was Nicola Masini, our architect. We had met Nicola some weeks before, when Roy introduced us, and we'd warmed to him immediately. An erudite and charming man, he spoke perfect English and was an expert on the Etruscans, the first settlers of what would become Tuscany. He loved the possibility of continuing some elements of their architecture in modern Italian homes, and so did we, but we couldn't imagine how he might manage this within the very simple scope of what we had planned for Poggiolino.

Winningly, Nicola took an immediate liking to the house, reassuring us that it was a wonderful purchase. He pointed at the arches in the hallway, and between the sitting-room and the dining-room. 'Typically Etruscan,' he announced.

Nicola seemed to wave away most problems with his hands, making everything seem possible. Agreeing with us that the dining-room was too dark he suggested that we install two oval windows high in the wall, to capture the sunset. 'Oval?' quizzed Lawrence. 'Would that by any chance happen to be an ancient Italian design?'

'Exactly,' Nicola beamed, oblivious to the amused look we exchanged. 'You see them in houses built around 500 BC.'

After he left, Teresa, who had come over to see how we were getting on, told us his ideas sounded very good; La Signora would approve. The house needed to change for its new owners.

We asked Teresa if she would continue her long association with the house by cleaning for us twice a week and looking after the animals when we were away working. She consented, with a gracious nod of her head.

When she arrived for her first cleaning session I found her in the sitting-room, busy with a broom and damp cloth on the floors and rugs, so I showed her the brand new vacuum cleaner we'd bought for her to use. She smiled politely and then carried on with what she was doing. By her second or third visit it became clear that it would never be taken out of its box. Her strongly developed sense of frugality wouldn't allow her to use an expensive Hoover when a broom would do. She couldn't bear waste of any kind. When emptying the waste-paper baskets in the house she would take out anything she thought wasn't quite finished – stubs of candles, shampoo bottles with just a little left inside, useful plastic bags – and put them back on the table for us to find. Over time she probably saved us the cost of the Hoover via these small reclamations.

She was intrigued by our arrangements in the house. 'Ah, you're putting the coffee table there? La Signora had it here, and her writing desk over by that window. La Signora had her grand piano there,' she went on. 'She would play it, and at her parties for the Music Society she would have visiting concert pianists play.'

In the dining-room the tales continued. Carol, it seemed, had a large dining table around which would be as many as sixteen guests, though that must have been a squeeze. She was meticulous about the seating arrangements; always a gentleman then a lady, and the closer you were to her the more favoured you were. In the summer, La Signora required a large vodka on the rocks every evening, on the terrace, at six.

Listening to Teresa's descriptions, I could only hope we would live up to the considerable legacy left by our predecessor. Our lives must appear somewhat dull after a grand society hostess. My fear that we might disappoint in this regard only increased when Teresa lowered her voice and said, conspiratorially, 'Every year, La Signora would ask me to clean especially good, then tell me not to come for two weeks. She had American friends coming . . . from *la Casa Bianca*.'

'Well that's great,' retorted Lawrence when I told him later, 'now we've got to live up to presidents.'

We were still musing over just who Carol might have invited over from the White House – was it one president or perhaps two or three that she had personally known? – when Todo leapt into action as the doorbell rang again.

It was the plumber Giovanni – a world away from Mad Matt, our plumber in London, whose foibles had included installing the shower upside down. Tall, quietly spoken, with a mop of curly hair and a pale complexion which seemed out of place among the ruddy local faces, Giovanni could have stepped out of a Renaissance painting.

Under any circumstances I would have found his presence pleasing but with the memory of that morning's tepid wash fresh in my mind, a man with a spanner in hand was a welcome visitor. Getting some hot water was becoming a priority. This was his third visit, and we were increasingly anxious. The first two times he had announced that there was much work to be done and he would have to come back. This time he once again poked suspiciously at the rusting orange monster which was the diesel boiler, before stepping back, stroking his chin and scratching his head for quite some time.

It didn't seem encouraging.

'I think I can start work in two weeks' time,' he said finally.

'Can't you do anything now?' I tried not to sound too whiny, but I was desperate for a shower and two weeks seemed like an age.

He looked at my pleading expression, shrugged and headed back into the boiler room.

'What is this white cylinder?' asked Lawrence who had followed him.

'Ah. That's an immersion heater, I hadn't noticed it before. Let's see what happens.'

He threw the bright red switch and we heard clunking, gushing and whirring sounds.

'*Ecco là!*' he announced triumphantly.

'What does that mean?'

'It means it's done,' hissed Lawrence, through tightened lips. 'If it was that easy, why couldn't he have done it the *first* time he came?'

I didn't care. Running my hands under the tap in the utility room I could feel warm water. It was a small victory, in the scale of things, but at that moment it felt wonderful. I would be able to have a shower that evening. And then, perhaps, a vodka on the rocks on the terrace?

Anything seemed possible. Now we just needed to rustle up some visiting dignitaries . . .

6

Officially Ours

Todo's joy in life seemed infectious, as we discovered when we took him out and about with us. Everyone loved to stop and chat with him and it was through Todo that we had our first introduction to many of our immediate neighbours. Most of them remembered him as a puppy but assumed he had left Poggiolino after Carol died. Our neighbours farmed the fields and land around us, living in houses that their families had owned for generations and continuing a way of life which has gone on in rural Italy for centuries. They were clearly bemused by the odd English couple who had descended into their community, but having Todo gave us an instant connection. Very few other local dogs were walked and we became known for our curious habit of taking a daily *passeggiata con Todo.*

Our favourite walk took us beyond Teresa's house and up the hill, passing the field with the horse and sheep, a smattering of neighbours' houses and some abandoned farm buildings, before we came to a small ridge from where it was possible to take in the whole of the Compito Valley. The scene was spectacular. We looked out over a vista of olive groves and vineyards, fields of cereal crops and golden sunflowers. Beyond them lay the village of Montebello and behind it the dramatic peaks of the Alpi Apuane.

With Todo, we set off on this walk most days, after we had finished work in our makeshift office. It was now well into June and with the midday temperature usually pushing 35°C, our trudge up the hill involved a number of extra pauses to 'admire the view' as we wiped the sweat from our brows.

Todo seemed cheerful enough, trotting along beside us, but with his thick fur we knew he must be very hot. We'd noticed that most of the local dogs, including Teresa's two excitable mongrels, Lulu and Borsi, had recently been clipped and it was clear that Todo needed a haircut too. Judging by the rough and ready nature of Lulu and Borsi's coiffure, we guessed that it had been done by Silvano, but since neither of us fancied having a go with the kitchen scissors, we decided to hand the job over to the professionals.

Our village, San Francesco di Compito, is very small; just a collection of houses, a church, a school, a trattoria and bar and several agricultural shops, including the *agraria* which became temporary home to our furniture on that first day. The next village along, Fontanella, is just a mile or two away, with several useful shops and services, so we often find ourselves there.

Once home to the grand villas and summer residences of princes, cardinals and dukes, Fontanella now has a newsagent, a couple of enticing bakeries and, most importantly in our current situation, a vet, with a *toilette di cane* – a grooming parlour – next door. This was where, a couple of days later, we arrived with Todo. The girl in the shop, who told us her name was Monia, smiled and nodded, patted Todo, slipped a chain over his head and told us we could collect him in an hour. He looked terribly worried as we left, as if we were abandoning him forever. We could only stroke his head, tell him we'd be back soon and hope he would appreciate the benefits once it was all over.

We passed the hour savouring the delicious pastries and coffee at the local *pasticceria*. Like so many in the surrounding villages, this was a family-run business where the staff seemed to enjoy any reason to celebrate a *festa* or special day, decorating the shop and making mouth-watering cakes and sweets for the customers, all of them known by name. We had only visited once before, but were greeted like regulars. 'Ah *l'inglese*. How are you?' asked one of the charming waitresses. 'No dog today?'

I attempted to explain that he was having his fur trimmed, which elicited a giggle.

'I think you might have just told her our dog is at the hair-dresser's,' Lawrence whispered in answer to my puzzled look.

When a smiling Monia showed us into the little anteroom beside the clipping area an hour later, we barely recognised Todo. We had expected a gentlemanly trim, but there he sat, eyes bright, button nose glistening, clipped almost to the skin and now silver-blond with a dark streak down his back and legs. Even his furiously wagging tail was shorn of its fur, apart from a little pompom of grey at the very tip. He looked like a large puppy with a No. 1 haircut.

Thrilled to see us again and beside himself with excitement, he leapt to his feet, executing a perfect turn, as if to show off his new look, and then chased the pompom on his tail round and round in a dizzying whirl. Laughing, I called him and he ran to me, jumping up and putting both paws on my legs. 'Todo, don't you look beautiful, and so young.'

He strutted proudly around the room, basking in the praise

we heaped on him, watched by Monia and the two lady vets who had heard the commotion and come to see him.

As we left the shop, a tall, elegant man held the door open for me. Seeing Todo he burst into loud laughter. We had no idea why and didn't understand what he said to us, but he greeted Todo like an old friend. It was only later that we discovered he was Signor Martini who had bought Villa Carola and had known Todo since he was a puppy. I suspect he had never seen him looking quite like that.

For the rest of the day, Todo skipped around in high spirits. He hadn't been pampered for years and he seemed to revel in all the care and attention. Now that he had been shorn of his long fur, we could see a strange mark on his groin. It appeared to be man-made and Lawrence thought he could make out numbers. The mystery was solved a day later when Teresa arrived.

'It's his registration tattoo, so he can be identified and his owner traced if he goes missing. All dogs have to have them in Italy.'

'Will it matter that he's no longer Carol's?'

Teresa frowned and gave a shrug. 'Maybe . . . maybe not. Perhaps it would be best to inform the Comune.' She explained that there was always the risk, if Todo were to wander off, that without a traceable owner he could be sent to the municipal pound or maybe even put down.

We'd tried hard so far to have little to do with the Comune, the local council governing Lucca and the surrounding area. We knew we'd have to eventually, but Italian officialdom and bureaucracy is daunting enough for Italians, let alone inexperienced foreigners with an imperfect grasp of the language. Neither of us would feel at ease until we had sorted this issue out though, so we set off that afternoon for the Azienda USL Lucca which deals with all health matters for the city and surrounding area, including dog registration.

We had an address on the Via di Tiglio, but when we found the road we discovered it perambulated for several miles beyond the city. We drove for twenty minutes, Lawrence counting down the numbers, until we passed under a motorway.

'Hang on, we've just had 153 and now it's 179. How did we miss it? Did I fall asleep?'

'You must have,' I grumbled. 'I'll have to turn round . . . again'. Lawrence has never driven and persuading him to learn now we were in Italy was one of my major goals. Instead, he had consistently proved himself a worthy navigator, even if he sometimes failed to bark out instructions in time. Perhaps he thought telepathy would work.

We headed back towards the outskirts of the city, with Lawrence peering at the buildings to either side of us.

'That's it.'

I screeched to a halt and swung hard left into the car park, sending poor Todo flying from one side of the back seat to the other. Unperturbed, the moment we opened the door he jumped out and headed towards the entrance.

'Do you think he recognises it?'

'He's clever, but not a genius,' Lawrence replied, though he eyed Todo with some doubt as he said it.

From the outside, the Dog Office, as it came to be known, was a rather ugly modern building, but inside, the marble entrance hall and sweeping staircase were impressive.

Finding our way to the section dealing with *Animali* we sat and waited in a long corridor lined with countless closed doors. As the minutes ticked by, Lawrence remarked that not one single person had yet appeared from any of them. 'It's like the Mary Celeste. Do you think we should choose a door and knock?'

On cue one of the doors opened and a stern-looking man poked his head around it.

'*Sì?*'

Lawrence had consulted the phrase book in advance. 'We're here with our dog. We think he needs to be registered.'

'Mmm, do you have your documentation?'

We handed over our passports and the contract for the house sale – the only documents we could think of that might be relevant.

'Is he your dog?'

'Yes,' said Lawrence.

'Do you have proof?'

'Er . . . he lives with us.'

'Mmm . . .'

Lawrence attempted to explain our situation in his very best Italian. Todo seemed to understand, looking at the official whenever his or Carol's name was mentioned, but I could barely make out the flow of the conversation. *Bought the house last month . . . the previous owner . . . inherited the dog . . . Lucca Music Society . . .*

'We need a letter from Mrs MacAndrew.'

'That could be a problem. She's dead.'

For goodness sake, don't start being sarcastic in Italian, I thought.

'From a relative, then.'

'There aren't any.'

This time his 'mmm' was followed, worryingly in my view, by a 'tut tut' and roll of the eyes. 'We'll need a copy of her death certificate. Come back with that and we'll see if we can do anything.'

'*Grazie, grazie mille, molto servizievole.*' Thank you, you've been very helpful. It was a phrase Lawrence had learned early in our language classes back in London, figuring he'd need it for multiple situations as we forged our new life, but on this occasion I didn't feel his heart was quite in it.

We left, Todo and I picking our way carefully down the marble steps, Lawrence stomping ahead, muttering a few choice words I doubt Todo had ever heard before.

'Tomorrow, we'll do it tomorrow; I've got bloody Telecom Italia this afternoon,' he grumbled. 'I don't know whose idea this "dream house in Italy" business was anyway.'

It won't be the last time we hear that phrase, I thought, smiling at Todo.

The following day we went through the papers we'd found in the house. Carol's death certificate wasn't among them, so we set off for Lucca again, Todo prancing from one side of the back seat to the other, delighted at the prospect of yet another outing.

The first stop was the Office of the Comune, which deals with births, deaths, residency and all matters relating to *stranieri*, or foreigners. If it all worked out we'd get back to the Dog Office to change the registration and be out in time to visit the Esselunga supermarket. Lawrence had finally worked out the grill setting on our microwave, and we had decided to celebrate Todo's registration with a nostalgic meal of bangers and microwave mash.

Our high spirits evaporated, however, as soon as we entered the Office of Registration (Humans) in Via San Paolina. We were tenth in line and nobody looked happy.

The three of us sat down, preparing for a long wait. But Italy is a surprising country and unusual things happen all the time. Lawrence was still staring at the number 079 on the ticket he'd taken – I told him the number wouldn't get any smaller just by looking at it – when a very stout woman appeared.

I stared in fascination at her pink leather ankle-boots, leopard-print dress and blonde beehive as she made her way along the queue, muttering and nodding to each person in turn.

'Why are you here?'

Lawrence answered gloomily that we needed a death certificate.

'Then why are you sitting here? You need Window Five. Didn't anyone tell you when you arrived?' She pointed to her left and to our delight we saw there was nobody at Window Five.

We made our way over and Lawrence smiled at the bespectacled woman behind the glass. 'I'm sorry to bother you; this is rather an unusual request.'

Don't be so English, I thought. *Get on with it.*

'We have bought a house and need a death certificate for the previous owner . . .'

His explanation was cut short by a brisk, 'Name, date of death and address?'

'Carol Cofer MacAndrew, 18 June 2005, San Francesco di Compito.'

She rattled away on her keyboard and then looked up. 'Have you got the *bollino*?'

'Excuse me?'

'It's €14.64; you need a *bollino* for that amount.'

Lawrence looked blank and she sighed. 'Go to any shop selling newspapers and you can get a *bollino*. It's a tax stamp.'

'And the certificate?'

'It'll be here when you come back.'

We hurried out of the office and, feeling we'd discovered some magical new world where everything worked, found a nearby newsagent. 'Er, we need a *bollino* for €14.64.'

Without blinking an eye the man produced a glossy, decorated postage stamp from a large book and handed it to Lawrence, who paid. 'OK?' he asked.

'*Sì*,' came the reply. 'That's it.'

Minutes later we were back at Window Five.

'*Bollino?*'

'Here,' replied Lawrence, pushing it through the small gap.

After a short burst of activity with three different rubber-stamps she handed us the certificate. I put it carefully into the folder we had brought; our first triumph over officialdom.

'Come on Todo, one more job to do and then we can go and find those bangers.'

Back at the Dog Office we climbed the marble stairs again, Todo attempting – not always successfully – two at a time.

This time Lawrence knocked firmly on the door from which our man had appeared the day before, only to have it opened by someone different. Introducing himself as Signor Martucci, he beckoned us all into his office and offered us chairs.

Taking the certificate he examined it before starting to type into his computer. 'Ah, yes, here we are.' He turned the screen to face us and there we could see an entry for *Mrs Carol MacAndrew: dog type, lupetto cross; age, not known; size, medium; colour, brown*. While this brief description did our beautiful boy no justice whatsoever, I smiled at the thought that around eleven years ago Carol had sat in this very same office with a young Todo while another Comune employee had entered these details.

'Unfortunately his registration number is missing. No problem, let's check it now.'

Todo looked indignant as Lawrence picked him up, cradling him in his arms, his golden belly visible to all. Signor Martucci walked around his desk to us and peered at the tattoo. 'It's a little faded,' he mumbled, pushing up his glasses and moving closer to the spot. 'Yes, I can see . . . 9, 7, 5 . . . No, I can't make out the rest. Let me call my colleague.'

Todo waited patiently in Lawrence's arms as a call was

made, and seconds later the man we'd seen the day before entered. With a thin smile and perfunctory '*Buon giorno*' he leaned down towards Todo's groin. He had a small magnifying glass which he held just above the mark.

'Take this down: 9759 . . . 4, no 8 . . . Harrumph.' He moved the glass and his face still closer and Lawrence and Signor Martucci did the same.

Poor Todo seemed resigned to this unseemly attention and had wisely chosen to direct his gaze out of the large window at the trees outside and the distant hills, as if to say, *I'm a senior citizen, this isn't becoming. Was that a pigeon? Damn, could have got it.* Meanwhile the three men were peering at his private parts, occasionally pulling the skin on his belly as they tried to make another digit clearer. So far they'd reached agreement on seven numbers.

'There should be twelve,' said Signor Martucci.

'I thought it was ten,' replied his colleague.

'No, it switched to ten after the year 2000, this pre-dates that.'

'Are you sure? I can go and check.'

Oh for goodness sake, get on with it. I didn't say it, but I so wanted to.

'No, Carlo, no need.'

I looked over to see whether Signor Martucci had miraculously deciphered the final digits, but he was telling Lawrence to put Todo down.

'It's impossible to get it all. I propose we insert a new micro-chip. We'll start again.'

We nodded gratefully while he went to the other side of the office, returning with a small electronic contraption. Todo was as good as gold, standing completely still as Signor Martucci placed the machine between his shoulders and pressed.

'There, it is done.' He patted him. 'Todo, now you have a tattoo and chip; I think you are unique.' But we *already* knew that.

Smiles broke out, we handed over €15 and handshakes were exchanged before we descended the marble staircase and emerged into the sunshine, Todo skipping along excitedly beside us. He knew he was special. And now he officially had three owners: Carol MacAndrew, Lawrence Kershaw and Louise Badger, all of the same address. It seemed the perfect outcome.

7

Dinner with a Princess

We had now been installed at Poggiolino for five weeks and little by little things were beginning to fall into place. In between delighting in our brave new world and dealing with the inevitable frustrations that came along with it, we woke every morning to that enchanting view over the Tuscan hills and began every day with Todo's cheering presence by our sides as we sipped a steaming espresso on the terrace.

Our plans for the house were advancing. In addition to the two oval windows Nicola was so keen to install in the dining-room, these included a new kitchen, a new boiler, repair of the small summer house next to the terrace, an overhaul of the electrics, re-modelling the wall between the kitchen and dining-room, knocking down the wall in the second down-stairs bedroom to create an office, enlargement of the sewage system and the installation of a gas tank. Like most rural prop-erties, Poggiolino had mains water and electricity but no mains gas. For that we would need to have a *bombolino* (gas tank) sunk in the garden. Carol had used diesel oil for heating and hot water, but the thirty-year-old diesel boiler, once no doubt a state-of-the-art piece of engineering, was now silent, cold and far too scary to meddle with. Over seven feet high with very few controls, neither of us had the courage to turn it on as we were sure it would take the house with it. So for the moment we were managing with the small immersion heater, our microwave and a barbecue, and as the builders could not start until late June, our temporary arrangements would have to continue for some time.

Acquiring the barbecue had been no mean feat. The last time we bought one we had simply gone to John Lewis, but barbecuing doesn't seem to hold the same fascination for our neighbours that it does for the English, and no one we asked knew where to get one. It was Umberto who came to our rescue once again. We hadn't seen him since he helped with our removal crisis at the *agraria*, but one afternoon we bumped into him in the village. He asked us how the house was coming along, and we explained that our main problem was no kitchen, and that we needed a barbecue. He scratched his head at this odd request, and then recommended a large agricultural shop where, once we'd found the place, a box was brought out. It wasn't much like the sophisticated gas one we'd bought in London. Lawrence spent several hours cursing and swearing as he struggled to put it together, but once assembled it made a very welcome change from the microwave.

It also proved to be a source of intense delight to Todo, who sat beside it whenever it was in use, his eyes fixed on that evening's dinner, in the hope that a morsel might somehow wing its way in his direction. We had discovered early on that he was food-obsessed. Soon after we arrived I had left a bag of croissants on the outside table and then wondered why Todo flew past a little later with a white flag in his mouth. It was the paper bag, as I discovered when he reappeared, licking crumbs from his snout and looking very pleased with himself.

He didn't have many bad habits – he liked to get things out of the waste-paper bins in the house: sweet wrappers, bits of paper and, disgustingly, old tissues – but apart from this his one real vice was food. Anything edible – apart from grapes, apple and lettuce – left within his reach was likely to disappear unless we kept a close eye on it. The cats' bowls provided another source of extra treats; we had to make sure Todo was out of the way when they were fed or he'd beat them to it.

His fixation with food was so funny – and occasionally frustrating – that we invented a new word for it, *snuvare*, to describe the action in which Todo devoured any food in front of his considerable snout in a matter of milliseconds, using suction at the power of which Messrs Hoover and Dyson would marvel. We got as far as conjugating the verb, following the rules set down since the days of Dante, the father of modern Italian: *io snuvo*, I snuver; *tu snuvi*, you snuver; *noi snuviamo*, we snuver. When Lawrence began conjugating more tenses – *ho snuvato*, I snuvered, the past participle; *io snuverò*, I will snuver, the simple future – I told him he was being a smart-arse. He told me it was Todo's idea.

We forgave Todo his misdemeanours, even though he frequently deprived us of food we were about to eat. How could we stay cross with that enchanting smile, or those big brown eyes that looked at us with such evident delight?

One morning, not long after the life-enhancing acquisition of the barbecue, Teresa rang the doorbell. This was unusual, as she had keys and used them when she came to clean. But the purpose of this visit was more formal.

'Silvano and I would like you to come to dinner.'

'That would be lovely, Teresa. *Grazie mille*.' Our first dinner invitation. 'When would you like us to come?'

'Tomorrow evening, at eight.'

I was startled. In London, even with close friends, we'd usually set up dinners for several weeks ahead, co-ordinating diaries and availability with endless telephone calls and emails.

'I've invited Signora Albertina.'

I smiled gratefully at this news. I was keen to expand our little social circle and especially to meet Albertina, to whom Teresa had referred a couple of times in glowing terms.

'Shall we bring Todo?'

'*Sì*, of course. La Signora always brought him. And, besides, Diego adores him.'

We'd briefly met her grandson, an angelic-looking boy of eight, with his father Maurizio, Teresa's son, and his mother Barbara, a pocket battleship of energy who talked nineteen to the dozen with barely a pause for breath. As for Teresa's husband Silvano, he was without question the happiest man in the whole of Tuscany. Tall and solidly built, with hands the size of buckets, he was the quintessential farmer, permanently ruddy-faced from outdoor work, a broad smile never far from his lips. Our exchanges so far had mostly concerned the weather, how the Compito Valley and indeed the whole of the Lucchese hills were the most beautiful part of the region and how lucky we all were to be living here. I got the impression that nothing would faze Silvano; he was content-ment personified and I looked forward to getting to know him better.

The moment Teresa left I rushed inside, told Lawrence about the invitation and searched for my Italian textbooks, anxious to brush up on my verbs and conjugations before sitting down to dinner with an Italian family.

'I think it's a little late for that,' Lawrence laughed. 'Anyway, I'm pretty sure Albertina speaks English.'

Teresa had told us that Albertina Castoldi had been Carol's greatest friend, one of a tiny handful who stuck by her as her health deteriorated and who attended her funeral. She sounded a fascinating woman, a garden designer and traveller who had lived for many years in Chile. We were looking forward to meeting her, even more so when we realised that she must have known Todo since he first arrived.

By the morning of the dinner our excitement was tempered by a fair amount of trepidation. We couldn't really expect Albertina to translate for us – would our Italian stand up to a whole evening of conversation? And what would she think of us, the new residents in her old friend's house?

Arriving a few minutes after eight, as everyone did in London, we could see that Teresa's other guest was already there, sitting at the long outdoor dining table, cigarette in hand. As we approached she spotted Todo.

'Todo, how are you my old boy? You're looking well. Your new life clearly agrees with you.'

She looked up at us. 'Hello my dears, it's lovely to meet you. Teresa has told me so much about you and now you're living in dear Carol's house. I'm amazed you were able to move in so quickly, the house must have been in a terrible condition after all this time?'

Lawrence smiled. 'We had a lot of cleaning to do but most things work very well. Even the awning over the French windows works; I flicked the switch and – first time!'

'Ah, that was Carol,' she replied. 'Things done properly, all to the very best standard. Everything.'

Teresa appeared with wine and a plate of antipasti – salami, bread and tomatoes, olives and cheese – and the rest of the family arrived to join us. It was the beginning of a lovely evening. Albertina, who had to be nearly eighty, laughed, drank and smoked non-stop. Quite short and a little portly with dark grey hair combed into a smart and sculpted style she regaled us with a stream of stories about Carol and Jim, Poggiolino and life in Italy.

'I'm so glad Teresa is still cleaning the house. You won't find anyone better, she's a marvellous person. Carol could be beastly to her but she never missed a day. I don't know what dear Carol would have done without her.'

As she talked, switching from English to Italian and back again, Teresa hurried between table and kitchen, bringing successive courses each more delicious than the previous one, as her family smiled and nodded and passed around the plates of tomato, meat and mushroom crostini, a zucchini risotto flavoured with a wild herb from the garden and succulent spit-roasted chicken with beetroot and potatoes.

Lawrence, agog at the splendour of it all, complimented Teresa. 'This chicken is so fresh, so much flavour.'

'Yes,' she answered making a wringing motion with her hands. 'This morning, six-thirty.'

'Can't get much fresher than that,' he said, peering across at the chicken coop on the other side of the yard.

I couldn't help thinking of the first pet I ever had in Australia, a pretty white hen called Pip. I loved her and took her every-where with me, tucked into the basket on my bicycle. I decided it was probably best not to mention it. What a soft touch Teresa would think me.

Silvano was in great spirits. He joked and laughed, mostly about my dreadful Italian: 'You've been learning *how* long?'

Maurizio, who had his father's open and friendly face and his mother's reserved manner, occasionally interjected with a carefully pronounced English phrase, while Diego, whose angelic face could have adorned the dome of any of the great Italian cathedrals, sat silently, perhaps overawed by the presence of three outsiders. Barbara, who had met Maurizio when she came on holiday from her native Poland and had never returned home, helped Teresa with the food before joining in the conversation, firing off a round of speech so fast we had no hope of comprehending, particularly as the kick of Silvano's homemade wine set in.

We asked Albertina what she remembered of Todo's early days.

'Carol really didn't like him at first, but . . .' she looked fondly at him as he lay beside us, 'how could you resist him? Before long they were inseparable. She knew that he was a special dog and deserved the lovely life that she could give him. That is why I was so insistent that he was looked after when she passed away. I phoned the President of the Music Society and told him, "This is dear Todo, Carol's dog, and after everything she did for us we must take care of him. He doesn't want to leave Poggiolino so we will set aside €200 per month for Teresa to look after him there."' She slammed her fist on the table, 'There will be no argument!'

And I'm sure there wasn't, I thought, as I pictured the President of the Society on the other end of this call.

Todo thumped his tail lazily on the floor.

'Yes, that's you we're talking about, you gorgeous hound,' Lawrence teased.

I had been dying to ask Albertina a question about something she'd said earlier. As the others launched into a loud conversation, I leaned across to her. 'You said Carol was beastly to Teresa. What did you mean?'

Leaning back and roaring with laughter she translated my question into Italian for the rest of the table and everyone joined in.

'Oh she could be a real witch. And her temper! Carol liked everything done just so, very precisely, *her* way!'

As Albertina described some of Carol's more fastidious demands, Teresa and Silvano added their own tales. It seemed that the table had to be set exactly as she wanted, all her linen washed and folded the same way, after cleaning all the furniture had to be replaced within a millimetre of where it was before, and after the 6 p.m. vodka, dinner was at 7.30 p.m. 'Never 7.32!' Teresa said, pointing her finger at us in mock admonition.

'She even made Teresa work on Christmas Day,' Silvano added. 'And when Teresa was ill, La Signora came to the gates and demanded that she get up and go to work. She could not manage without her.'

'Did Teresa go?' we asked in amazement.

'Oh yes,' Silvano nodded, smiling affectionately at the memory. 'She went.'

'She was very lucky to have Teresa run errands for her at the drop of a hat,' added Albertina.

'Errands?' I asked.

'Oh, yes: *fetch me my medication from the farmacia; I need a copy of* Corriere *immediately!*'

Lawrence and I looked at each other, puzzled, as we knew Teresa rarely ventured far and didn't drive. 'How could she get to the *farmacia*?'

Albertina chuckled. 'Teresa hasn't told you? For many years she drove a Vespa, one of those *Roman Holiday* scooters.'

I tried to conjure up an image of Teresa astride an Italian scooter, *à la* Peck and Hepburn. 'But she always seems so . . . cautious.'

'Well she was nervous, poor thing, of all the crazy driving, so she just drove through back ways and across the fields.'

I would spend much of the next few days, when walking with Todo, picturing Teresa – headscarf protecting her newly permed hair – navigating her solitary way through these same fields, doubtless waving cheerily to neighbours as she passed, avoiding the many pot-holes and streams, before returning with a basket full of whatever medicines Carol had requested, along with the newspaper and a warm slice of focaccia for La Signora's lunch.

I wondered aloud how Carol had kept any friends. 'Ah, but she was generous to a fault and she helped people whenever she could,' Albertina insisted. She told us Carol had worked tirelessly for the Music Society and had inveigled her into writing letters to local banks asking for financial support as well as overseeing the new system of buying tickets by subscription. 'The first such organisation in the whole of Italy to do this. All Carol.'

'How is the apartment in Rome?' asked Silvano, changing the subject.

'Oh fine,' Albertina replied. 'I went there to supervise some decoration.'

Rome! I was envious, 'How long have you had it?'

'Oh it belonged to my mother, a legacy from the Palazzo days.'

My gaze was blank, so Albertina continued. 'It was my mother's when she lived at the Palazzo Borghese.'

'Your mother?'

'She was the Princess Santa Borghese.'

I choked on my last piece of almond and cherry tart. The closest I'd ever come to Princess Borghese was when I bought some of the cosmetics range of the same name in Selfridges.

Albertina laughed. 'Oh, you don't have to curtsy, my dear,

she was a princess by marriage so the line doesn't carry through to me!'

She may not have inherited the title, but the tale explained Albertina's unmistakeably aristocratic bearing. I mused over this meeting of worlds – the daughter of a princess, people of the land and a couple of Londoners enjoying dinner together. Italy seems to produce these incongruities with effortless charm.

The evening was drawing to a close, night had fallen and a full moon shone down. With no artificial street lighting, the myriad stars were bright and clear and the hills surrounding us, north to the Garfagnana and south to Pisa, were shadows in the moonlight.

We rose to say our goodbyes, and Albertina took my hands. 'I'm so glad you've come to look after Carol's house and Todo, and that you're keeping Teresa on. You know, you really have to thank her. There had already been two other offers for Poggiolino but she wasn't having any of it.'

I was about to ask her what she meant, but Silvano had taken Lawrence off to look at something and now Albertina turned to them. 'Are you showing him your guns, Silvano?'

Lawrence, fixed grin threatening to slip at any moment, was holding an extremely large rifle and trying to look as though he was a) interested and b) understood what Silvano was saying as he explained in minute detail what it was for. As Silvano urged him to come along one day and try out the guns, Lawrence began to look ever so slightly desperate.

It was Todo who rescued him, getting up and padding over to his side.

'Hello Todo, were you thinking of heading home? Oh yes, goodness me, just look at the time . . .' The relief in Lawrence's voice was palpable.

We said warm farewells, leaving Albertina still chatting as

we closed the big wooden gates behind us. The cicadas, invisible in the olive trees, were singing their nightly chorus as we walked the short distance home, Todo trotting happily beside us, stopping only to sniff at a patch of wild mint.

I was still pondering Albertina's comment. 'What do you think she meant by that? We have to thank Teresa?'

'I'm not sure,' Lawrence replied, 'but I guess we'll find out. Teresa wasn't just a housekeeper; I think she must have had a lot of influence on Carol.'

'I'm certain she did. But did she have a say over who could buy the house?'

I was longing to know the whole story, but it would have to wait.

As we rounded the bend in the road and Poggiolino came into sight, Todo broke into a run.

'Nothing like home, eh, Todo? I couldn't agree more.' Lawrence unlocked the gate and we filed down the steps, Todo in the lead.

Early the following morning Umberto stopped by. Dropping in was just not done in the middle-class enclaves of London we had left behind, but here it was an everyday thing, and I enjoyed the informality, even if it did occasionally mean being caught in my pyjamas.

Thankfully on this occasion I was safely dressed for the day and we chatted, while wandering around the garden. Though there were still signs of its former splendour, the years of neglect during Carol's illness and after her death had taken their toll and tall weeds and wild plants overwhelmed areas where beds of roses, irises and lilies had once been. I was itching to get to work on imposing some order and freeing our thirsty London plants from their temporary pots.

Umberto was well known; his name would elicit an approving nod or '*Sì*' then '*Un vero contadino,*' a true man of the land. He had mentioned when we met that he had worked for Carol, and now he explained more about their arrangement, which had been in place for more than twenty years. As was common practice in the area, he maintained the olive grove without charge, carrying out the twice-annual pruning, feeding, pest-control to ward off insects if the weather was especially hot and, of course, the harvesting. In the case of Poggiolino's hundred or so trees, this last task took two people about ten days. Umberto would take the baskets of olives to the old *frantoio*, or press, just beyond the church of San Martino on the hill opposite, and would keep the bulk of the fresh green oil produced, but would give Carol two large flagons which kept her plentifully supplied for the next year.

He asked if we would be interested in continuing this arrangement. I wondered whether I should consult with Lawrence before I gave Umberto an answer. I could just imagine visions floating in his mind of us climbing trees in the autumn sunshine, beating olives to the ground before gathering them up and pressing them ourselves, rounding off the day with several glasses of local red wine, before sinking crusts of freshly baked bread into bowls of our own perfect day-old oil; the gentleman and lady farmer!

On second thoughts ... Back in the real world I was only too happy to recognise we knew nothing about this practice, and telling clients, 'Sorry can't talk to you at the moment, I'm up an olive tree,' wouldn't go down well.

I turned to Umberto. 'Yes,' I said firmly. 'We'd love to continue the arrangement.'

He seemed pleased, and said he'd back later in the week as the trees needed a little pruning. As we made our way to the bottom of the garden, where the weeds were still higher and wild brambles grew up the fence, Lawrence and Todo arrived to join us.

Reaching down and patting him, Umberto said he had first met Todo just days after Carol had reluctantly taken him in. He reiterated what everyone else had told us: La Signora was not pleased to begin with and the little dog roamed free in the garden with Teresa appearing every now and again to see to him or encourage him in for some food. 'He had such spirit,' he laughed. 'You can still see it all these years later. I knew it wouldn't be long before he was at home here.'

Todo was sniffing away at the fence marking the end of the garden. 'Perhaps he can still smell the *orto*?'

'*Orto*?' asked Lawrence.

'You know, a garden for vegetables, salads, tomatoes. La Signora liked fresh food.'

We looked at one another. There had been a vegetable garden!

'Can you do it again, for us?' I asked.

'Of course; I'll start when I come back.'

That evening, over yet another microwave meal, we fantasised about eating our own fresh food. 'Pasta with *cavolo nero*,' Lawrence mused. 'Or a salad of fresh spring veg.' We couldn't wait.

By the time supper was cleared away Todo was already asleep in his basket. As I made coffee, Lawrence rooted around in some of the smaller packing cases that had been stowed in one of the bedrooms. 'Found it!' he said, producing a CD, before collapsing onto a sofa and pressing start on the remote. Horns and trumpets roared out of the speakers and a broad smile spread across his face. I knew he was contented when Schumann's Third Symphony was brought out and, with the closest neighbour a hundred yards away, he threw open the French windows and let the music soar, as if announcing to the whole world that life was good.

The sound startled Todo, who was now standing beside Lawrence, staring intently at the stereo. He walked over to the speakers and sniffed, before haring outside then back in again, once more to the speakers, then to his room where he threw himself into the basket, only to immediately emerge again and go back to the stereo. We'd seen him excitable many times, but this behaviour was unusual. He continued his odd ritual until finally he settled at Lawrence's feet, his head resting on them for the remainder of the symphony.

Lawrence looked down at Todo. 'You know what?' he said. 'This dog's got taste.'

8

A Long Way from Tuscany

O ur first trip back to London was fast approaching and it hung like a cloud over our heads.

We both knew that regular trips to and fro were the price we would have to pay for our new life, and something we would need to get used to. But after less than seven weeks, with so much still to sort out and with Todo just beginning to settle, it felt much too soon. How were we going to leave him?

Our trip would take us away for six days. Lawrence had several meetings with artists to attend, as well as an opera first night for one of his singers. As for me, I had two events requiring the services of a celebrity to add glamour and sparkle. These occasions are fun, and at the same time fraught with potential – and actual – hitches, dramas and last-minute changes. I'd been fielding calls backwards and forwards for a couple of weeks now, all with our far from adequate phone and Internet system – we were still in fraught negotiations with Telecom Italia and relying on mobiles and data cards. At least in London we'd be able to catch up with our communications backlog.

It wasn't only our concern for Todo that made it hard to leave. There was still so much to sort out in the house. Negotiations were ongoing with the builders, who we hoped would start shortly after our return. Then there was the leaking water pipe at the back of the house. Its discovery led to a hunt for the water meter; we'd been horrified to see the dial spinning round at an alarming rate. Teresa had told us that utilities in Italy were very expensive and we dreaded to think how many hundreds of euros were running down the drain each day. And we had yet to change the ownership details for electricity, water and Comune services, each of which would involve complex negotiations and multiple trips to Lucca.

Teresa had promised to come in a couple of times a day to look after Todo. We agreed that she would let him out in the morning, give him his food, leave him outside during the day and then come back in the evening to put him in his bed and lock up. But how would he adjust to being alone again? He would have the cats for company but we knew he would miss us and we dreaded the thought that he would feel abandoned again.

Counting down the days to our departure, we watched him more closely than usual. Did he sense our worry? Was he robust enough to cope with our leaving, or would he think we were two nice strangers who had dropped in for a bit and taken off again? In the short time since our arrival we'd bonded so much; he already appeared very dependent on us and as I contemplated his distress at being left again my spirits sank.

Lawrence tried hard to cheer me out of this melancholy state. 'He's a smart dog. We've brought an entire house full of furniture and three cats; he'll realise it's only for a few days.'

'You're right. So much has changed; he won't think we're leaving for good.'

But neither of us was convinced.

The night before our flight we packed, but left our cases in the bedroom, not wanting Todo to see them. Dogs always know when change is in the air, and we didn't want to alarm him, but the moment I went downstairs I could see that he'd already realised something was up. His tail down, he pattered around the house after me, like a clingy toddler.

I sat on the sofa and he came and stood next to me, putting his head in my lap. I stroked his face, which he loved. 'Don't worry, Todo, it's only for a few days, then we'll be back. And Teresa will come in every day and see you, and she'll bring Diego so you can go for walks.' I kept stroking him and Lawrence joined me, talking gently to him all the time. He explained that this was how things had to be, we had clients who needed us and the small flat we were renting in South London so that we had a base when we went back still required some setting up.

'That's the price of our Tuscan dream,' I told him.

After a few minutes he padded slowly off to his basket and lay down. Did he understand that we would not be leaving him for good? We could only hope so. That night I slept fitfully. I knew that there was no alternative – this was the deal we'd made – but at that moment it didn't feel any easier.

In the morning Lawrence brought the cases downstairs while I sat in the garden with Todo, reassuring him. He seemed brighter but every time one of us made for the door he'd look up as if this was the moment we were leaving.

Finally I couldn't linger with him any longer. Lawrence was hopping from foot to foot. 'C'mon, the plane won't wait for us.'

I bent down to give Todo one final hug. He followed us up the steps to the gate, hoping that he might be coming with us in the car, but he knew that this time he wouldn't, and offered little resistance when I pushed him gently back inside. Driving away, I tried hard to concentrate on the little road which would take us through the olive grove, past Teresa's garden and down towards the cemetery. Lawrence looked back once and I could tell from the tears in his eyes that Todo was sitting at the gate as he must have done for almost two years, waiting for his owner to return.

We stepped off the plane at Stansted Airport into sunshine. London looked at its brightest and best and it felt good to be back, but we had no time to go for a leisurely lunch or walk in the park. This was a business trip, full of meetings with clients and colleagues, the joys of city driving and the Underground.

'Does it still feel like home?' Lawrence asked me one morning.

'Yes, it does, and it's nice to understand what everyone's saying.'

'And your English is *so* much better than your Italian! Are you missing Italy?'

I nodded.

'Missing San Francesco or Todo?'

I didn't need to answer that one. I could hardly bear to think of him, sitting at the gate. That evening, even though I knew Teresa would think me silly, I asked Lawrence to call her and check how things were.

Ten minutes later he reappeared.

'All good; the builders came round with Nicola to do some measurements and they think they'll start the day after we get back.' I looked at him in exasperation and he grinned. 'Oh, and Todo's fine, eating like a horse and Teresa and Diego took him for a long walk this evening. No need to worry.'

I felt relieved. He might be missing us, but he wasn't pining, and in a few days we'd be back with him.

The rest of our trip passed in a whirlwind of activity, every day filled with two or three appointments, numerous calls and meals eaten on the hoof. Our tiny rented flat felt anonymous, like somewhere you stay when you're away on business, which was exactly what it was. By the time we headed back, getting up at 4 a.m. to catch the 6.30 a.m. flight to Pisa, I was desperate to be in Poggiolino with Todo. London might still have felt like home, but it wasn't where I wanted to be. My heart was taking root on a hillside in Tuscany.

Thankfully, Pisa Airport is small and efficient. We could be through passport control, the baggage area and out into the car in fifteen minutes. As I drove up from the coast into the hills, I had to try hard to contain my excitement. I hit the road for San Francesco at a speed bordering on reckless. Jolted from his Valium-induced doze, Lawrence clutched the side of his seat as we whipped around yet another tight bend. 'Steady on,' he muttered. 'Let's get there in one piece.'

As the car rounded the little church of San Martino, then the cemetery and finally our road, I wondered where Todo would be. In the garden? Or maybe the summer house? Or was he stretched out in the ramshackle pergola which afforded shade from the mid-afternoon sun?

Thirty yards from Poggiolino, I heard him bark. The first sight as we pulled into the driveway was his smiling face up against the fence, the pompom on his tail lurching frantically from side to side.

As I opened the gate he rushed out and jumped into my arms – an impressive feat, given his age. After doing the same with Lawrence he turned and tore down the steps to the house, taking the final three in one bound before barking at the front door and then running back up to us. It was the happiest, warmest and most wonderful welcome we could have hoped for.

For the rest of the day he smothered us with affection, and we returned it, the three of us enjoying our reunion as we toasted the success of our first trip back with a rich Chianti and one of Esselunga's finest pre-made lasagnes, while watching the sunset from our terrace.

As a special treat we'd bought a piece of gorgonzola dolce, our favourite piquant cheese, made locally. 'Don't put it in the fridge,' advised Lawrence, 'it needs time to breathe.' I left it on a plate on the dining table, and after the lasagne was cleared away, I went in to get it.

It wasn't there, and neither was Todo.

A few minutes earlier he'd left our sides for the first time since we got back and when I found him in his basket, chewing blissfully on the last piece of sticky blue gloop, I could see why. He had clearly decided the gorgonzola was his homecoming present. As he looked up at me, licking his chops appreciatively, his 'Who, me?' expression was the picture of innocence, and I could only laugh.

I called to Lawrence, 'I think it's *stopped* breathing now!'

9

The Chicken Thief

The following Monday morning was a momentous one. The builders were coming.

The evening before had seen us in a fever of expectation. Who would have thought you could get so worked up about having walls knocked down, windows poked through and a kitchen put in? But we had been living in a state of semi-camping for almost two months; eating microwave meals, tripping over wires and cables in our temporary office and using a bucket for a sink. After that, a builder seemed the most heavenly sight on earth.

Or so we thought, until the bell rang at what felt like a very unearthly hour. We had been luxuriating in being an hour ahead of the UK and therefore able to take a little extra time in bed in the mornings, surfacing gently and getting to our desks by ten. So when the bell sounded at what turned out to be 7.40 a.m., it was a rude awakening.

Peering through the window I mumbled, 'The builders are here.'

'Tell them to go away; I'm happy with the house as it is,' said Lawrence, pulling the sheet more firmly around his ears.

Our team of workmen had arrived together. First came Daniele, head builder and foreman, a great bear of a man, and the spitting image of one of Lawrence's favourite actors, James Gandolfini, of Tony Soprano fame. He greeted me and Todo with a cheery smile and introduced us to his assistant Eduardo, a good-looking young man with a dark complexion and the physique of an athlete. Next came Giovanni the plumber, whom we already knew, and finally Roberto the electrician, a dead ringer for Dennis Hopper – shortish, tanned and full of wiry charm and energy.

'Wow,' I reported back to Lawrence when I'd shown them in. 'Two film stars and two Italian gods. Not bad for a Monday morning.'

Todo seemed delighted to see them. He welcomed each one with a friendly sniff and an abundance of tail-wagging, and as they got to work he trotted cheerfully from one to the other, as if to inspect progress and offer encouragement. Teresa had told us that Carol had Poggiolino decorated every other year (we gulped at this, having thought a fresh coat of paint every five or six years was more than enough), so he was clearly used to having workmen around the place.

Teresa also explained that there was a list of Carol's favoured artisans to deal with every aspect of the house among her papers. We'd found it and tried calling some of them, but a combination of discontinued numbers, retirements and, in one or two cases, deaths had rendered the attempt fruitless. Instead we'd taken on men recommended by Nicola, all of whom knew one another and were used to working together.

That first morning I offered tea or coffee, preparing for the endless round of brewing that would be expected in England, but to my surprise the men politely declined.

Daniele gave us the already familiar, 'We take lunch at twelve and return at two.'

'And will you start at this time every day?' I asked nervously.

'No,' he replied. 'Today we were a little late. We will be here by seven-thirty in the morning and will finish at six.'

My 'Any chance of making it eight?' produced a roar of laughter as Daniele threw back his head in amusement. 'Eight? The day's almost over by then.'

Great, I thought. *No more lazy mornings for us for a couple of months.*

Daniele had a list of the works to be done and we agreed that they should start in order of urgency. That meant the leaking pipe first and then the alterations to the kitchen and dining-room, in preparation for the installation of the gleaming new kitchen we had ordered from a supplier in Lucca. After that the wall had to be taken down in the room that was to be our office, various other more minor alterations made, and then the new gas tank installed in the garden.

'Fine,' Daniele beamed. He was a bit like an overgrown schoolboy, all legs and arms and constantly on the move. He rarely stood still except when there was a problem, at which point he would push back his well-worn cap and rub his chin as if it was a magic lamp and might somehow provide inspiration. He spent most of each morning on the phone, often disappearing to check on jobs at other houses, while Eduardo dug and drilled and sweated away. In the afternoons Daniele would join him on whatever tasks were in hand, and we would hear him calling 'Ed-uaar-doh, Ed-uaar-doh,' as his put-upon assistant scurried around after him.

Giovanni and Roberto did their own thing, sorting out the

plumbing and wiring, respectively, occasionally crossing paths with one another or the building team but mostly beavering away in separate parts of the house.

Although we longed to get the work done, we hadn't looked forward to sharing the house with workmen for several weeks, but in fact it was as close as possible to builder heaven. There were no breaks for coffee, no endless cups of milky tea and not a moment wasted. Apart from lunch, they worked incredibly hard, and did their best not to disturb us, though they'd all pause when Todo came up to inspect their handiwork and I often heard them asking, 'Do you approve?'

I was amused to find that all questions were addressed to Lawrence, unless they involved something of a more decorative nature, such as the colour of tiles, the location of the washing machine or whether the towel rail should be right or left of the basin? After years of supporting the feminist cause, and apologising mentally to Simone, Germaine and Gloria, I accepted that any attempt to confront this was going to be a losing battle. Italy has many wonderful qualities but it remains a male-dominated society, even if the matriarch is still head of the family unit.

It was a discussion over the positioning of a new sink in the utility room – now known as Todo's room – that brought home to me just what an uphill struggle I faced in being taken seriously.

Giovanni wanted to put it in the most convenient place to connect with the original plumbing. Convenient for him, that is, but it would mean putting the fridge behind the door, which would then not open fully.

I knew exactly where I wanted the sink – on the other side of the room. As I stood in my chosen spot, with Giovanni in his, one by one Daniele, Roberto and Eduardo wandered in and went over to stand by him. I looked at Lawrence for support. Would this be an England vs. Italy stand-off? He shrugged at me as if to say, 'What can I do? My manhood is at stake here,' and joined the other four, at which point Todo, no fool when it came to odds, ambled over and sat with them.

As all six of them looked at me expectantly, I knew I was beaten. 'OK,' I hissed at Lawrence, through pursed lips. 'But don't blame me when the door bangs into the fridge every time you open it.'

While Daniele and Eduardo battled with the alterations and Giovanni pottered around with a length of piping in one hand and a tap in the other, Roberto got to work on the electrics. His arrival came not a moment too soon. Where once elegant wall lights had been in place, as we'd seen in Teresa's photos, we had been left with bare wires poking through the plaster like bony, lethal fingers. Lawrence, calling on handyman skills which had previously lain dormant, had managed to put in a few vital light fittings and to adapt our electrical equipment to Italian power. This hadn't been easy given that there were three different voltages used in fittings around the house. More than once I'd heard him, lying on the floor, screwdriver in hand yelling, 'Here's an idea; have just one!'

To Roberto, Poggiolino resembled a large jigsaw puzzle and he took great pleasure in stripping out and replacing all the electrics and getting the lights and power points working. The house contained an industrial-sized fuse box straight out of the 1970s, which we gladly agreed to replace with a new one a fifth of the size and a great deal more user-friendly.

We had already discovered that every light in the house could be turned on from three or four different switches in each room. Even in the small passageway from the sitting-room to Todo's room – just eight paces long – there were three switches, one on each wall, for one overhead light. Was this an American fad or just Carol's whim? We suspected the latter.

Roberto was so concerned about getting everything right for us that one day he brought his pretty daughter Roberta, who spoke good English, acquired working in one of Lucca's liveliest bars. His love for her and fatherly pride was evident and he concluded the discussion with, 'OK, we agree. My English is good, yes?!' while shaking with laughter.

Every now and then Nicola arrived to inspect the progress of the building works. He would confer with Daniele, and then look carefully at what had been done, nodding in approval.

One of the bigger jobs we had decided upon was to knock through the top half of the wall between the dining-room and kitchen and to install a door between the two rooms.

The original kitchen/dining set-up was bordering on the bizarre. Carol might have left the grand Villa Carola, but her standards hadn't been allowed to slip. Servants were not to be seen, and she had designed the ground floor so that Teresa could come and go from the front door to the kitchen without ever being observed. The only entrance to the kitchen was hidden under the stairs in the hallway next to the front door, and there were serving hatches to the dining-room and sitting-room.

Teresa had been the most devoted and caring servant, friend, companion and carer for Carol over many years, but during La Signora's heyday at Poggiolino she was hidden away, hard at work in the kitchen. Teresa explained that for the grand dinner parties she would pass successive courses – invariably four – to Carol through the hatch. When chocolates, petits fours, coffee and liqueurs had been served, she would exit Poggiolino without having once been seen by the esteemed guests.

I had no such desire to hide my chef (i.e. Lawrence) from our friends, and anyway the dining-room was quite dark, so with Nicola's guidance, we planned a large archway – Etruscan in style, naturally – in the top half of the connecting wall, to open up the whole area.

We were no strangers to knocking out walls; in our London house we'd taken out several and each time the process was hideously long, expensive and complicated, with planning permissions, inspections from the local council and a studious structural surveyor who referred constantly to a PhD-thick sheaf of papers full of calculations. Temporary props and heavy steel joists had been put in place before the wall could be removed. All in all these were not happy memories. So when Daniele announced that it was time to take the wall down and asked Lawrence to accompany him to inspect the site, we naturally girded ourselves for a complex process. However, when I followed Lawrence into the dining-room – my presence was not officially required but I was curious – I could see no sign of any props, joists, paperwork or even plans.

There was only Daniele, with a thick pencil in his hand. As we watched he drew a horizontal line halfway up the wall, measured a point in the middle from which he drew another vertical line about two metres high. Drawing two more verticals at either end, about six inches shorter than the middle line, he joined the two outside lines to the middle one with a perfectly symmetrical, gently curving arc.

Stepping back a moment to assess his handiwork he nodded with satisfaction, before turning to us. '*Va bene*. OK?'

Lawrence broke our stunned silence. 'Er, it looks fine; yes, that's what we had in mind.'

He glanced at me, as if to say, 'I don't know what's going on here. Help!' But the only things I could think of saying, such as, 'Did Nicola draw up plans for this?' or 'Are you sure we don't need permission from the *comune*?' seemed a little redundant, especially as at that precise moment Daniele picked up a heavy hammer and swung it at the middle of the wall, sending plaster and brick in all directions. 'Ed-uaar-doh!' he bellowed, '*Continua!*'

Thus our first major alteration began. The noise sent poor Todo scurrying to his room but he emerged shortly afterwards to pick his way over the heap of debris on the floor, as light emerged between the two rooms.

I decided that it would probably be less alarming not to watch the wall coming down so, leaving the builders to it, I went to talk to Teresa who had just arrived. There was something I had been meaning to ask her for days.

'Why are there so many bricks and breezeblocks along the bottom of the garden fence?'

'Ah, to keep Todo in.'

'Really? Didn't the fence keep him in?'

'When he was young he got out of the garden all the time. He would make holes in the fence, or dig under it. La Signora wasn't strong enough to walk him, and she couldn't stop him digging, so she covered up the holes with the bricks.'

Lawrence, looking slightly pale, as befitted a man who had just witnessed a sledgehammer being taken to his property, now joined us. Behind him Todo, all breezy unconcern, padded past, wandering out into the garden and the field next door. As Lawrence chatted to Teresa I watched Todo trot across the road and under the fence into her garden. For the next few minutes I watched closely, wondering whether I should go over and retrieve him.

'What happened when he got out?' I asked Teresa.

'He would take himself off for long walks. Once he got lost and the Carabinieri had to bring him back. They found him because of his tattoo.'

At that moment I spotted him rushing back across the road. He was running fast, so I couldn't be sure, but it looked as if he had something in his mouth.

Teresa, oblivious to what was going on, continued talking. 'Sometimes, when he was very young and naughty he would steal one of my chickens, but now he's old he doesn't do that anymore.'

A split second later Todo shot past the fence. The 'something' in his mouth was a *gallino*, or small chicken, hanging limply from his jaws, which were clamped firmly shut.

I hadn't the heart to say anything to Teresa.

IO

In Carol's Footsteps

To our immense relief, Todo never repeated his audacious snatch-and-grab raid. Perhaps it had been one last hurrah, proving to himself that there was life in the old dog yet. Since we were spoiling him rotten he had no real need to go hunting, and thankfully he very soon gave up his habit of escaping from the garden.

For the most part he was indifferent to other dogs, but one day we discovered he had a friend. Returning from a morning walk, having left the gates wide open as there were builders everywhere, we found a brown muzzle staring back at us. This was no mongrel but a beautiful, pure-bred hunting dog, tall and long-limbed, his coat a sleek and shiny white with brown patches. His noble profile was reminiscent of dogs in aristocratic portraits, the kind that stand beside their grand masters, staring out of the paintings with piercing eyes.

No more than a year old, a teenager in dog terms, from that first meeting he and Todo played together excitedly like old pals. They would take turns chasing each other and Lawrence pointed out how fair the young dog was; he could easily outrun old Todo, but he never did, sportingly allowing himself to be caught every time.

Umberto told us that the new dog's name was Varco and he lived nearby. We never knew exactly where, but each morning when we opened the gate to take Todo out, Varco would appear and they would rush off together for another game of chase. It was great exercise for Todo, who clearly enjoyed having company. Umberto later told us that Varco's owner was disappointed with him – he was too gentle and playful to become a useful hunting dog. Perhaps this explained the link between them: neither was able to cut it as a hunter. It seemed touchingly appropriate that somehow these two friendly and sweet-natured boys had found one another.

In the meantime we had a practical problem to deal with – we needed to install a catflap. We'd bought one, but we didn't want to cut a hole in the magnificent three-inch-thick chestnut front door. All the other exterior doors were glass and we possessed neither the tools nor nerve to cut into any of these.

We explained the situation to Daniele, for whom no problem was without a solution. He summoned Roberto and the two of them walked around the house, examining potential locations, until they reached the French windows in the dining-room. Muttering to one another they turned to Lawrence. 'We think this is the best place for it.'

'Oh, so you have glass-cutting equipment?'

Roberto grinned and produced a large claw-hammer. I caught my breath: surely he wasn't about to use this on a thirty-five-year-old window? Almost in slow motion, and before I could even begin to construct 'You can't do that!' in Italian, he swung the hammer, smashing through the bottom pane of glass.

Stepping back, he explained that he would call a glazier friend to provide a new piece of glass with the *porta del gatto* pre-fitted. Problem solved. Two days later Bob gave it a successful trial much to the consternation of Todo, who was shocked at seeing his ginger pal appear as if by magic through the door.

While some of their solutions were a little rough and ready, most of the builders' work was meticulous and it was a joy to watch them bringing new life to the neglected house. All of them took great pride in their labours, and several times Roberto came to find us so that we could admire his handiwork. 'I like this Carol MacAndrew of yours!' he declared. 'This copper wiring; *benissimo*, the best quality.'

The following morning Daniele introduced Carlo, who arrived on his digger and set about removing tons of red clay soil from the garden, ready for the installation of the gas tank. Carlo, a De Niro lookalike with shoulder-length hair and a large Romanesque nose, was a charming addition to the team, an assembly so stunning looking that it didn't take a great stretch of the imagination for me to see the house as a movie set and the *muratori* – workmen – as the cast. Lawrence, I was pretty sure, would envisage himself in the role of a Scorsese, directing the whole thing.

I was shaken from this rather pleasant daydream by Daniele. 'We're going to have lunch at the local trattoria; do you want to come?'

It was an offer I couldn't refuse . . .

We were later to discover that our neighbours considered us completely mad to have moved in to Poggiolino before the repairs had been carried out, but having survived far worse

97

with our previous home, we hadn't given it a second thought. And now that the house was in good hands, we were happy and relieved to see the transformation in progress. But while we knew it would all be worthwhile and – hopefully – look wonderful when it was finished, in the meantime we had to live with plaster dust over everything, including our clothes and hair, and chaos in every single room. We struggled to keep working, timing our phone calls around the thumps, bangs and crashes echoing through the house, but it wasn't easy. So when Teresa arrived one morning with Mario, another neighbour, and announced that the day had come for them to take us to visit Villa Carola, we were grateful for the chance to escape.

We had seen Mario, a stocky man with a shock of white hair and a big smile, once or twice on our walks, pruning, feeding and clipping the trees in the grand villa's gardens, and we'd stopped to say hello. He took to calling us *gli inglesi con il cane* and would wave and smile whenever we passed. He told us that the current owners, the Martinis, were in the process of moving, the villa having become too much for them to maintain, just as it had for Carol and Jim. Mario was acting as caretaker, which included showing prospective buyers around and, on this occasion, sneaking us in for a quick peek.

We passed the field next to Teresa's and stopped to pet the horse, an elderly palomino with a light sandy coat, blonde mane and big, beautiful long-lashed eyes. A gentle and docile creature, she shared her field with four large sheep and a lamb.

'*Ciao Bella*,' said Mario cheerily. I wasn't sure whether this friendly greeting was for me, but he saw my puzzled expression, laughed and said, 'No, *this* is Bella, the horse. She has lived here many years and these are her friends. They belong to Amy and Enzo who live up the road.'

Bella had appeared to recognise Todo when we'd first

walked past, pushing her large soft nose through the fence as he brushed against it on the other side and we had enjoyed the thought that Todo had his friends too.

We walked on to the villa, full of mounting excitement at the prospect of finally seeing Carol's original home, about which we had been told so much. From the road it is hidden away discreetly behind a high hedge, stone gateway and large iron gates.

As Mario opened the huge double front door, a burst of sunlight hit us from the full-length windows opposite. We wandered around, marvelling at the beauty of the decorative tiled floors, the symmetry of the rooms, the tall, graceful windows with their painted shutters, leading onto stone balconies. Arranged over four floors and with a spacious cellar, the house was generous but not intimidatingly huge. Its origins went back to the seventeenth century when it would have been a summer residence for one of the great Lucchese families.

Images flashed through my mind of the life Carol must have led here. This long table graced by candelabra was where she and Jim would have eaten. She would have written her daily correspondence at the marquetry bureau, read the latest novel on the chaise longue and sipped her evening vodka beside the hand-turned wrought-iron table on the balcony as the reddening sun dipped below the tall cypresses.

The garden was still preserved faithfully as Carol had established it in the sixties. There was the long pergola, planted with white wisteria and strawberry grapevine. We had found among her papers photos of friends here at lunch; ladies wearing wide-brimmed summer hats with long cigarette-holders in one hand, cocktails in the other, and men in linen suits and silk ties, all of them seated on wicker chairs around a table covered with a lace cloth and laden with plates of food.

The topiary was old and immaculate; I wondered if Salvatore, the treasured 'man of all work' whom Carol talked of in the newspaper interview, had planted these. Still clinging to the stone and flint walls were caper bushes full of vivid purple fuchsia-like flowers. *She'd be cross*, I thought. *They've not picked the buds early enough so there will be no capers.*

As we continued our walk through the garden I noticed patches of roses and other plants all white in colour, then beds of iris, both blue and white, and another of day lilies, some still bearing their burnished orange flowers. A thought struck me and I turned to Lawrence. 'This is just like Poggiolino.'

He laughed, 'I think the sun's got to you. Have you seen the state of what passes for our garden recently?'

'No, look, there's the white garden, then the iris and the lilies, the coloured and scented roses and those steps and stones. She copied all of this at Poggiolino, on a smaller scale. Even the wisteria's white like ours; everywhere else in the area it's blue.'

Nodding, Lawrence could see what I meant. 'Have you seen that tree? A false acacia, just like the one in front of our house that Umberto wants to cut down.'

Walking back through the villa we began to notice other similarities. The main sitting-room windows faced south to catch the full journey of the summer sun; the exits onto the garden were through French windows and the pebbled area at the front was the same as ours at Poggiolino.

'Do you think she hated leaving this place, even though she knew it was getting too much for her and Jim?' I wondered.

'She kind of took it with her,' smiled Lawrence. 'It's not just Todo we inherited, is it?'

We thanked Mario and headed back down the hill, our minds full of scenes from a more elegant age.

We may not have met Carol, but we were beginning to feel

we knew her well. Her presence was there in everything connected with Poggiolino. In the garden, the roses she planted had been in full bloom for several weeks. Prince among them was the rich burgundy Papa Meilland, which we'd just seen at Villa Carola. Carol's love of music was eclipsed only by her passion for flowers and she had been adventurous and ground-breaking in both areas. Meilland was only born in 1963, around the time she moved into the villa, so she must have been one of the first to acquire it, and forty-four years later we were still enjoying its beauty and sweet fragrance.

I was standing beside the roses the day after our visit, looking out over the valley shimmering in the heat, when Teresa arrived to deliver a message. Excitement and delight in her voice, she explained that finally, two years after her death, La Signora was to be recognised properly in her adopted city with a memorial concert at San Martino Cathedral, featuring music by her favourite composer, Rossini, conducted by her great friend, Maestro Herbert Handt.

'It's about time, too. The Maestro has been trying for a long time to arrange it. Will you go?'

'Of course. We'll look forward to it,' I assured her, and I could see from her broad smile that she was pleased.

'And you?' I asked.

'Maybe, we'll see.'

I got the impression that she wouldn't, perhaps a little daunted at the prospect of all those grand people, and it saddened me. No one else knew or cared for Carol more. I hoped she would change her mind and come.

Telling Todo he was going to Lucca with us for this occasion, I marked the date in my diary. It would be fascinating to meet Herbert Handt, the co-founder, and some of the other members of the Music Society. And it would be lovely to have an excuse to dress up. For weeks we'd worn nothing but work clothes, since we'd been busy tackling the weeds and over- grown grass in the garden or getting on with jobs in the house that we could do ourselves. Every now and again I'd gaze longingly at the rails erected in the upstairs *sottotetto*, from which hung my small selection of evening dresses and floaty jackets and Lawrence's linen suits and Armani shirts and ties. Shoes with heels and bows were arranged underneath, along with the evening handbags and purses I'd collected over the years. I really enjoy dressing up, but there had been precious little opportunity in the weeks since we moved, so when the day of the concert arrived I felt like a little girl waiting to get ready for a party.

As I stood in the unplastered room – bare electric cables running along the top of the walls, floor tiles stained with years of grime – looking over my 'best' clothes in the limited light afforded by the one small, unfinished window, I imagined Carol as she must have prepared for a night out, in the dress- ing-room at her villa, surveying her Rosetti shoes and Ferragamo handbags, designer gowns hanging neatly in antique inlaid wardrobes.

I smiled. There was no competing with that, but I was deter- mined to put on the best show I could manage. I picked out a favourite grey chiffon jacket and applied make-up which hadn't seen daylight in weeks. Lawrence shaved for the first time in days and put on a suit, while a freshly clipped Todo sported a new red collar bought especially for the occasion.

Decked out in our finery, we got into the car. Todo, sensing the excitement, bounced joyfully across the back seat from window to window as we headed for Lucca.

We had discovered that the city is the shape of an oval lozenge with the historical centre contained within the extraordinary seventeenth-century walls, which are still completely intact. They were built of specially commissioned red bricks, and made so wide that a narrow road runs along the top, where the Lucchese and visitors walk, cycle and jog underneath the shade of tall plane trees while looking down on the city spread below. Many Tuscan towns had walls built around them to keep out marauding enemies, mostly from other Tuscan towns. Lucca's foes were the Pisans and Florentines, who waged regular war against the little city. But we preferred the local myth that tells how the walls were originally built to protect a Lucchese girl from the amorous advances of the god Jupiter. He had sent Venus and Apollo down to find the most beautiful woman on earth and they discovered her in Lucca. Lavinia was indeed more beautiful than Venus, but she loved her husband and wanted none of Jupiter's attentions. Desperate to have his way, Jupiter sent Mars with his army to capture her, but the whole city defended her honour, building the walls to protect the virtuous and faithful wife.

The cathedral of San Martino is in the centre of the city. Most of the car parks are outside the walls, so after leaving the car, we walked through the courtyard of the Palazzo Ducale then crossed the grand Piazza Napoleone, heading up the cobbled streets past the Teatro Giglio and down Via del Duomo. 'It sure beats the route past the Shell Centre to the Royal Festival Hall,' Lawrence joked.

We stopped in front of the cathedral, its three beautiful arches more than eight hundred years old. Lawrence had boasted for years about his home city's *two* cathedrals, but despite being a fraction of the size of Liverpool, Lucca had an astonishing *three* – all of them historic masterpieces.

Waiting for us outside we spotted the President of the Music

Society, Signor Parducci. As we made our way towards him an elegant woman in a black evening dress stopped us. 'Is it really Todo? No, it can't be!'

'Yes, it is.'

'Well that must make you Signora Luisa and Signor Lorenzo. We're pleased to meet you. My husband and I were old friends of dear Carol. We've heard so much about you.'

Lawrence, who adored being addressed by the Italian version of his name, bristled with pride.

After a brief exchange we went over to Signor Parducci, who was delighted to see Todo. 'You were quite right to bring him,' he said. 'Carol loved the dog very much.'

He went ahead into the cathedral to greet other guests and another smart couple stopped us, the man bending to pat Todo. 'Have you come to pay respects to your old mistress? Good evening, I'm Signor Pasquinelli. I met Carol when she first moved to Lucca.'

Lawrence was charm personified, shaking hands and acting for all the world as if they were gracious and long-lost acquaintances. I, feeling a little tongue-tied as usual, had to rely on friendly smiles.

'Ah, *buona sera* Todo, how lovely to see you,' declared another guest. Each time the initial greeting was to Todo, as if he was host for the evening, and he carried off his duties in exemplary fashion, his tail going like a windmill as he lapped up the attention.

The concert was due to start at 8.30 p.m. It was now 8.40, which meant, in Italian time, we had ten minutes or so to go. Lawrence went inside to find our seats while I took Todo back to the car park. Charmed as everyone was to see him, he couldn't come to the actual concert.

'Bravo Todo, you were lovely to all those people. Wasn't it

nice they all came to see you?' He lay down on his blanket in the back seat and I kissed his head, 'I must go and say goodbye to your dear Carol.' As he buried his face between his front paws, slowly closing his eyes, I could have sworn he understood.

We were touched and a little taken aback to find that we had been given seats in the VIP area. Close by, waving to us from her seat with the other members of the Music Society committee, sat Albertina. She had written a moving and occasionally mischievous tribute to Carol in the programme, and though much of it was beyond our rudimentary Italian, I smiled when I spotted a reference to the Papa Meilland rose.

The speech Maestro Handt gave before the concert was full of warmth towards Carol and the audience applauded enthusiastically. The programme began with two short pieces of funeral music, the second composed on the death of Lord Byron. I thought the choice particularly poignant as he had adored Italy and spent a year in Pisa, just half an hour from Lucca. Like him, Carol had also left her native land for a new life in Italy and now so had we.

Rapturous applause greeted the close of the final part of Rossini's *Messa di Gloria* and as everyone rose to go we spoke briefly with Albertina and then the Martinis, before heading towards a queue of people waiting to speak to Maestro Handt.

When our turn came, Lawrence stepped forward. 'Bravo Maestro, we enjoyed it very much. We are the couple who have bought Poggiolino.'

'Ah, the most peaceful house I have ever known. I have very fond memories of it and of Carol.' His accent retained its New York roots, but lilted like Italian. 'And I hear you have her little dog.'

'Yes, we brought him along; he's waiting in the car.'

'Probably best,' he smiled. 'I don't think Rossini is his cup of tea. Now Schumann, there's a different thing altogether! Did Signora Teresa come?'

'Sadly not,' Lawrence replied, 'but she asked us to send you her best wishes.'

'What a wonderful person; Carol couldn't have found better. We should get together soon. My wife Laura would love to meet you.'

Walking back to the car we were in buoyant mood. Everyone seemed to have heard that we'd bought Poggiolino, and the fact we'd taken on Todo appeared to have generated a great deal of warmth towards us.

'I think we're becoming a part of this community,' Lawrence said, squeezing my hand.

'I think you're right,' I smiled. 'It was a really lovely evening.'

If further confirmation of the rightness of things was required, the little face smiling back at us through the car window was all we needed.

'Todo, I think you were as much the star of the show as Carol tonight. Thank you for helping us come here.'

Halfway home, Lawrence's mobile rang. As he listened his smile faded and his face filled with concern. 'When's the next flight? Was yours cancelled or did you miss it?' One of his young singers was due to travel from London to Lyon but something had gone wrong at Heathrow; it was difficult to understand exactly what through her tears and the poor telephone reception.

We rushed home so that he could call more easily. It was a difficult conversation, not least because she had already tried phoning several times but with no success, so panic had set in. Lawrence managed to calm her and sort the problem out, but our blissful mood evaporated completely. The whole episode exposed just how out of touch we were. It was all very well to revel in living our Italian dream but in between the highs there were the stressful lows. We were still without a landline, in spite of Lawrence's numerous calls to Telecom Italia, and this lack of communication became increasingly burdensome as each day passed. We were just a two-hour flight from London, yet a world away. Our livelihood depended on our being at the other end of the phone or having instant access to email, and in that we were failing miserably.

11

Our Very First Mazurka

We had been trying to push our anxiety over the communications problems to the backs of our minds for weeks when that late-night phone call left us feeling ruffled; but our worries were about to get much worse.

The following morning I woke late after a disturbed night's sleep and wandered downstairs to see what everyone was up to. Roberto was fixing power sockets in what had been Jim's rooms but would become our office, once the dividing wall had been taken out and the longed-for wiring was up and running. The others were cutting through terrace tiles at the side of the house, where the leak had finally been located. To replace the existing pipework would be time-consuming and expensive so a new one was being laid, fractionally cheaper but still threatening to take us well over budget. As the family accountant, I knew – but hadn't yet told Lawrence – that we were going to have to find more money from somewhere.

He was already at work in the temporary office, amid the blue chintz of Carol's old rooms. I put my head around the corner to say hello, only to find him staring blankly at the mailbox on his computer screen. Something was wrong.

'One of my conductors has emailed; he's leaving the agency. He thinks the move to Italy has been disadvantageous for us and therefore, of course, for him.'

Lawrence spoke quietly; he looked dazed. I reached for his hand.

Clients go and new clients come, we both know that's the way it is for a company like ours. In our ten years as a business we'd been lucky, suffering far less changeover than many other agencies. Some of our existing artists had been with us since the very beginning. But inevitably some move on. Lawrence has always taken such events calmly and philosophically in the past, so I was shocked to hear how gloomy he sounded this time.

'The thing is, Lou, I think he's being unfair in going at this stage. We've done well for him in the last couple of years and the next twelve months are pretty full too; he's got debuts in Spain and France and a tour at home. But he doesn't think I've been as attentive as I should have been since we came here – and the trouble is, I know he's right. I'd like to explain to him that we've had problems but they'll be fixed soon but, you know, I'm beginning to doubt it myself.'

It was unnerving seeing him so low; he was usually the one geeing me up when things didn't go well. I did my best to sound optimistic. 'Most of our clients have been great about the move, haven't they?'

'Yes, but how many of them are having secret doubts? They all know that getting hold of us on the phone or by email is more difficult at the moment, and we're not always able to be in touch as regularly as we were in London. If we don't get a proper phone and Internet connection soon, we're going to lose more of them.'

'Why don't we go into Lucca and see Manuela again, to find out how things stand with the phone line?'

'I'm not sure I can face another visit there today. In any case, all she said last time was that she would try. That was weeks ago and there's been nothing since. The last time I phoned Telecom Italia they didn't even know who we were.'

There was no cheering him. And I found it hard to sound convincingly upbeat. We both knew that the technical problems were crippling us. Though neither of us said it, the fear that we would never be able to work effectively from Italy was feeling increasingly real. And if we couldn't run our business, we would have to re-think everything.

I looked at Todo, sitting patiently beside us. To leave him would be unbearable.

Lawrence's mood didn't improve when an hour or so later Roberto told us he'd have to hack into the walls of the new office to install the casings for the telephone extension. Lawrence sighed, then swore – universal language which everyone understood. Roberto slipped out of the room and Daniele, passing by the open door, smiled sympathetically as Lawrence said bleakly, 'What's the point anyway? There'll never be a telephone line for it to carry.'

Our evening walk with Todo cheered us a little. The heat was cooling and he trotted close beside us, straying less frequently than usual. He always loved to investigate sounds and smells, to say hello to Bella the horse and her sheep pals. Normally he would criss-cross the road, tempted by the cluck of a chicken on one side, or the scent of a dog on the other.

But tonight he remained with us, as if he felt it his duty to keep an eye on us in our hour of need.

'Bless you, Todo,' I whispered, stroking his head, as Lawrence announced, a little more cheerfully, that he would light the barbecue when we got home. 'I think you've managed to brighten him up.'

Todo responded with an appreciative wag of his tail, and was rewarded a little later with a couple of stray sausages from the evening meal. But even he couldn't entirely lift the melancholy that had descended on Lawrence in the wake of his client's defection. It was as if all his worst fears were coming true.

That night neither of us slept well. I'm not sure Lawrence slept at all. I woke frequently to see him sitting, head in hands, on the side of the bed or pacing in and out of the room. After waking for the fourth time, at 4.30 a.m., I stopped checking the clock and eventually drifted into a light sleep.

A shrill squealing noise roused me, hours later, and I turned to see Lawrence dragging himself out of bed. 'What the hell is that?'

We had no builders coming until later that day, as they had to collect materials, so I had hoped we might make up for lost sleep with a later start. I peered at the clock. It was just before eight.

The squealing continued.

'It's coming from the sitting-room,' said Lawrence. 'I'll go and check.'

He plodded downstairs and I stared after him, my sleepy brain only half engaged. It sounded like . . .

'Oh my God. Lawrence . . .' I shrieked. 'It's a PHONE!'

Suddenly awake, I shot out of bed and after him in time to hear him pick up the receiver on the handset in the sitting-room.

'Hello. I mean . . . *pronto*.'

There was a few seconds' pause.

'No, I'm sorry, Signora MacAndrew is not here.'

What on earth was going on? Was this some other-worldly call for a deceased woman on a phone that had no connection?

There was another, longer pause, followed by Lawrence's '*Sì*' twice, and then '*Buon giorno*.'

He put down the receiver and turned to me, a mixture of delight and disbelief on his face.

'That was Telecom Italia; they wanted me to let Carol know they've re-installed her phone line.'

Lawrence was like a child in a sweet shop. He spent the next few hours calling as many friends as possible to inform them we were connected and give out our new *Italian* phone number. His excitement almost boiled over when, later in the day, the same shrill squeal rang out again.

This time he was ready. '*Pronto!*'

'Er, no Signora MacAndrew is . . . not here now.'

'Well it's not actually a lie, is it?' he whispered, hand over the mouthpiece as I rolled my eyes. '*Non, grazie*, we already have another company to provide our Internet but thank you for asking.'

'Typical!' He put the phone down indignantly. 'The first call and it's a sales one.'

Why the telephone line had been reinstated neither of us could work out. Perhaps they'd finally taken pity on us. The fact that the line was in Carol's name and not ours didn't worry us at all. It was a phone line – more precious to us at that stage than our own weight in gold. It was only one piece of the jigsaw – we still needed the Internet – but it was a big piece.

Lawrence thought we should go into Lucca to thank

Manuela, but while I appreciated his considerate wish to thank her in person, I suggested that, given how much we had to do, a phone call might suffice.

As he hummed cheerfully over the goat's cheese salad he was making for lunch, the despair of the day before was forgotten. It was always the way with Lawrence; his moods changed as fast as the Italian weather, when a morning of brilliant sunshine would be swept away within minutes by a tropical downpour and gale-force winds, to be replaced in turn by a warm and mellow evening.

I often found it a little harder to recover my equilibrium and I couldn't quite shake the image of him sitting, head in hands, on the edge of our bed. The contradiction kept re-presenting itself: that our very ability to continue in this paradise and make it a success depended on our business – at least from the outside looking in – changing very little, when in reality change was all around us. Could we square this circle?

And then there was the money, which we were spending at an increasingly alarming rate. The overspend on the house was heading towards €10,000 and I had no idea where we were going to find it. Every time Daniele suggested that a really skilled colleague of his could come and repair the glass in the summer house, or an expert in intricate wrought-iron work would be the best man to make the new dining-room windows, I winced. When Daniele told us, 'Yes it'll cost more but you'll appreciate the extra quality,' I knew he was right. He and the other builders were doing a brilliant job and the house would be lovely. It was just that we couldn't afford it!

Each bill that arrived was a little higher than the budget we'd put aside for it. The process of receiving and paying bills was itself charming; Daniele would sit us down, going through everything line by line, detailing that this material had proved more expensive, but he'd not needed an extra builder so we'd saved there. Then at the end, after we'd handed over the full amount, he would count it all slowly and methodically, so that I found myself mouthing the numbers along with him, after which, grinning delightedly, he would round it down to the nearest hundred and hand anything over back to us, as if it was we, and not the workers, who had earned a bonus.

'Two thousand, four hundred and sixty-seven Euros: here, you take the sixty-seven, go and have a nice dinner!' Or, 'Lorenzo, a new tie!', 'Luisa, a pair of earrings.'

It was a delightful way of doing business, a win-win style that left both sides feeling valued and appreciated. But sadly the 'extras' that Daniele handed back weren't going to cover the shortfall we needed. It seemed that while yesterday had been Lawrence's low point, today it was my turn to panic. I couldn't stop weighing up everything we now had to lose.

In so many ways our Great Italian Adventure had been good for us. Lawrence especially had adapted seamlessly to our new life and seemed to fit in, and not just because of his rapidly improving language skills. He was one of the lads with Daniele and crew, at ease chatting and making little jokes, as though he'd known them for years. It was the same wherever we went; at the supermarket he joked with the cashiers – 'We're English, we need chips!' – and in the *agraria* he and Beppe shared their hopes and aspirations for Liverpool and AC Milan in the forthcoming football season. He'd taken to everything: the weather, the pace of life, the food and of course the three daily newspapers devoted entirely to sport. I found myself speculating there'd been some Italian connection long ago in his ancestry, maybe a seventeenth-century nobleman who followed one of the famous composers to London or perhaps a silk merchant who found himself at the great port of Liverpool on business one day and with time on his hands one evening . . .

Settling in had been harder for me. I still missed things about London: pottering around the West End and a really good department store, catching the 88 bus to see a film in Leicester Square in a language I knew, and the ease of old friendships. Slowly and surely though, the Italian way of doing things was becoming familiar and it felt more and more like home. It was hard won, and it made me proud of myself, and of us. I couldn't bear to lose all that we had achieved.

And then of course there was Todo. He had given us a purpose above and beyond a change in our way of living. We had grown to love him, he needed us, and I knew we needed him too – he had become our reason to go on when things got tough, and his sweetness and trust always comforted us if we were down.

We had to make it work, I knew that. What we needed – at this moment, anyway – was the Internet and ten thousand euros.

Lawrence didn't get involved in the money side more than was absolutely necessary, mainly because he hated dealing with it and struggled to take it seriously. Our accountant still recoils in horror when telling stories of him arriving at their smart offices with a plastic bag of assorted receipts. But although I managed the day-to-day budget, when it came to the big stuff – decisions that affected our lifestyle and business – we had always made them together. Sitting in the sun on the terrace, while the glow of the newly acquired phone line was still making all things seem possible, I raised the subject of our finances.

Lawrence didn't blanch and his calm helped to reassure me. He suggested we see our always helpful Turkish bank manager back in London on our next trip. The idea of a loan didn't appeal but he was right that on paper at least our finances looked better, and as he'd been with the bank for twenty years, he felt sure they would help.

From time to time I would take out Carol's papers and envy the way she and Jim lived without money worries. Her day-to-day accounting had been meticulous, all income and outgoings were noted in her tiny, neat handwriting. Every month showed a surplus, even after treating herself to a shopping trip to Florence or Milan or throwing a lavish party for forty people at Poggiolino. She had good financial sense and it was to prove invaluable in the last three years of her life, when she could afford round-the-clock care from three private nurses and, of course, from Teresa who supervised the whole process and took on a great deal of responsibility so that Carol would be saved the indignity of going into a nursing home.

Reading through these financial records, I sighed. If only our situation seemed as straightforward. It sometimes felt as though we lived on a knife edge, relying on so many uncertain factors, from the future of our business to the cost of air travel and our ability to learn fully-functioning Italian.

As I sat in the blue chintz office pondering these imponderables, I heard the gentle tick-tick of Todo's paws on the tiles in the hallway and a moment later his sweet face pushed open the door. He looked at me expectantly before coming over and pressing gently against my side.

I smiled and stroked his head. He knew when it was time for his evening walk. But more than that, he knew when one of us was down, and his constant presence and unwavering affection sometimes felt like the only absolutes in a world of chaos.

I stood up. 'Come on, let's hit the hills.' Todo's tail went into overdrive and together we went to find his lead and call Lawrence.

As we walked my spirits lifted. Who could remain burdened with cares in the face of that stunning view? I thought about Todo, and how much he had taught us. Not least, the value of distractions. For him this was usually finding the last bone he'd buried – *Did I leave it under the seventy-sixth olive tree or the seventy-seventh?* – or chasing his tail on the grass in the afternoon sun. Like him, I decided, we needed something to take our mind off the chaos of our unfinished house and unresolved work problems.

I turned to Lawrence. 'What about a night out?'

'Nice idea. Why don't we try Daniele's Sagra? I think it's this weekend.'

Over the previous weeks we had seen signs posted on the roadside for various Sagras. Each one had a food in the title, as in Sagra di Zuppa di Frantoiana or Sagra di Funghi Porcini. Unable to find the word in any dictionary, Lawrence had asked Daniele what they were. 'Ah, they are festivals of food, music and dancing. Everyone from the local area joins in and they all have a good time. We have one in my village Gallicano, the Sagra di Rigatoni.'

When we got home from the walk we checked. Yes, the Gallicano Sagra was on Saturday, two days away. Food, music, dancing; could one ask for more?

With something to look forward to I felt brighter, and by Saturday evening the excitement was growing. We set off, leaving Todo with a couple of extra biscuits as compensation for not taking him, and followed the signs to Gallicano, which took us some way off the main road. With the light fading, we could barely see the signs, but eventually we reached an expanse of red tape slung between metal poles, indicating the car park.

Heading towards the sound of music and voices we turned

a corner to discover a magical scene. The local park, small and very ordinary by day, had been transformed with coloured lights strung between the trees, bunting, balloons and long trestle tables covered with bright cloths. The backdrop of the dark woods behind the park made the lights glow even more brightly; the whole picture was enchanting.

Though quite early, the place was already packed, the crowd ranging from young children rushing around, trying to persuade mothers or grandmothers that candyfloss was absolutely essential, to elderly couples dressed smartly but casually and taking up the spot they'd had since the first Sagra, over twenty summers ago.

As outsiders, we felt a little shy as we stood on the fringes. This was not a tourist event, but a true village celebration.

'Come, come,' a smiling woman beckoned us over. 'Sit, take some food, enjoy.'

It took us a while to work out how to do things. We learned, after wandering around for a bit, that you didn't pay for food where it was served. To speed things up you had to queue at the log cabin, tell them what you wanted, pay and get a succession of tickets which you then redeemed at the serving hatches.

The food at Sagras is simple but delicious; the signature dish generally just one of several starters and the main courses usually comprising of roast pork, sausages or steak grilled over open fires of olive wood. Neither of us could remember anything like it, though Lawrence talked, a little wistfully, of hotpot suppers at the church hall in Huyton where he grew up, followed by a local folk group, kitted out in cable-knit sweaters, fingers in ears, trolling nasally through ancient sea-shanties or tales of lasses, shepherds and unrequited love.

Here we had Sylvia and her Red Hot Orchestra! During the summer months, the roads and motorways of Italy are filled with battered transit vans crammed with a singer, several band members plus instruments and PA system, the livery announcing *Live Music, Live Dancing!* The term *orchestra*, we soon discovered, was defined somewhat liberally: not a violin or contra-bassoon in sight. Instead there were two guitars, keyboard, bass, drummer and one other, whose role encompassed tambourine shaking, handclapping and occasionally a burst on an out-of-tune trumpet.

Sylvia would haunt my dreams for some time to come. Pushing fifty – and none too slowly – the gold lamé hot-pants she squeezed into might have been a good fit thirty years earlier but now strained at the seams to contain her ample curves.

As for her voice, I'm not sure she would have got past the first round of *X Factor*, but what she lacked in accuracy she more than made up for with her spirit and enthusiasm. Starting out flat, her voice would sink lower and lower, until she and the band were in different keys altogether. Then she'd clap hands above her head, unleash what appeared to be a star-jump, yell 'Hey!' and resume the song somewhere near the original bum note. But did anyone care? Not a bit. The music played, the lights twinkled, the food was delicious and the mood joyous. And as soon as everyone had eaten, chairs were pushed back and the dancing began.

This was where we really came into our own: several months of ballroom dancing lessons finally paid off. I had always wanted to learn, and when we took on a client two years earlier who was a professional dancer, I became even more determined. Watching him and his partner glide around the room at star-studded events, wearing stunning outfits and making it look effortless, I felt embarrassed that we couldn't attempt a single step.

I had broached the issue with Lawrence one wet weekend.

'Can we go to ballroom dancing classes?'

'Hmmm, I'm not sure I fancy that.'

I was ready. 'It's up to you,' I smiled sweetly, 'but bear in mind that if you don't come with me, the marriage is over.'

'Well, cha-cha here we come!'

I found a teacher, Douglas, and before long we were kicking lumps out of each other in a studio in North London, lacking style, grace, finesse and indeed any semblance of talent, but enjoying ourselves. Over the course of several months we wrecked every dance known to man; we waltzed in four rather than three, our jive owed more to Johnny Rotten than John Travolta, our quickstep was too slow and our foxtrot too fast. But Douglas had the patience of a saint and we stuck with it, and in the end we did at least master the basics.

And now, finally, our moment had come! As we finished our last sip of wine, we rose to our feet and strode with purpose to the dance area – a tarmac circle in the middle of the park.

'Cry God for Harry, England and St George,' yelled Lawrence as he whisked me onto the floor to begin our first ever public foxtrot.

I wish I could claim a perfect ten from all four judges but, in truth, *Strictly* this was not. Our greatest achievement was avoiding trampling each other or our fellow dancers.

We arrived, breathless and laughing, back at our seats. 'Was that as bad as I think it was?' I panted.

'Worse, I suspect.'

'I don't know why the Fred and Ginger moves in my head don't quite translate to my feet. I think it's because I some-times get confused between left and right. Or perhaps it's my shoes. Or the wine.'

Lawrence grinned. 'Or maybe . . . face it, Lou, we're rubbish. But who cares? Let's tango!'

We did, with vigour, our energetic performance every bit a match for Sylvia, strutting her not inconsiderable stuff on stage. Luckily no serious injuries were sustained and Lawrence had mastered the art of dragging me away from the racks of speakers just before Sylvia went for the big-finish high note. As it rang out, I suspected even Todo could hear it five miles away, and I imagined him in his room, paws over ears and head under the blanket.

As the evening wore on, the wine flowing and more dancers joining the throng, we no longer felt like the worst dancers there as we swirled around the floor, heady with success. We even managed a perfectly (well, almost) co-ordinated New Yorker step during our rumba: '. . . *two, three, four, out; two, three, four, in* . . .' Lawrence whispered, 'Douglas would be proud!'

We paused for coffee and grappa and then danced on until the crowds began to disperse and it was time to go home. Arms draped around one another in a final waltz – or was Lawrence just propping me up? – I looked around at the beautiful setting and the people of all ages enjoying simple pleasures and thought, *This is why we came to Italy*.

As always, the moment we opened the front door, Todo rushed out to greet us. I tried to explain to him about our night out, but I sensed I didn't have his undivided attention when he turned his back on me to sniff greedily around my handbag where I had the remnants of two Tuscan sausages tucked into a napkin. I'd planned to give him one and keep the other for breakfast. But confronted by his most winning expression – all big eyes and pleading looks, with just a hint of a desperate whimper escaping his trembling lips – I caved in and gave him both.

Meanwhile Lawrence was quickstepping round the kitchen.

'Let's go to the Sagra at Aquilea next weekend. Vegetable soup!'

We did, and we loved it just as much. Visiting Sagras became one of the highlights of our summer, then and each successive year; a wonderful way to relax and enjoy ourselves and forget about our worries.

Our dancing improved with practice and we felt quite proud of ourselves. But there was one dance which was beyond us. We watched poised Italian couples swirling and spinning their way through what seemed to be a very fast Viennese waltz and longed to have a go, but to our untutored eyes it looked alarmingly difficult. Still, we promised ourselves we'd pluck up the courage to try it one day, and eventually, after three years, just before we were due to leave the Sagra in Aquilea, we heard the orchestra strike up the quick three tempo and looked at one another.

'Come on, this is it,' Lawrence said, grabbing my arm. 'Now or never.'

We hit the dance floor and were off. Five minutes later, after what felt like a major cardio workout, we whirled to a grand and flourishing finish.

'*Bene, bravi,* very good. Well done.' It was the voice of one of our neighbours, Claudia.

We laughed. We had done it – our very first mazurka.

12

I Think La Signora Would Be Very Happy

That was all in the future. Back in June 2007, our first outing to a Sagra had lifted our spirits but not magicked away our Internet problems. Lawrence, our one-man IT department, was still on the case.

'Yes, I've tried all that but still nothing. It's definitely right at your end, is it?'

He was in the middle of a prolonged technical conversation with our Internet provider. His third or fourth that day. And while I couldn't make out the detail, the gist was easy to follow, not least because of the increasingly agitated look on Lawrence's face.

'*Grazie, arrivederci.*' As he put down the phone he shook his head. 'They're as puzzled as I am about why it won't work, but apparently an engineer will be with us tomorrow to run a check on the line and equipment.'

We both knew that if the Internet company was anything like the phone one, it was unlikely that they would actually show up the next day. We just had to hope that 'tomorrow' meant sometime reasonably soon.

In the meantime, and partly as a distraction from telecom issues, Lawrence started on the task of removing the frankly hideous wallpaper from Carol's room in readiness for its conversion into the guest bedroom. Our office was moving to Jim's old room, where the interconnecting wall between bed and bathroom had now been removed, creating a bright, double-windowed room with an inviting view of the olive grove next to ours.

We had always known that getting the wallpaper off would be a challenge, but it was only when Lawrence started that we began to realise quite what we were up against. Not only was the thick, blue chintzy paper over absolutely every surface, but . . .

'Oh my God, there's newspaper underneath it.'

Lawrence had painstakingly scraped off a few inches of the blue stuff, only to find that the walls had been lined with newspaper which, over the years, had almost merged into the plaster work, forming a seal so strong that, as we soon found, no amount of steaming and scraping would shift it.

Lawrence stood back, hands on hips. 'It's like Carol. Tough, stubborn and doesn't want to be moved.'

One by one, each of the builders came in to investigate, lured by the sound of vociferous swearing. Picking up a scraper, each one had a try for a few minutes before puffing, shrugging his shoulders and leaving Lawrence to it. 'Italians don't use wallpaper,' said Daniele helpfully, pausing a moment to read the sports page of the 1975 *Corriere* and smiling when he saw that Inter Milan had won that Sunday.

Lawrence descended the stepladder and surveyed the very small amount of paper lying at his feet. 'Is that all I've got to show for the past two hours? We'll never get it off.'

Todo nosed the offending material which had lined the walls of his beloved mistress's room. It was in this room that she had died in June 2005, the same night she was released after a brief stay in hospital.

Teresa always spoke in hushed tones when describing the final events of Carol's life. She had fought valiantly, but eventually her doctor informed Albertina that nothing more could be done, and advised she return to Poggiolino. Albertina phoned Teresa to tell her La Signora would be coming home. Knowing that Carol was close to the end, Teresa dismissed the nurses. 'La Signora wanted privacy and only her friends.'

The nurses had always shooed Todo from the house, believing that it wasn't hygienic to have an animal around a sick person. So he'd spent a lot of time outside, only slipping into Carol's room in rare moments. Now that they had gone, Teresa welcomed him inside and told him that his mistress would be home soon.

She had prepared a light supper, and after they had eaten Albertina and Teresa helped Carol to bed. Settling onto fresh pillows she smiled and uttered one word, 'Todo?' In seconds he was at her side, delighted to be allowed there again as Carol stretched out her hand to him.

As Albertina left, she said, 'Teresa, do you want me to come and sit with her tomorrow morning?'

She shook her head, 'No, Signora Albertina, I will take care of everything.'

Teresa stayed for another couple of hours, busying herself with some cleaning and tidying, but in truth just biding her time until she could be sure that Carol was no longer awake. Checking every few minutes on the darkened room she would gently ask, '*Signora, ancora sveglia?*' Are you still awake? Then, as Todo raised his head, '*Totino, tutto bene?*' Little Todo, all OK?

When she was absolutely sure Carol had fallen asleep, she went to the side of the bed, '*Buona notte, Signora.*' She patted Todo. 'Good boy.'

At 7.30 a.m. the following morning, as she had very nearly every morning for the last thirty years, Teresa slipped through the gate to Poggiolino. It was a perfect Compitese day; the summer sun already warm in an unbroken blue sky, the only sound the birdsong coming from the olive trees, their branches laden with fruit – the sort of day La Signora adored.

Unlocking the shutters and door to the *cucina di cane*, Teresa stopped there for a moment, listening. There was no sound at all and she nodded. Although she knocked at La Signora's door it was only out of respect, because she knew no answer would come.

'She looked so peaceful, just as I'd left her, asleep, her hand still resting on Todo's head.'

I was deeply moved to think that Todo had been the one to remain with Carol at the moment of her parting. He and Teresa had been faithful to the end. Now, standing in Carol's old room, I bent to hug the dog she had loved so much. Todo's instinct for cheering us up kicked in and he returned my affection, licking my hands.

The following day the doorbell rang, sending Todo scurrying out to the gates, where a van had parked. Lawrence went to speak with the two men who got out. 'You're here to check the line? Great, come in.'

'Where is it?' asked one of the engineers, brusquely.

Lawrence pointed to the telephone socket but the man shook his head. 'No, I need the point where the line enters the house.'

A search ensued, headed by Lawrence who would occasionally break an increasingly stony silence with, 'Well, it's got to be here somewhere!'

Roberto, who was working on sockets for bedside lights in Carol's room, pointed out that the telephone cable ended at the large pole immediately outside, so it must come in through the wall of her room.

The two of us, three builders and both engineers began scouring the walls, feeling across the expanse of blue for any sign of a telephone point. After twenty minutes we were in despair, especially Lawrence who feared the engineers might leave at any moment.

Todo came to the rescue. I don't know if a biscuit had dropped in that exact spot, or whether he really understood our predicament, but he started sniffing and scraping at the skirting under the window. Roberto saw him first and, bending over, cried out '*Ecco là*. The dog's found it!' We really shouldn't have been surprised at the sight before us; the plate covering the wiring had fallen victim to the same blue wallpaper. Carol was nothing if not thorough.

The joke was lost on our two engineers who went to work, one inside the other out. A few minutes later they announced portentously, 'We will have to return.'

'Of course you will,' Lawrence muttered.

As they roared off down the road we both worried that they might never appear again, especially as they hadn't given us a date for their next visit. But to our delight, their grumpy faces peered at us from over the front gates only two days later. Stepping over the piles of dislodged plaster – Roberto was finishing the casings ready to carry the line from the back of the house to the new office – they made their way to Carol's room where for the next hour there followed a scratch of the head, a stroke of the chin, much tapping of the box and testing with multimeters, until one of them suddenly got in the van and drove off.

The other pulled at the wires protruding from the box, staring intently at the thick copper he held in his hands.

'Looking at it won't make it come back to life,' Lawrence managed, through gritted teeth.

The van re-appeared and the two men stood on the terrace by the front door staring at the sky as if looking for divine inspiration.

'That's it,' said the first one. They hadn't introduced themselves and not even Daniele knew their names.

'That's it; it's fixed?'

I thought Lawrence would explode.

'No, not fixed. The fault is in the cable coming from the junction box down the hill.'

'Great, so you can fix it now?'

The engineer began shaking his head ominously. Then there was a sharp intake of breath. What is it with the sharp intake of breath? It transcends all boundaries, be they land, language or nationality. Is it part of the basic training to become a builder, engineer or plumber?

Then, '*Ah buon giorno, Marco!*' came a familiar voice.

'*Signora Teresa, buon giorno, come va?*'

'Very well, Marco, how is Giovanna?'

I don't know why I was surprised Teresa knew the telephone engineer. She seemed to know everyone in the immediate area and they her; then again she had lived there all of her married life and before that in the neighbouring valley.

Marco introduced his colleague, Alessandro, and the three chatted amiably for some minutes, after which Teresa, perhaps reading the despair on our faces, appeared to ask questions and Marco and Alessandro pointed to various parts of the house's exterior.

By the time Teresa had finished, Marco was a different man.

'Of course we can do it today. It'll take a couple of hours but Sandro's the best we have. Then we'll test it and I'm sure it'll work before we leave. If your Internet company is good you should be connected by tomorrow.'

He only narrowly avoided a hug from Lawrence, not normally the most effusive of men.

'You know, La Signora was the first person here to ever have a telephone line?' said Teresa as we walked together into the house. It was an extraordinary thought. At the same time as this momentous event in San Francesco, England was enjoying The Beatles and Enfield became the first London suburb to have an ATM machine installed. By all accounts the arrival of the phone line had been something of a local celebration; the whole process only completed on the third day, having required the erection of a completely new telegraph pole. All the villagers took turns to wander up the hill and marvel at this modernity and Carol even invited some favoured ones in for a demonstration. Previously each village in Italy had a local telephone point, often attached to the Post Office, where residents would go to make calls. Everyone had to queue, waiting their turn to call family in Milan or Sicily, or maybe even abroad, and while they chatted the village would be usefully informed of all their news.

As Teresa continued with the story, it became clear that the phone was not the only innovation Carol had introduced to San Francesco. 'She was the first to have water from the mains; imagine not having to draw it up by hand!'

What must the local people have made of all this? It reminded me of one of Carol's photos, large crates of olives being carried away from the villa on a wooden cart . . . pulled by a donkey! Running water, international telephone calls, glamorous parties and Hermès scarves but a biblical animal still needed to help at the end of the olive harvest. Mercifully, perhaps, La Signora hadn't quite managed to modernise everything.

The next morning, Lawrence went to the new telephone socket and plugged in the ADSL cable and then the broadband router. Daniele and Roberto stopped work and came to stand next to him; all three of them staring at the little grey box sitting next to one of our computers. The first blinking green light came on, then the second – the line was installed. Moments later a third indicated the ADSL was functional, then after an agonising wait, the fourth light blinked on. We were connected.

'Call the neighbours, haul out the bunting; we have the Internet!'

We settled for handshakes all round, as we connected our equipment to the magic grey box.

'Look, Todo; it's the Internet!' Lawrence pointed to the router, but Todo was having none of it. Modern technology could wait – he wanted breakfast.

For two days we immersed ourselves in a backlog of emails and calls. Oh the bliss of seeing our in-boxes full again and revelling in emails pinging back and forth. Lawrence had to stop me from hitting 'Send and Receive' just for the hell of it. But as the end of the week approached we downed wallpaper scrapers and computer keyboards to smarten ourselves up for a lunch date with Albertina and the Handts.

Albertina's house, a restored hay barn just down the hill, was a triumph of architecture and style. The outside had been painted a vivid yellow, and inside we were astonished to find a central atrium with a ceiling three floors high. The sitting- and dining-rooms were on the ground floor with a wrought-iron staircase leading to the next two floors, bedrooms opening off an internal balcony circling the atrium.

We were delighted to discover that Teresa had been invited as chef for the day. During the laughter and greetings that followed, we learned that Albertina always engaged someone to cook for her guests, and of course there could only be one person who was perfect for today's gathering.

Maestro Handt and Laura arrived shortly after us and I noticed how warmly they greeted Teresa.

Herbert, smartly dressed in a green tweed jacket and brown fedora, pulled Lawrence to one side. 'I'm so pleased a musician has bought Carol's house. Tell me what you thought of the memorial concert.'

As they discussed the wonderful tenor's high C and legato line, Laura sat beside me on Albertina's elegant sofa. 'So, do you like it in Carol's house?'

Her voice was a rich American drawl and in a full-length black skirt and fitted velvet jacket, her grey hair elegantly short, she cut a glamorous figure.

The conversation over lunch was punctuated by laughter, especially from Albertina, who sat at the head of the table puffing on her favourite cigarettes while stories were swapped. As Teresa brought out one delicious course after another, we learned more about each of these three feisty octogenarians, and their relationship with Carol.

We had thought that Carol had co-founded the Music Society but Herbert politely but firmly corrected this misunderstanding. 'I first met her in 1960 when we moved from Rome to Lucca,' he said. 'When I formed the Music Society I realised we needed some help and asked her to become the first president.'

Prior to that, Herbert, Philadelphia born then Juilliard

trained, had been a successful tenor, singing in great opera houses from Vienna to New York, Milan and Chicago. Turning his hand to conducting, he worked with the famous Toscanini and performed with all the major opera companies in Italy. After settling in Lucca he set about transforming the music scene there, running opera festivals at many of the wonderful villas in the region.

'Without Carol we wouldn't have been so successful,' he said. 'She knew everybody there was to know and helped us raise money. But she never interfered with my artistic planning.'

'No one would dare,' chimed in Albertina. 'Not even Carol!'

Teresa placed a mouth-watering joint of pork on the table, with dishes of cheese-infused polenta and a fresh salad. I wondered, was she pleased to hear us discussing La Signora, and perhaps a little sad? Her features gave nothing away, as she slipped back into the kitchen.

Lawrence asked about the beautiful painting of Carol reproduced on the front cover of the Memorial Concert programme.

'That was one of mine,' Laura smiled.

'Goodness, I thought you were a sculptor.'

'Well I am mostly, but I like to paint whenever I can and Carol was a very good subject.'

'Did you ever paint Todo?' I enquired. Everyone laughed but Laura told us she had, in fact, painted and sculpted dogs, including two Dalmatians she and Herbert once owned.

Laura too, had made the pilgrimage to Italy. She had arrived in Rome in 1949 as a Fulbright Scholar, to study with the great Pericle Fazzini. She was delighted when Lawrence told her we had seen Fazzini's masterpiece 'Monument to the Italian Resistance' on a trip to Ancona.

'He did that much later, in fact after we moved here,' she said.

Laura's own work had been exhibited throughout Italy and America and she reeled off, in a matter-of-fact manner, a few of the private collectors who had bought her works.

'Oh . . . Rockefeller' – 'JD and Nelson,' interjected Herbert – 'Thomas Messer, he became Director of the Guggenheim the year we moved to Lucca, and a few others.' She had also been taken up in England by the esteemed Jacob Epstein and befriended Henry Moore.

It was an extraordinary catalogue of achievement. She told us she'd had a studio in the orangery at the imposing Palazzo Pfanner, immediately within the city walls, which had been renovated for her. But after the buzz of Rome she'd felt lonely and isolated, so moved to a studio in nearby Pietrasanta, a renowned centre for sculptors and artisans.

I listened transfixed by their stories: what extraordinary lives they'd lived. My mind wandered to a favourite film, *The Talented Mr Ripley*, about glamorous young Americans living in Italy in the fifties, drawn by the wonders of old Europe. Herbert and Laura, Carol and Jim had done it for real, and had beaten a path we were following fifty years later.

'Albertina, how is the house in Bologna?' asked Herbert.

'I was there just last week; it's always so nice to get away.'

House in Bologna, I thought, *as well as a Rome apartment and this place! She certainly is the daughter of a princess.*

Teresa put a rich peach tart and a bottle of chilled sweet wine on the table and Albertina poured generous measures. 'To Carol,' she toasted, 'without whom we wouldn't be enjoying each other's charming company!'

I hesitated. 'Where is Carol buried?'

'Oh, in San Martino,' Albertina replied. 'Alongside Jim. They were so devoted to each other.' She raised her glass once more. 'To Jim, he gave us all so much fun.'

'We'd love to know more about him,' I ventured.

'Jim was a lovely man,' said Herbert, 'the most gentle and refined fellow you could hope to meet. He never did learn to speak Italian, but he managed to communicate with everyone.'

'He was talented too,' Laura continued. 'He had been a successful commercial artist back in the States but do you know he was almost completely colour-blind?'

'There were a couple of paintings of his left in the house,' Lawrence said. 'We've kept them on the walls.'

'Oh, Carol would be so pleased to know his work was still on show.'

'He was the most tremendous support to dear Carol,' Albertina said. 'She may have been the fine hostess, the one with her name in the press and on the Music Society note-paper, but I don't think she could have done it without him. He'd often be on the end of her scolding but she appreciated all he did for her. It's so sad he left her so early; twenty years is a long time to be without your closest companion.'

As the meal drew to a close, two things happened which were to delight and intrigue us – as well as solving a mystery which had been puzzling us since the dinner at Teresa's.

Laura touched me on the arm. 'Teresa's very fond of you.'

Her comment warmed my heart. Teresa was a woman who would give her approval only after careful appraisal, so to hear that she liked us meant a great deal.

Albertina had heard and she laughed. 'Well, of course, she liked you from the very first day. She saw the way you fussed over Todo when you came to see the house and she called me immediately after you left. *A very nice English couple has just been to Poggiolino. They were kind and gentle with Todo and he liked them. I think La Signora would be very happy.* Well I knew what I had to do, so I phoned Marcello, the President to tell him, *if they put in a good offer, it's what Carol would have wanted and what Teresa would like.*'

So that was what Albertina had meant, when she said we had Teresa to thank!

There are many factors that can affect the outcome when you set out to change your life but for us, it seemed, the most significant had been the opinion of our dream house's former owner's housekeeper, and her dog.

As we said our goodbyes I spotted Teresa, standing at the kitchen door removing her apron, her eyes dancing and the largest smile I'd yet seen illuminating her face.

13

Summer Holidays – For Some

We spent a couple of days basking in the happy glow left by our delightful lunch at Albertina's, not to mention the huge relief occasioned by our triumphant rejoining of the Internet-connected world. But lurking in the back of my mind was the thought of the €10,000 gap in our finances; and of course the blue paper still mocked us, stubbornly clinging to the walls of Carol's room. After several days of cursing, pulling, yanking and, occasionally, kicking, Lawrence realised he was never going to get it off with a scraper.

The builders looked on with some amusement as attempts to dislodge the layers welded to the walls resulted variously in dismal failure, a round of expletives and a red-faced Lawrence stomping out of the room swearing never to attempt another decorating job in his life.

'It's not as though I haven't done this sort of thing before,' he grumbled. And he was right; in our London house we'd had plenty of experience of stripping walls. More, in fact, than either of us ever cared to remember. But we'd never come across anything like this. 'What did they put it on with,' he snorted. 'Superglue?'

'We need a wallpaper stripper,' I suggested helpfully.

'Fine,' Lawrence sighed. 'Goodness knows where we'll get one of those.'

We set out to find one, but as virtually nobody in Italy uses wallpaper, our quest was in vain. After a long, hot and fruitless afternoon, we decided we would have to bring one over from England. We were due to make a short trip back – our second – the following week.

This time, although it was hard to leave Todo, we were less worried, as we were only going for three days, and in any case the builders would be in the house, so for much of the time he wouldn't be alone.

The stripper – one we'd been assured could remove absolutely any paper from any wall – proved a horribly awkward object to pack. In the end it took up most of our suitcase, and all of the baggage allowance, leaving us to cram our clothes and papers into the few spare inches of space.

Once again Todo gave us a glorious welcome, and this time we rewarded him with a couple of his favourite Joki Dent chewing sticks to occupy him while our *gorgonzola dolce* was left to breathe well out of his reach.

After breakfast the following day, Lawrence brandished the wallpaper stripper triumphantly. 'This will do the job,' he declared confidently, striding into Carol's room *à la* Schwarzenegger. 'This time it's personal . . .'

I settled down to work in our half-finished office. The sight that met me when I took Lawrence a mid-morning coffee was not a happy one. He stood, hands on hips, looking at the stripper, which lay on the floor at his feet. 'It's dead! It tried valiantly for half an hour then it just died.'

'Round two to the wallpaper then.'

'Ha, ha. Seriously, what are we going to do?'

It was Nicola, on a brief site visit later that day, who suggested that we try to burn the paper off.

'Well, it survived trial by water so we might as well try fire. It'll be just like the *Magic Flute*. Carol loved her opera; she'd get the irony,' Lawrence said. 'Do you have a blowtorch handy?'

Nicola promised to talk to a friend and two days later he returned with a blowtorch and a protective mask.

'Round three,' said Lawrence, grimly, as he donned the mask and disappeared once again.

It was hideous work, especially in the late July heat, and he'd emerge from behind the safety mask looking like a newly boiled lobster. We took it in two-hour turns, and it did the trick. Within three days, the walls were bare and the room transformed.

'It's a really lovely room. Nicer than I had realised.'

I stood amazed. The blue chintzy paper had made it look so much smaller, almost claustrophobic. But a pretty, well-proportioned room had emerged. And with the paper gone, I was keen to get painting. 'Go to the *Fai da Te*,' Daniele advised. We had seen the name a few times, but had no idea what it meant. Lawrence went off to leaf through our pile of diction-aries and phrase books and came back laughing. 'It means Do-It-Yourself, they're DIY stores. You'd think we'd have worked that one out sooner.'

We found our nearest *Fai da Te* and chose a lovely soft cream. But when we got it home and opened the tin the paint was so thick it was almost impossible to apply. Time after time we dug our brushes into the almost solid gloop and attempted to transfer it to the walls, but it was like trying to spread custard and, as Lawrence said, not the nice kind: 'The custard we used to have at school!'

After a couple of days of hard labour, two large tins of paint had only covered one wall.

'We'll have to get some more,' I said.

'At this rate it would be cheaper to re-paper the walls.' Lawrence caught my horrified look. 'Only joking. C'mon, let's get to the *Fai da Te* before closing time.'

'What are you painting, a palazzo?' the friendly assistant asked, as we lined up three more pots of paint.

'Hardly, but it doesn't go far, does it?'

'Are you using the right mix of paint to water?'

'Water?'

'Yes, for one pot of paint, seven pots of water. All paint here is like this.'

'But it says on the tin "*pronto all'uso*" – ready to use.'

We looked at each other, red-faced.

'Er, I think we can put a couple of these back. One more might do it after all.'

Outside the shop we both started laughing.

After that, the painting was a joy. And the room took on new life. No longer a boudoir, it became a lovely space where we could welcome family and friends when they came to stay.

Having Carol's room finished was a huge hurdle overcome. Suddenly we glimpsed the possibility – just – that we would eventually have a completed house and functioning office.

A couple of days later, Nicola arrived to announce that he and Daniele were ready to make the dining-room windows.

We'd been delighted by his suggestion of two small, Etruscan-inspired, oval openings high up in the wall. Surely this time there would be some structural drawings, or at least some very precise measuring, particularly as the wall was more than a foot thick. So when we found both men taking turns to draw the outlines of the windows on the wall in thick pencil we were, despite the previous sledgehammer incident, somewhat taken aback. We knew how this was likely to go, and the prospect was alarming.

The ovals were re-drawn several times as they argued about it.

'Too high?'

'Not big enough.'

'Are they even?'

How on earth would they know which of the lines criss-crossing one another was the right one?

We left them to it. They knew what they were doing. Didn't they?

A few minutes later, sitting in the office, we heard the smash of sledgehammer against brick. 'They've decided, then,' said Lawrence not even looking up from his keyboard, where he was bashing out an email about a baritone and *The Marriage of Figaro*.

I was standing on the terrace, the following afternoon, when Daniele came out and joined me.

'Beautiful, eh?' He inclined his head towards the distant hills.

'Yes, it's lovely. We enjoy the view very much.'

'Holidays soon.'

'Not for us, I'm afraid. We've got too much work to do.'

Daniele looked shocked. 'No holiday?'

'Being here is our holiday.' I attempted a convincing smile.

'Me, I need my holiday. I'm going to the seaside, with my family.' He looked happy.

'That sounds nice. When?'

'Next week. For three weeks. Eduardo, Roberto, Giovanni too.'

It was Thursday. They would work for one more day and then disappear for three weeks. My heart sank. We would have to endure three hot, miserable weeks, with no progress at all. And though they had worked hard, virtually none of the jobs in the house were finished. Every room had something still to be done; the dining-room windows were just open holes – albeit perfectly oval ones, the half-wall to the kitchen had to be completed, the tiles were waiting to be laid on the floor of Carol's room and we had no kitchen. Worst of all, the boiler still didn't work, and the old immersion heater which had kept us going so far, showed distinct signs of fading rapidly, its red light blinking on and off as our hot water supply dwindled to a trickle each morning. Getting from one room to another was an obstacle course, around the as-yet unpacked boxes, over the heaps of bricks or pots of paint or piles of tools. And as for the garden, it had been savaged from laying the new sewer pipes and tanks and what was left had been burnt dry by the sun. It looked like barren scrub, and even my optimistic mind struggled to see a way forward, let alone the possibility of creating the glorious garden of my dreams.

I went to find Lawrence. 'Do you know what Daniele's just told me . . . ?'

'Yes, he was just in here.'

'I wish we'd had more notice.'

'I don't suppose it would have made much difference.'

'And in the meantime we have to wait.'

'Yup, that's about the size of it.'

It wasn't an easy prospect. I had been longing to get the work done and our lives in some kind of proper order. The thrill of barbecue living was wearing thin and I fantasised about constant hot water, a real sink to wash up in, a dining-room we could eat in, a house that didn't smell of brick dust and paint.

With the builders gone, the house felt very quiet. Teresa still came in to clean and I asked her if she too would be going on holiday.

'No,' she said firmly. 'I went to the seaside once but I didn't like it. Too much sand. Silvano goes, with Diego, but I prefer to stay here.'

We'd hear her chatting constantly and gently with Todo as he followed her around. '*Buono cane,* Todo. Are you behaving yourself, *vagabondo*?' That she adored him was obvious but I knew it went deeper than that; he was her link to the past, to a time when she'd worked for La Signora with such pride and care. My heart skipped a beat the day I heard her tell him, 'I told you everything would turn out right.'

August brought no relief, the summer heat intensified, the temperature at night barely cooler than it had been during the day. I grew ever more envious of the tourists thronging the narrow streets of Lucca. We'd see them when we rushed into town to go to the bank, look for paint or shelves, have another argument with the shop that was supposed to be delivering our kitchen ('*Sì, sì,* soon it will come, soon . . .') or, on one occasion, race from one end of the city to the other, trying to locate the Canon photocopy centre, only to find it closed for the *ferie* (the long Italian summer holiday). Virtually all Italians depart to the coast during August leaving the hot city centres to the foreigners and pigeons. The tourists we passed would be enjoying lazy holiday lunches, basking in the sun and looking as though they had all the time in the world.

'Do you remember when we used to be like that?' Lawrence sighed, as we passed a laughing young couple, sitting under a tree, their table laden with food and wine.

'Laughing?'

'Young.'

It felt like another life. We'd loved our holidays in Italy so much that we had moved our entire lives here, only to find that we no longer had time to do the very things we'd enjoyed so much in the first place. Would we ever explore the winding streets or sit in the shade of the Botanical Gardens or even just stop for a cool drink, I wondered . . .

'Come on,' Lawrence urged. 'No time to daydream, the kitchen shop will be closing soon.'

We sped on, hot, bothered and up against the clock.

But despite occasional pining, we knew that while we might no longer have all the leisure time enjoyed by tourists, we had something more precious. It hit home a couple of days later after accepting Herbert's offer to come and see him conduct *Tosca* at Villa Oliva.

Laura was at the gates to greet us when we arrived, 'I must introduce you to Signora Oliva, the owner; she was very good friends with Carol.' But as she scurried off to find her Lawrence walked me back out, stopping us right in front of the gates at a poster on one of the imposing stone posts, advertising the concert.

'Just think; less than a year ago we stood in this very same spot debating whether to go to the performance of *Don Giovanni*. The Music Society . . . Herbert Handt; who would have thought . . . ?'

Lawrence could be pithy when he became emotional and I

143

could tell that this resonated with him. Last August we had no claim on the area beyond the fact that we liked visiting it every year, enjoying the sights, the food and the music. Now we were on the inside, about to meet the villa's owner; to be introduced as the people who'd bought Carol's house and taken on her dog.

Of course, it was a joyous occasion but a melancholy overcame me too, standing in the still-warm evening sun staring at Lucca's great and good assembled before us in their summer finest, men in cream linen suits and open-neck blue shirts, ladies in bright silk floral dresses and scarves. While we had stood here last year, full of *joie de vivre*, the notion growing stronger in our heads that we could become more than mere interlopers, just a mile or so away a loyal dog kept watch over his mistress's house in the middle of his second summer without her. Teresa would have come with his food earlier that morning, doubtless fussing over him while she attended to some cleaning in La Signora's Poggiolino. Italian schools were closed so perhaps she'd brought Diego with her, which would have meant an extended walk and some extra petting and attention.

Who cares about Tosca, I thought, *when there's Todo?*

But as the long, hot days of summer continued, the reality of our Italian dream felt like a bump down to earth. Of course we'd known there would be obstacles, but did there have to be so *many*? It felt as if each time we achieved something that had looked as if it would be the solution to all our problems, such as connecting to the Internet, another hurdle presented itself.

Adding to the pressure of the never-ending To Do lists, I faced an even tougher issue: my painfully slow grasp of Italian, a huge disappointment to me and a source of frustration to Lawrence. I had thought that with lessons in London before we moved and continued practice with my language tapes I would improve rapidly once we were living in Italy, but I had underestimated the task of learning a language properly. In every book and film we had read and seen about others who had made a similar journey abroad, they all seemed to be fluent half an hour in. Could that really be true? Was I the only one to stumble and fall over every linguistic hurdle?

I tried to remind myself to laugh about my mistakes as much as possible. That was easier on some occasions than others. One night we went to a favourite restaurant, a place we'd been visiting for years, since long before our move. The owner bustled over and asked for an update on the state of the house, in between rattling off the menu for that night's feast. I stopped her as she launched into the list of main course dishes.

'I've been dreaming about your steak.'

'I remember you liked it last time. *E com'è il cane?*'

'*Medio*, please.'

I didn't understand the shocked and puzzled look on her face at my response but Lawrence did and spluttered on his glass of prosecco before explaining to Stefania that 'Luisa thinks you asked how she wanted her steak done.' Her laugh rang loudly through the little dining-room. Stefania had forgotten to ask earlier but was now enquiring after Todo. The Italian word for dog is *cane*; steak is *carne*. By missing that one little letter *r* I had inadvertently ordered our dear Todo well-done.

Calm was restored, my embarrassment eased and my reputation as a dog-eater repudiated. Red-faced, I whispered to Lawrence, 'Thank goodness Todo didn't hear.'

'Oh, I'll tell him,' he replied, 'but he'll forgive you if you save some of the steak for him!'

★ ★ ★

It wasn't always possible to remain upbeat about our difficulties, though. On holiday we had felt a sense of achievement with our ability to order a meal (most of the time!) or comment on the lovely weather, but living in the country we quickly came to realise just how limited our vocabulary actually was. Dealing with utility companies, builders and services exposed our limitations – mine in particular – but with the pressure of work and the demands of each day it was very hard to find the time to sit and practise.

Like many men, Lawrence experiences stress physically and by the middle of August he was suffering with sleepless nights and occasional mild panic attacks. His greatest fear was that he would wake in the night with a heart attack and I would end up ordering a pizza instead of calling for an ambulance.

There was nothing for it but to keep going, with the house, with the Italian, trusting that our progress towards fully-fledged insider-dom would continue, even if it wasn't a continuous upward trajectory.

In late August we had to make another trip to London, this time for a week. We had clients appearing in open-air concerts and a number of meetings. Todo had begun to accept that this was how life would be, our disappearances a hiccup in an otherwise settled existence. This time, with an early start, we did bring our suitcases downstairs the night before. He sniffed around them and walked away a little droopily, tail down, head hung low, but after that he cheered up and came and leaned against my leg as I sat reading a book by Paul Gervais, an American who had moved to the area and restored a splendid garden and villa. I shrieked with delight when I came across a section on Carol, Jim and Poggiolino – their friendship, their lunches together in the garden; Carol greeting them warmly, wearing a wide straw hat and dressed immaculately. Calling Lawrence, I read the passage to him. It seemed extraordinary that everywhere we turned there was another reference to her.

Back in London I missed Todo dreadfully, though we resisted phoning Teresa, afraid of appearing too soppy. England was cooler than Lucca, and we relished the fresh feel of the air after the sweltering heat. But as we settled down to enjoy the first of the open-air concerts, the skies opened. The audience struggled gamely on, under their umbrellas and macs, as our artist sang, smiled and joked bravely through the downpour.

Another day, another concert, another downpour. Muddy fields and portaloos. The most important items for an English summer concert are clothes pegs, to hold the music in place on stage, mops for the dressing room floor and strong-armed chaps to carry divas and dresses through the mud. The final event saw the heavens throw in a force ten gale for good measure. We could only laugh and look forward to returning to the sunshine, and our little companion.

Two days later we headed for the airport, arriving home in the early evening, to much leaping, barking and wild excitement. A week had felt too long for all of us.

The next morning we took Todo for a quick walk before work. The air was a little cooler and we felt cheerful knowing the building crew were due to return the next day and that we'd been promised our kitchen the following week. After the long pause of August, life would be up and running again.

'Is that a cough?' asked Lawrence, as we roamed the fields beyond our garden.

'What, from Todo? Yes, it is. Not much, but definitely a bit of a cough.'

Todo seemed his usual energetic self, but something wasn't

quite right. On the way back to the house we stopped to see Teresa, who seemed unconcerned. 'It's normal for an old boy. Maybe he swallowed a little grass from the fields.'

She was more perturbed about the situation with the electricity. Apparently for several days there had been short power cuts at the house – though strangely neither she nor any other neighbours were affected. Maurizio, a whizz with electrics, had investigated but could find nothing, even when a cut occurred while he was there. It had been two days since the last blackout but Teresa wanted us to know about the problem.

'Daniele is back tomorrow,' Lawrence said. 'We'll ask him to see about getting Roberto to come and check it.'

Giovanni arrived early the following morning to start putting in the new boiler. Always quieter than the other workmen, that morning his greeting was very subdued. 'Terrible news about Roberto,' he said quietly.

'Sorry, we've been away, we didn't hear anything.'

'He died last week, a heart attack. Just fifty-two.'

I caught my breath. We'd known Roberto for only two months but he'd been a huge presence and having him in the house had been enormous fun. He often had all of us shaking with laughter and we had been delighted when he brought his lovely daughter to translate.

When Daniele arrived he too was sombre. 'Roberto was complaining of feeling unwell for a few days last week but thought nothing of it. Then Friday morning he died suddenly.'

I froze. *That was the day Teresa said the power cuts stopped.* I mentioned this later on the phone to Nicola, who had liked Roberto greatly. An intelligent and level-headed man, his reply surprised me. 'You never know; I believe in such happenings.'

The power cuts remained unexplained and since Roberto's

death the electrics have worked perfectly. We like to think he is with us to this day. Every time we flick on a light or replace a bulb I see his face or hear his wicked laugh and smile at the memory of a man who was a joy to know.

Daniele and the others had returned from their holidays tanned and relaxed. Over the next few weeks one by one the jobs around the house were finished and our home began to emerge from the chaos. After all our fretting during the long hot August, when it felt as if progress would take the rest of our lives, tasks were completed so quickly it left us giddy and excited.

The day we settled into our new office we felt like throwing a party. It seemed only right that we invited the other member of the household to join us. Todo soon became an integral member of staff, so much so that we'd move his basket in with us after our morning walk. It's remarkable how satisfying, even comforting, the company of a dog is during one's working day.

'You're offering how much?! No, we could never accept that fee.'

'What do you mean, he didn't get the job?'

'Great, I look forward to the contract.'

It was all like water off a, well, dog's back to him; each exclamation, and the occasional profanity, greeted with nothing more strenuous than the lifting of one lazy eyelid, as he lay with his face pressed between two golden paws.

Finally there was just one more job left for the builders. The kitchen had been ordered in March but despite our many calls and visits to the suppliers, it remained no more than a set of lovely drawings pinned to the wall. Todo was enjoying the barbecued sausages, steaks and pork fillets which were our staple diet, but for Lawrence and I the thrill had long since worn off and we yearned for somewhere to cook proper meals. Daniele had Eduardo and two other builders waiting to install the units, and he needed to move on to another job.

'I'm sorry, Daniele, they keep promising me but . . .' Lawrence spread his hands wide, in a gesture of helpless frustration.

'Lorenzo, would you like me to speak to them?'

'Yes, please; let me give you their number.'

Daniele laughed. 'Bah, telephone. I'll go see them.'

Two days later, Todo ran to the front gates through the open *cucina di cane* and stood barking at the small van pulling up outside.

Lawrence had dashed after him, 'Todo; *basta, basta*. Be quiet.'

'Signor Lorenzo?' It was the kitchen. *Grazie* Daniele!

Three days later we waved goodbye to Daniele, Eduardo and Giovanni and celebrated the completion of our home over the first meal cooked in our own kitchen. We had spent quite some time admiring the blonde wooden cupboards and the marble work surfaces, not to mention the pristine stainless steel sink, after which Lawrence surpassed himself with a meal of pasta Genovese, followed by *petti di pollo*; grilled chicken with braised finocchio. He reminded me it had been our menu at the lunch we'd had just half an hour after seeing Poggiolino for the first time eight months before.

'*And* meeting Todo; don't forget him.'

'Who could forget Todo?'

He sat attentively at my feet, awaiting the next 'Oops!' as another morsel dropped to the tiles. At the mention of his name he looked up, swished his tail from side to side across the floor, and nudged my knee with his nose, as if to say, 'Never mind the nostalgia, I'm right here. Is that chicken for me?

14

The Hunters Arrive

At 6.15 a.m. one mid-September morning we were woken abruptly by a volley of gunshots.

Lawrence sat up in bed. 'What the hell was that?'

'It must be the hunters.'

'It sounds like a war zone out there. I'm going to see what they're doing.'

He went out to investigate. Ten minutes later he was back.

'They're in the field next to ours and they're not just passing through. It looks as though they've set up camp.'

We'd known they were coming. A few days earlier we had been out walking with Todo when he began barking with a fervour we'd not heard before. We could see nothing for a few moments, until a gun dog appeared, followed by a large man in camouflage gear carrying two rifles. Much to our amazement, our gentle Todo started to growl ferociously, hackles raised. Ignoring him, the hunter soon disappeared from view. It was the only time we ever saw Todo show any signs of aggression, and he remained agitated for some time afterwards. We'd also seen the many shops selling guns, ammunition and macho hunting apparel and Teresa had told us that many of the older *contadini* still liked to hunt. But we'd imagined they would keep to the woods and forests, looking for boar and wild game – we had no idea they would come so close to us.

After breakfast, ears ringing, I went to look for myself.

On the other side of the stream at the bottom of our field there is a wide open space of grassy land. It was here that two hunters had set up a cruel contraption for luring birds, while they lay in wait in a makeshift hide, cut into the tall dry reeds which lined the edges of the stream. The contraption was a small motor with long wires spreading out from the centre and fake birds attached to the ends. As the wires whirred round, the birds appeared to be flying while others had been placed on the surrounding grass. To birds flying over it would appear to be a flock, circling low over a source of food. There were more of these elaborate decoys stuck into the ground and in what appeared to be small trees but were in fact large branches planted in hollow metal rods.

I made my way back to the house feeling puzzled and very alarmed by all this. The hunters had gone to quite a lot of trouble to set it all up.

Lawrence was as horrified as me. 'Why would they want to shoot these birds? Are they after ones they can eat, or is it just for sport?'

'Heaven knows.'

When Teresa arrived later that morning, she enlightened us. 'The hunters can go anywhere they want. Some keep to the woods, others prefer the fields.'

'What can they hope to catch down there?'

She gave one of her signature rolls of the eyes. 'Birds. To protect the crops and for food too.'

We knew, of course, that guinea fowl and pheasant were eaten, but it seemed that much smaller birds were also considered delicious. Aware that Silvano still hunted regularly, though mercifully he'd not yet followed up his invitation to Lawrence to join him, we trod cautiously when discussing it with Teresa.

'Can anything be done about the people firing so close to us?'

'Mmmm.'

It was never a good sign when she did that.

'Some people have talked with him, but . . .' she shrugged. 'Still it's not every day and will finish soon.'

Well that was a relief, at least. The shooting in the field was coming in bursts of three or four shots, every twenty minutes or so. Surely they couldn't keep that up for more than a few days?

If it was an intrusion for us then it was far worse for poor Todo. We knew he'd been bred for hunting and he remained a remarkable tracker, his sense of scent infallible in finding the game birds that make their homes in the woods and fields surrounding us. During those early months we had often wondered why he had been abandoned. But when the hunting season began it became all too clear. He was absolutely terrified of the shooting. He bolted upstairs and hid under our bed, curled into a trembling ball and even the offer of a treat couldn't persuade him to come out.

At intervals, one of us would go upstairs and kneel down to peer under the bed.

'C'mon Todo, there's nothing to be afraid of. No one will hurt you. Why not come downstairs to the office with us?' But he wasn't to be moved and eventually we'd have to give up and go back down to work. He didn't come out until well after the shooting had ended.

We thought it would only last for a week or so. But we were sadly wrong.

'How soon will it stop, Teresa?' I asked, when she came the following day.

'January.'

'What!' Lawrence and I looked at one another in horror. How on earth could we put up with this, from six in the morning until three in the afternoon, five days a week for four months?

It seemed we had no choice.

As for Todo, there was no possibility of taking him on our usual morning walk, or even coaxing him out onto the terrace.

'Can you imagine what it must have been like for him when he was here by himself?'

It was painful to think about how frightened he must have been, with no one to comfort him and only the boiler-room to escape to, where the open door would have offered little protection against the ferocity of the shots. If he had hated the shooting as a puppy, his trauma could only have worsened when he had to endure two hunting seasons alone. No wonder he retreated to our room.

It wasn't just Todo we were worried about. I had dreadful visions of the cats being shot accidentally down in the olive grove where they spent most of their time. I couldn't relax with constant gunfire going on all around us and the occasional shell bursting into the garden. We cursed every hunter and every shot and found ourselves obsessed with the noise throughout the day. After two weeks of shooting, nine hours a day, we were at our wits' end.

'Surely we haven't come to Italy to put up with this?' Lawrence exploded. 'If we'd known about it, I'm not sure we'd have made the move. There must be something we can do to get them out of the field.'

We started talking to our neighbours. The culprit, it seemed, was one stubborn hunter. Nobody in the area approved in the slightest of what he was doing, not least because they had all avoided disturbing the peace in the village, heading further up the hills to carry out their so-called sport, while he persisted in staying in the field at the bottom of the valley, driving everyone mad while he peppered shots into any poor songbird that had the misfortune to fall for his decoy.

As friends told us, direct action is just not the done thing in Italy, which is why bars and cafés are filled daily with the sounds of customers bemoaning their lot, convinced there is nothing they can do about it.

But we aren't Italian.

The following day, Lawrence marched down to the field to confront the shooter. Tired and angry after another early morning barrage of shots that woke us and sent Todo whimpering under the bed, he had had enough.

The conversation didn't get very far before it escalated into shouting which, on Lawrence's part, was rather more Anglo-Saxon than Latin-based. He arrived home shaking with fury and I struggled to calm him down.

'He just laughed at me. He knows we can't touch him. It's infuriating. Why won't someone around here do something?' He went over to stroke Todo. 'I'm sorry we couldn't help you this time. But we'll keep trying and I promise you we'll make it stop one day. We just have to be patient. You know all about that, don't you?'

Our glorious Tuscan paradise had turned into a firing range.

We couldn't believe that such senseless cruelty was allowed to take place in such a tranquil and beautiful place. Our only shred of comfort was knowing that hunting is slowly dying out in Italy as the younger generation of men have little or no interest in sitting out in wet, cold fields all day for months, simply to slaughter thousands of small, almost inedible, birds. One day Teresa invited us over to share in a feast she had prepared, using the birds Silvano had shot. Forty birds for ten people. It was the only time we declined her hospitality; we simply couldn't face it.

We did know that the hunters were not supposed to come within a hundred metres of our fences and on occasions Lawrence confronted those that came too close. But we had to accept that we were the newcomers and foreigners. It was a hard lesson in 'put up and shut up' and we longed for the days to pass quickly. The toll on the wildlife was even more distressing than the noise and my greatest joy in January, when the shooting finally finished, came when watching great swirling clouds of birds fill the skies, catching the winds that took them off for their long journeys home; these were the survivors and I blessed them all as they swooped past our trees in a breathtaking rush of noise and chattering excitement.

As the days progressed, we managed to coax Todo out from under the bed, but we had to resort to a lead for his daily walks, otherwise at the sound of the first shot he would run back home, tail between his legs, not daring to venture out again for several hours. Even on the lead it was often impossible to take him far, he was just too miserable and we had to give up and turn back.

His paralysing fear of the hunters was not our only worry. The cough we had noticed a few weeks back was not going away, and we decided to take him to the vet. We'd been to the *toilette di cane*, the grooming parlour, in Fontanella to get Todo clipped, but this was our first visit to the vet's next door. We announced our presence to Dottoressa Viviana, a delightful blonde with flashing blue eyes who radiated energy. 'Do we need to register? We've just moved here from London. Besides Todo we have three cats.'

'No, no,' she replied, after she had deciphered my Italian. 'If an animal is sick, you come! Now, how is this old boy?'

I explained about the cough which Todo refused to demonstrate though he behaved impeccably, relishing the attention as Viviana checked him over, pausing to pat him or shake the blond fur which was growing back under his chin.

'Todo, I'll give you some tablets and you come back and see me in a week if it's not better.'

Slightly concerned that she might have directed her words to Todo thinking he would understand better than I did, I was relieved when she handed over a prescription. 'Where do we get the tablets?'

Her pitying look made me feel even more of a dummy. 'From the *farmacia*,' she said, pointing out of the window at the chemist over the road.

'Just like humans?' asked Lawrence.

'Of course,' came her reply.

A week later the cough was, if anything, worse, so we returned to the vet's. The waiting-room was full and several '*buon giornos*' were exchanged as we entered. '*Sono l'ultimo*' (I am the last), a large lady clutching a yapping dachshund informed us helpfully.

We had to wait for some time, so chatted to the other patients and their owners – a wonderful opportunity to practise our language skills – and discovered that the surgery was home to a number of damaged and abandoned animals that loved to be fussed over by the many visitors. There was a small tabby cat who had been dreadfully injured by a grass strimmer; she'd lost a paw and wounded others but had survived to live a contented life. The most recent addition was Gaea, an affectionate, handsome dog who had been hit by a car and left for dead. Her back legs were badly damaged, but with physiotherapy and the help of a little wheeled contraption she had regained some movement.

We realised that Todo was by no means alone in his terror of the hunters and their noise. The board on the wall, like the one in the pet food shop, was filled with notices imploring people to take in unwanted dogs and puppies. Each included a photo and a little story about the dog, many of which had been abandoned after proving inadequate as hunters' mates.

After almost an hour – each patient was afforded as much time as necessary – a vet popped her head round the door, '*Prego.*' It wasn't Viviana. *We'll have to go through the whole thing again.* Sighing, Lawrence began to explain but she interrupted, 'Ah, *l'inglese*, the dog with the cough. Viviana told me; I am Dottoressa Tiziana. So it's not cleared up?'

The opposite of her colleague, Tiziana was dark haired, cool and calm, but equally affectionate with the animals. She went through the same thorough examination as before, lingering at Todo's chest, listening intently with her stethoscope.

'How old is the dog?'

'We think he's around ten or eleven, but can't be sure. You see, we inherited him when we bought the house and no one can remember exactly when he came.'

'I think he might have a bronchial condition, maybe with his age . . . I'll give him two medicines, and you should inject him twice a day with the first one.'

Inject! As in, syringe and needle? I pointed at the sharp object in her hand.

'*Sì*, injection. You have done it before?'

Tiziana shook her head in amazement as Lawrence explained we most certainly hadn't, nor did we think it was even legal in England.

She laughed. 'It's normal; you'll do fine.'

As we went back through the waiting-room I spotted a wall-chart detailing the comparative ages between dogs and humans. Looking up Todo's eleven years, his size and weight I breathed a sigh of relief. 'According to this he's only just hit sixty; he's a kid!'

Leaving the pharmacy, this time with a much bigger bag, Lawrence seemed preoccupied. 'She didn't seem worried about the bronchial condition. Should we be?'

I wanted to say something reassuring. I looked down at Todo trotting along happily with us. 'He seems fine; perhaps it's just a legacy from being outside so much. Let's hope it's nothing but a cough.'

We both wanted to believe it.

Giving Todo his injection was a comedy of errors and bumbling inaccuracy. On the first morning he stood still, as good as gold, while I lunged at him wildly, eyes almost shut. 'It's not pin the tail on the donkey,' yelled Lawrence. It wasn't much better the second morning, and by the third it was hard to know who was more nervous, me or Todo. I think Todo shaded it, though he held his ground bravely while I stabbed at the fleshy part of his thigh.

'Are there any reactions to the injections?' asked Viviana on our next visit.

'You mean apart from him running a mile and our hands shaking like jelly?'

'*Medical* reactions,' she continued, '*vomito* or *diarrea*?'

Finally; two words I understood! 'No,' said Lawrence, 'he's been fine and the cough is clearing up.'

'Keep an eye on him and come back if it returns.'

'Did you have any more thoughts about the bronchial thing?'

'Well, at his age . . . you say he's eleven? It's something we should check, you know, make sure it doesn't develop into anything more serious.'

We promised to watch him closely. I could hear the concern in her voice, but with the cough gone – Lawrence suggested we'd forced him to get better in order to avoid our campaign of terror with the needle – Todo seemed full of energy and eager to get on with the fun things in life, like searching out the next snack.

Over the next few weeks his daily walks – when no hunters disturbed us – were a source of delight, and even more so when the ebullient Varco joined us. I marvelled at the sight of him bounding through the fields like a canine Tigger. His speed was remarkable and the joy he took in this athletic grace, infectious; Lawrence and I both lost weight attempting to keep up with him and it did Todo the world of good too.

One morning a large brown beast with wolf-like ears, a long pointed nose and perfectly white teeth ran towards us, screeching to a halt in front of Todo, who looked tiny next to him. Varco tried to shoo him away but Todo followed after the pair of them, albeit at a pace rather more in keeping with his age. By the end of that walk they were the best of friends and I laughed at the sight of the two bigger, younger dogs, bounding away together as we headed down the steps while Todo, tired after all his exertions, making a beeline for his water bowl.

The newcomer's name, we later discovered, was Rex, a German Shepherd cross who lived up the road. He was a gorgeous chestnut colour and quickly became one of the gang, the loveable rogue to Varco's elegant leader of the pack. Having these two pals seemed to give Todo courage. The next time they joined us on our walk, although Todo flinched when the shots rang out, rather than head home, he stuck close to his friends, who didn't seem to notice the noise at all.

15

We've Had a Wonderful Time

'**W**hat if they don't like it?'

The hunters for once forgotten, we were preparing for our first dinner party, with Teresa, Silvano and the rest of her family.

'Calm down, you're a great cook. They'll love it.'

'But these are Italians; their food is the real deal. I've never cooked for natives whose own cooking is so good.'

I had seldom seen Lawrence so nervous. He stood in the kitchen, surrounded by heaps of vegetables, breads, olives and herbs, looking doubtfully at the menu he'd chosen. The night before he'd spent hours poring over all his favourite cookbooks, agonising over whether to prepare them English food or compete with Teresa's sublime creations by keeping the menu Italian. In the end he'd decided on a compromise that avoided a full-blown attempt at *cucina Italiana* and gave a nod to both England and Italy: creamed fennel soup, roast herb-crusted loin of pork with braised Umbrian lentils and an orange and almond cake.

Normally Lawrence is in his element when cooking, singing along to music or yelling at the radio presenters who *never ask the politicians the right questions*, while happily chopping, beating and blending. But this afternoon he was quiet and I thought he looked pale.

'They'll love the meal; you'll see. Now don't worry. I'm going back to the office.'

It was a Friday afternoon and things were quiet at work. I had a few emails and letters to write, a couple of calls to make and then I planned to call it a day and give Lawrence a hand with the preparations.

The phone rang. It was a colleague in London, someone I'd become friendly with as we brokered two separate book and video deals for one of my clients. During the preceding weeks, a row had been developing about the contracts and I knew there could be trouble ahead. She was ringing to warn me that the production company involved with the video had decided that the book sales could badly affect their chance of success, despite being previously convinced that the two would only enhance one another's sales. I felt my stomach tighten at her words.

'They're really not happy,' she added. 'Best to get onto it Monday morning.'

Thrown into a mild panic I briefly pondered trying to sort it out over the phone straight away, but time was getting on, all the relevant people had finished for the weekend, and besides, I needed to lay the table and tidy up before our guests arrived.

Never mind, I thought, *nothing's going to happen over the weekend. I'll deal with it first thing next week.*

I pulled out our beautiful new cream and olive tablecloth. I'd spotted one in a shop in the Piazza Anfiteatro, a dazzling example of the Romans' genius for building and design right

A puppy Todo at
Poggiolino.

Our first sighting; life would never be
the same.

The boiler room, where Todo slept
for two years after Carol's death.

The *Associazione Musicale Lucchese*
1964, Herbert Handt front row,
first left; Carol MacAndrew centre
of attention!

Signor Jim with previous
canine incumbents.

1960's olive harvest at Villa Carola.

Three generations at Poggiolino:
Carol, Signora Teresa and her
grandson Diego.

Not the outdoor living we'd
envisaged . . .

Daniele; *Is THIS where you wanted it?*

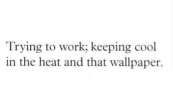

Trying to work; keeping cool
in the heat and that wallpaper.

Pampered pooch – Todo's first
haircut.

His seat in the car – how many times
did we see that smile?

Singing for Carol?
Sunday morning ritual.

Three London cats in Italy,
home away from home.

From garden to table, couldn't be fresher.

Each olive checked personally by Bob . . .

. . . then drizzled over garden-grown courgettes.

Poggiolino.

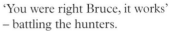
'You were right Bruce, it works' – battling the hunters.

Remembering Carol – heading off to her Memorial Concert in Lucca.

Todo's first taste of fast food – such concentration.

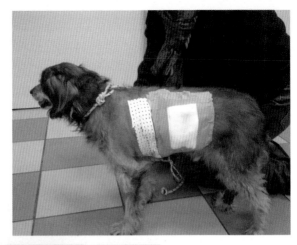

'He's a strong dog' – just three days after surgery.

And still searching for that one extra treat.

Post operation – but still young at heart.

Todo in Tuscany – the dog and land that captured our hearts.

in the heart of Lucca, just after we'd signed the final *rogito* to buy the house. I loved it, but it was too small for our table. 'Not a problem,' said the shop owner. 'Leave us your measurements and we'll make one up for you.'

'We won't be back for two months, is that OK? Do you need a deposit?'

She laughed. 'Of course not, we'll see you in May.' Walking in two months later she looked up and smiled. 'Ah, you're back; I have your tablecloth.'

'Lou,' Lawrence mumbled from the kitchen. 'I'm not feeling too good. A bit queasy.'

He was prone to the odd bout of sickness, usually brought on by eating porcini mushrooms. Poor man, he adored them but his love was not reciprocated and a day out of action often ensued. But he hadn't eaten porcini this time. 'I think it might be the *valdostana* I had at lunch.'

Ah. We'd gone into Fontanella to collect supplies from the delicatessen and he'd stopped to try one of the delicious flat pastries, filled with smoked ham and mozzarella.

I stuck my head over the half-wall into the kitchen. He was grey.

'You look fine. Just keep chopping.'

The shrill ring of the fax machine sounded from down the hallway. Surprised that something was being faxed over on a Friday evening, I went to retrieve it and found a legal letter, addressed to me, seven pages long. I scanned it and my blood ran cold.

Serious breach of contract ... Our client will seek damages ... Clear conflict of interest ...

The production company was a great deal more unhappy than either I or my colleague had anticipated. They were threatening to sue us, and the implications were unthinkable.

I stood in the office, engulfed by waves of panic. Should I try to call a lawyer or wait till morning? And what about Lawrence? He was already stressed about the meal and afraid he wouldn't make it through the evening, but I had to tell someone.

He emerged from the downstairs bathroom, a hand clamped to his stomach.

'We're about to be sued and we could lose everything.'

'Well this just keeps getting better.' He attempted a grin before looking at the pages. 'Don't worry, they're just bluffing; all lawyers send these letters, it's part of the bluster. Let's get through this evening and we'll go from there. If I can avoid throwing up before the first course then everything else is a doddle.'

He was right; nothing else could be done. Our guests were due in half an hour and I needed to finish the table, get changed and wipe the panic off my face, at least for the next few hours.

The doorbell sounded as the last of San Martino's eight o'clock chimes rang out. Everything was in hand; the soup simmering, the pork roasting and Lawrence still upright.

Silvano was jolly even by his standards. '*Ah buona sera, Signori Inglesi!*' Teresa echoed his *buona sera*, Maurizio and Barbara settled for '*Ciao!*' Diego grinned shyly and handshakes were exchanged all round. Their arms were full of gifts: cut flowers, a beautifully scented lemon tree and two bottles of wine from Elba, where Maurizio and Barbara loved to holiday.

Teresa, making a rare appearance without her apron, wore a floral dress and smart shoes. I thought about all those dinners and lunches when she'd had to tiptoe in through the little arched doorway to the kitchen, hidden from view of Carol's friends except as a pair of hands emerging from time to time through the serving hatch, only to exit quietly once the meal had finished. The thought struck me suddenly that she would never before have been received at the front door, as a guest. Did this explain her obvious unease or had her impeccable sixth-sense already picked up on my stress, no matter how hard I tried to hide it?

We showed them into the living-room, offered drinks and passed round crisps and nuts. They looked politely puzzled. Of course, I thought, mentally kicking myself. In Italy people go straight to the table to eat, the wine is plonked in the middle and everyone helps themselves. There are no polite rounds of pre-dinner drinks or preliminary nibbles to wreck your appetite before the antipasti.

Oh God, there were no antipasti.

We went straight from the sofas, with our tiny glasses of prosecco and hands greasy from the crisp bowls, to the table and the starter. An air of politeness pervaded as we seated them according to our plan – what were we thinking of? A *seating plan*? And we'd put Silvano at the head of the table, which should surely have been Lawrence's place, as man of the house.

Carrying the soup tureen to the table, a short exchange was going on in my head: *serve it; let them serve themselves; serve it . . .*

The English host in me won out.

As I moved round the table, spooning polite measures of soup into their bowls, the silence was broken only by the clink of my ladle on china. Glancing up at Silvano, I thought I saw him look askance at this meagre offering.

'Ah, finocchio, *delizioso*,' he said enthusiastically, after his first spoonful. Bless him.

Was he trying to keep up the charade that they were actually enjoying the evening? *No time to find out; keep ladling. The more you're doing the less you have to speak!* Is it *abbiamo* or *siamo* for 'we have'? *Come on woman, that was our first Italian lesson!*

'I told you this was a mistake,' Lawrence whispered. 'They want proper food.'

'How are you feeling?'

'Don't ask . . .'

'Lorenzo, are you joining us?' asked Maurizio.

'*Sì, sì*, I just need to get something from the other kitchen.' In his rush to exit, he almost crashed into me – and my tureen of soup – with the swing door. Re-emerging moments later, his face the same colour as the soup and fixed smile in place, he joined us at the table.

In the unfamiliar 'dinner party' setting, the family were clearly uncomfortable and the conversation stilted, with long, awkward pauses. We talked about the weather; 'warm for this time of the year . . . aren't the trees turning a wonderful colour?' The olive harvest was approaching; 'I think it'll be a good year,' said Silvano and we both nodded and smiled before Lawrence leapt up and shot out of the room once more.

'He's preparing food,' I said, rummaging through my elementary Italian for useful phrases. I'm not sure that one fooled anyone; Teresa looked concerned and Silvano baffled.

When Lawrence returned it was clear that things were getting worse, his face now almost sheet white, eyes sunken with the beginning of red rims. Barbara shot me a look which suggested sympathy and I got up, taking his arm and ushering him into the kitchen, stopping to turn down the dimmer on the dining-room lights, privately blessing Roberto for installing it.

'Can you make it through or do you think we should bail out?'

'No, I'll manage; the least we can do is give them dinner, after everything they've done for us.'

Poor man, he was sweating profusely, but Lawrence is nothing if not a fighter. So we both squared our shoulders and pushed on.

I announced the next course, '*Il secondo, arrosto,*' to exclamations of appreciation. Todo, delighted by the prospect of all these people to feed him, had been hanging around under our feet, and now he did his best to hijack my progress around the table. 'No, Todo,' I said, 'this is not for you.'

'Well, maybe later,' retorted Teresa; it was one of the few times she spoke. Usually a central presence at any gathering, tonight she seemed like a lost soul, sitting on the edge of her chair. There were none of her funny, animated stories of La Signora and Todo, her hands were clasped firmly together unless she was eating. As Lawrence and I busied ourselves around the table, her eyes followed our every move; perhaps she was unsure of how to behave, or maybe she just longed to get up and take over. More than once I thought of asking her if she would.

The pork went down well, and so fast that I realised we hadn't made enough of it. At least there were plenty of lentils to go round and they could help themselves. Which they did, with such enthusiasm that I was convinced they would go home at the end of the evening with hunger pangs and Teresa would have to rustle up a huge pot of pasta.

Lawrence was off again. 'Sorry, something in my throat,' he croaked as he dashed for the door. This time he was gone for a while and I thought I heard some very unpleasant noises coming from the bathroom. Oh God. Should I switch on some music, or would it appear too obvious?

I looked around. The game was clearly up. '*Lorenzo ... non cosi bene.*' I patted my stomach and they nodded sympathetically.

It looked as though I was going to have to manage the conversation alone. 'Todo is very well,' I ventured.

'Ah yes,' they all said, latching onto a familiar topic. 'What a good dog he is.'

'That cough is much better.'

'His fur's growing well.'

'So you took him to Erasmo? That was La Signora's favourite restaurant.'

At the mention of Carol I felt an even bigger failure. Her dinner parties would have buzzed with sparkling conversation, English and Italian spoken fluently by her cosmopolitan guests as they enjoyed Teresa's superb food and Carol sat, effortlessly elegant, at the head of the table. At that moment I hated Carol MacAndrew. Wealthy, successful, bilingual, a lady of leisure, her parties the most sought-after invitation in Lucca. And with a husband who wasn't rushing off to the bathroom every fifteen minutes.

I dumped the dishes in the sink and mopped a light film of sweat from my brow before grabbing the next course.

Lawrence put in an appearance just in time to take the acclaim for his superb cake, rich and moist, the sharp tang of the oranges contrasting beautifully with the sweet creaminess of the ground almonds. Not that he tasted any of it himself.

'Perhaps a little fever,' he ventured weakly to the assembled company.

I sneaked a look at my watch. *How is it just ten o'clock? It's only been two hours.* Still, the rate at which they were tucking into the cake suggested they might not be here much longer. 'Diego, are you going to school tomorrow?'

'*Sì*, at eight.'

Inwardly I cheered. With such an early start they would soon be heading off.

'Coffee?' asked Lawrence, who appeared a little brighter after yet another bathroom dash.

'*Non, grazie*, we never drink it this late,' replied Maurizio.

'In fact,' said Silvano, 'we should probably leave, with Diego having to be up early.'

Their farewells were generous. They assured us they'd had a wonderful time; the food, the wine, the company, it had all been splendid. I knew it was a big lie, but as I closed the door behind them, I blessed them for it.

We had got just about everything wrong. Never again would we ask an Italian family to eat 'English' style. The relaxed jollity and abundance of Italian eating were infinitely preferable to the stuffy formality we had unwittingly inflicted on them, and ourselves.

I sank onto the sofa. Lawrence had disappeared, presumably for another attack of what Dr Viviana called *vomito*, poor man. 'Well, at least that's over,' I said to Todo, who had curled up at my feet.

Tonight had been traumatic but I didn't want to think about what lay ahead. In the morning I would have to call lawyers, arrange a hasty trip to London and try to find a way through the nightmare threatening to engulf us.

Though it was late and very dark I took Todo out for a stroll to get some fresh air and clear my head. Slipping past Teresa's house, hoping I wouldn't hear the sounds of her cooking, I headed up the hill. I breathed in the night air. It was still warm and the lights dotted across the hills formed a twinkling necklace. Whatever lay ahead, we would cope. And whatever happened, we would not leave Todo.

Back home I locked the door behind me and looked down

at him, waiting patiently in the hope of a goodnight treat. Lawrence hadn't yet re-emerged; I could hear low moans coming from the bathroom but headed up the stairs, Todo at my heels. It was breaking all the rules, but I didn't care. Just this once we both needed his comforting presence beside us.

16

The Blackest Week of Our Lives

Saturday in Tuscany. Our favourite day of the week; a day to put aside work and immerse ourselves in the joys of our new country. Since the renovations to the house had finished, Saturdays were delightful. After a late breakfast we might wander round the shops of Lucca or visit a palazzo or cathedral, followed by lunch in some little out-of-the-way trattoria we had been longing to try. Or we might drive up into the hills to walk and enjoy the breathtaking views, laughing as Todo cavorted like a puppy, before stopping in a café where the only other patrons were men as old as the hills, sitting over their drinks and their backgammon boards.

But not this Saturday.

On what was to be the first day of the blackest week of our lives, I got up early, having barely slept, and cleared up the remains of the previous night's dinner, before re-reading the letter and calling our solicitor, Alexander. I couldn't believe this was happening to me. I'd been an agent for ten years, had a good reputation and had never encountered a legal problem till now.

Alexander listened as I gave him the gist of the story. When I finished he was silent for a moment.

'Hmm. I think it's best if we meet. Come to my office first thing Monday morning.'

'Is this as serious as it sounds?'

'I'm afraid it is.'

'But surely they've jumped the gun – if they'd just talk to me, I know there's a solution.'

'Look, I don't want to worry you unnecessarily, but similar cases have led to damage claims in the region of £600,000.'

I put the phone down and stared at the handset. It was almost impossible to take in.

When Lawrence came in a few minutes later I looked up at him.

'I'm sorry, we'll have to cancel your birthday trip to Turin. I need to go to London. I've just spoken to Alexander and I think we're in real trouble here.' I began sobbing uncontrollably. Lawrence did his best to comfort me. He even managed the odd joke – 'Oh well, I've always fancied living in a tent and you can do wonders on a primus stove.' But his stricken face told the truth.

For the rest of that day and the next, there was a sense of unreality. I booked my airline ticket, packed and even managed a walk with Todo, who stayed patiently by my side, criss-crossing the path in front of my feet far less than he normally did. But a cloud lay over everything. I couldn't believe we had worked so hard, come through so much and found our little slice of paradise, only to lose it all. The sense that everything I had loved and worked for was threatened took over every aspect of my thinking and being. It felt as if I existed in a ghastly bubble and normal life remained on the outside, beyond my reach. In the course of our careers, we'd both had to deal with difficult and demanding situations but having the weight of a huge organisation and a major law firm thrown at us was on a completely different scale.

We had no hope of fighting the case in court; finding the kind of money involved was impossible and losing would mean having to pay damages as well as costs. We needed to find a non-legal solution, but even this – meetings with lawyers, letters back and forth and so on – would cost thousands. The renovations on the house had already left us in a precarious position. What we needed was a period of consolidation, not to be splashing out thousands of pounds we didn't have. The timing couldn't have been worse.

The following day I flew to London and headed over to the flat. Walking from Herne Hill station to the bus stop I bumped into a friend I'd last seen the week before the move to Italy, just five months ago. We picked up the conversation as though only days had passed and nothing momentous had happened in the interim. Minutes later, opening the front door, I experienced the strangest feeling. It was as though this little flat, full of familiar furniture and pictures, was home and nothing else existed.

Dropping my bag in the bedroom, I went to my desk. I needed to phone Lawrence, but realised I couldn't remember our Italian number. All of a sudden I felt as if Poggiolino wasn't there, that our move had never happened; life hadn't changed at all. And even with the sounds of children outside and the London street visible through the window, I felt disconnected and terribly alone.

I switched on my computer to find the number in a file and there, smiling on my screen, was a bright little face, floppy ears dishevelled from a morning run. Instantly I was back at home with Todo and Lawrence, walking past the vineyard next to our field, Todo dashing between trees in the olive grove and taking a drink from the stream that meandered through the valley, while we paused to talk about the harvest with Mario. To lose it all would break my heart. I wasn't going to let that happen if I could possibly help it. As for Todo, I tried to picture him living in the London flat and failed miserably. What on earth would he make of life two storeys up from the street, double-decker buses, London parks full of bikes and runners?

I picked up the phone. Lawrence and Todo were fine, so I turned my attention to the papers I needed to prepare for the following day's meeting.

Alexander was supportive and bullish and after an hour with him I felt a little better.

But even after his reassurance I knew that the legal costs, following on from the overspend on the renovations of the house and the drop in the value of the pound since our move, could ruin us. If the case continued for many weeks we would not even be able to afford to defend ourselves.

The week passed in a blur of activity. Meetings, more meetings and endless phone calls. In the meantime Alexander sent his reply and said we could do no more until the production company responded.

I had booked my return ticket for early Friday afternoon. First thing that morning Alexander phoned. 'Can you get over here? I've received their reply.' Too anxious to eat breakfast, I headed over to his office where, after sitting me down with a coffee, he told me that the reply was less combative and he felt cautiously hopeful that the matter might be put on hold. 'In other words,' he said. 'I think they'll wait and see what sales of the video are like and if they reach their target figure, they may quietly let the matter drop. We're not out of the woods, but there's room for optimism.'

The meeting over, I dashed to Stansted, desperate to catch

my flight back to Pisa. After such a ghastly week I longed to see Lawrence and Todo and to sit on the terrace with a plate of real food and a glass of wine. I arrived at the gate just in time to avoid the ignominy of hearing my name announced over the loudspeakers. Red-faced, I boarded the plane to find the other passengers strapped in and waiting to go. Sliding into my seat, I looked out of the window as we taxied down the runway. Relief washed over me; I would be able to tell Lawrence we had some good news.

I hadn't expected to see Lawrence until I reached home, but emerging into the tiny arrival hall there he stood, waiting for me. Silvano had kindly taken him to the station, then he'd caught the train to Pisa Airport. It was so good to see him. We hugged, then headed off to grab a coffee. Even without the caffeine injection of a double espresso, I was so churned up that Lawrence had to remind me several times to breathe.

Once I'd filled him in on the morning's meeting, we headed home to a joyous Todo. Never has anywhere felt more like a safe haven than Poggiolino did then. And Todo's loving welcome was exactly what I needed.

Over the next four weeks things were extremely rough. While there was room for hope, nothing was certain and ruination remained a very real possibility. Our world had turned upside down and we felt as though the future had been put on hold. We had to keep the business going, deal with our clients as normal, all the while knowing that an axe hung over our heads.

Inevitably the whole thing put an enormous strain on our relationship. Those weeks were the worst we'd ever been through together. Lawrence had been as kind as he could in the first week, but with time dragging on, no clear resolution and the threat still so real, I felt he began to blame me for having brought this on us. Even though we'd discussed these contracts, as we did everything, and he hadn't raised any of the issues which now confronted us, it was me who had agreed them. TV, videos and books were a long way from his work in the opera and concert world, the risks and pitfalls much greater. I felt guilty and miserable and although Lawrence did his best to stay calm, we were snappy with each other most of the time.

I knew that Todo sensed the tension between us. He'd only ever known Carol as a widow, Jim having died many years before she took him in, so it must have been a strange feeling that the two people who loved him so dearly, and whom he loved, were now at odds, resulting in terse silences or explosions of rage and frustration.

Everything depended on the book and video sales. If the video did as well – or better – than the book, the action might be dropped. Only time would tell.

In the meantime we could only carry on with the life we had been creating, and hope that it would not be snatched away from us. Walking in the hills, sitting on our terrace, meandering through the streets of Lucca – all of these helped to keep us sane in the face of a threat to the whole fabric of our existence.

We didn't tell Teresa all the details of what had happened – our Italian wasn't up to it, even if we'd wanted to – but it was obvious she understood we were facing difficulties, and her steady presence and quiet stoicism comforted us.

Umberto, another constant in our lives, came regularly to work in the garden and kept the *orto* stocked in preparation for the winter. Onions, aubergines, parsley and the late summer salads still remained and, although he hadn't as yet become overly proprietorial, the kitchen garden was Lawrence's pride and joy. He loved heading down to pick courgettes or tomatoes just minutes before cooking them for dinner.

On every visit Umberto would chastise me about the mock acacia tree Carol had planted in front of the terrace. 'I always told La Signora the tree was wrong for this area, so close to the house,' he would say. 'It needs to come down.' I had resisted for months, loath to cut down any thriving tree, but I could see it was too big. No doubt only a sapling when Carol planted it thirty years earlier, now it stood more than twenty feet high. Lawrence agreed with Umberto, so I decided to ask Teresa what she thought. To my surprise she concurred, so – to a cheer from Lawrence, who had tired of endlessly sweeping up leaves – I gave in.

By lunch Umberto had lopped off all the branches and in the afternoon he took down the trunk in two-foot sections, providing a wood supply for our fire that would see us through half the winter. When he called us to come and see the garden minus the tree, the sight greeting us was a thing of wonder. The entire vista had opened up; the garden felt so much lighter, brighter and bigger. Most magical of all, we now had a 180° view, starting from the hills of the Apennines, through little villages, including Fontanella, up to San Martino church and beyond. And where previously we'd had to go into the field next to the garden to see them, the rugged, wooded hills reaching far into the distance dotted with terracotta rooftops were now perfectly visible.

We were speechless, bowled over by the beauty of the panorama. Umberto laughed. 'La Signora got so many things right, but this she didn't. I think this might be the most beautiful vista in the whole valley and she kept it covered up.' Six weeks later the hard prune he gave the olive trees after the harvest opened up the garden even more, giving us an unimpaired view every morning of the hazy mist rising from the foothills opposite, dissolving to reveal the glorious russet reds and purples of autumn and early winter.

The removal of the tree held great significance for me. It had opened up a whole new world, and in my mind it somehow symbolised the obstacle that shrouded us in doubt and fear. I hoped and prayed that the threat of a court case would also be removed, leaving us with a bright, clear landscape – our future life in Italy.

17

Bandana Days

It had been the worst autumn we'd known. The threat of legal action had been a huge blow and the hunters remained a daily annoyance. We were still seriously frightened every time the fax machine whirred into action. But although I wished that none of it had happened, in a curious way it had also been a test of our resolve. Underlying our concern, there was a growing confidence that we had weathered the storm intact and could cope with whatever came our way.

Finally, after several weeks of suspense, in early December I received an email from Alexander confirming the legal threat had abated. Both the video and book were doing very well; as I had always hoped, they had complemented each other. The production company seemed happy with their sales figures. We were left £7,000 worse off, but we'd survived.

A couple of weeks before Christmas, Albertina, Herbert and Laura arrived for lunch at Poggiolino. It was the first time we had entertained since the disastrous dinner with Teresa's family and we hoped that in some way it might draw a line under the troubles that had arrived that evening.

'Goodness me, doesn't Todo look grand?' Laura exclaimed. Herbert, standing on the steps to survey the house and garden, agreed warmly. Albertina, bent over some of the plants, was in full flow, with Lawrence beside her.

'Oh look how well Carol's Sea Foam is doing,' she said, picking at the small-flowered white rose which had been in bloom since we'd arrived and only now looked as though it might finish. 'But, of course, really it was Jim's. Do you remember, Herbert, how Jim made an entire garden of white flowers?'

Herbert nodded but appeared distracted, lost perhaps in the memory of his last visit, days before Carol died. Not that this stopped Albertina. 'Except, of course, the Blue Waterfall,' she said, pointing at the campanula, cascading down the steps to the house. 'He was the first person to grow it around here; he gave cuttings to everyone they knew. You'll find Jim's flowers in most good gardens in these parts.'

The afternoon was a delight. Todo appeared very comfortable around our guests and I wondered if he recognised them from their many past visits. Lawrence excelled himself: in honour of our royal guest he presented *gnocchi alla Romana*, thick round slices of fresh pasta in a cheese sauce, followed by poached salmon with a saffron risotto. He had permitted me to make dessert and, inspired by the many versions we'd eaten in numerous *pasticcerias*, I attempted a strawberry frangipane tart. Just for once, Lawrence wasn't the only one to be complimented on his cooking! It was not a lunch for dogs, though Todo braved the slivers of fish quietly slipped to him by everyone around the table.

'Todo, I think you won the SuperLotto when Louise and Lawrence bought Carol's house,' said Herbert, reaching down to stroke the soft muzzle pressed into his lap. 'Do you know Carol would bring him in the car sometimes when she came to Lucca for meetings of the Music Society? Now and again, when we left, she'd joke to me, *he'd have made more sense than some of the people there if we'd brought him in.*'

The conversation turned to Christmas: we would spend our first in Poggiolino with a family of three cats and one dog while the Handts were heading back to Columbus, Ohio, Laura's home town.

'Albertina, will you go south to Positano?' Laura asked.

'Positano?' I quizzed.

'Ah yes, I have a house there, a charming place right on the sea. It can be very relaxing when the weather's cold up here.'

This was our third meal with her and we'd heard about a different home on every occasion. I wondered whether the count would keep on rising.

'Last time we toasted Carol and Jim,' said Herbert. 'Now I think we should toast dear Todo, without whom we wouldn't be here together.'

'Todo!' We raised our glasses, as Todo, happily oblivious, rolled on his back in the grass beyond the French windows.

Three days before Christmas the weather was still warm enough for us to have lunch outside. Tearing off pieces of ham for Todo and the cats, I threw a small slice to Cyd which landed accidentally on her head, making us laugh. We expected her to shake it off, but she didn't move, and looking at her more closely we could see something was wrong. A normal cat is held and stroked every day, so health problems are easy to spot, but it had never been possible to have that relationship with Cyd. The most beautiful cat we had ever owned, a small plump tawny with huge green eyes and a large soft face and paws, Cyd would have been an adoring lap-cat in another life but we had never once had a chance to stroke or cuddle her. This time, however, there was no quick dash away and no struggle when I went to approach her. I think Cyd knew she was in trouble and needed help.

We rushed her off to the vet's. '*Molto, molto grave*' was Tiziana's diagnosis as she shook her head sadly. They would keep her there to run more tests and get her under a heat lamp to raise her body temperature, which had fallen dangerously low. The following morning Tiziana was delighted Cyd had survived the night but told us she needed feeding by hand and, despite several efforts, neither Tiziana nor Viviana had been able to get near enough to give her the food.

But Cyd really seemed pleased to see us, kneading the blanket with her paws and lifting her head a little, and I realised in that moment just how much we meant to her. Despite her refusal to come near, we were the constant in Cyd's life and as I went over to her she seemed to have lost all her fear and I was able to pick her up and feed her gently by hand. We pushed the food into her mouth with a syringe, sitting with her for a long time, holding her tightly as she swallowed each mouthful. She managed to purr, which was encouraging, but we could see that Tiziana was not hopeful. She asked us to come twice a day to feed Cyd, which we promised to do.

That day was our twentieth wedding anniversary. A year earlier we had sat over a second glass of Armagnac in a busy restaurant in Borough Market, dreaming of a new life in a house in Tuscany. This time we had decided to splash out on the Michelin-starred restaurant La Mora, in Sesto di Moriano. We arrived to find the restaurant deserted. 'We could have brought Todo,' I whispered to Lawrence, as the owner explained to us that the Sunday before Christmas was the most popular time for visiting family, so nobody went out for lunch.

'I thought you might not be Italian when I saw the booking,' he explained, showing us to a table. Lawrence mentioned that it was a special celebration and two glasses of prosecco arrived. We went on to enjoy a delicious meal, even if having the entire restaurant to ourselves felt a little strange.

Our first Christmas passed with our days divided between the vet's and home. On Christmas Eve we walked across the fields to Chiesa San Martino for midnight mass, the hillside lit only by the moon, the air crisp and cold.

For many Italians the Church continues to be at the heart of daily life and at Christmas time the buildings come alive with the *presepi* – nativity scenes which are created year after year in all different shapes and sizes. The attention to detail is remarkable, as are the individual choices made by each creator about which parts of the Christmas story to tell; Fontanella's contained a gruesome depiction of Herod carrying out his decree of murdering each first-born son personally! My favourite could be found housed in the tiny chapel by the side of Villa Carola, made from paper, with toy animals, a small stable and the cast of Mary, Joseph, baby Jesus and three Wise Men. With the doors to the chapel open each morning, we were reminded of the story every time we passed by on Todo's morning walk.

For the mass, San Martino was filled with candles, flowers and its own *presepio* and we felt lucky to be there, with friends and neighbours, even though Lawrence complained about the guitar, electric keyboard and lack of rousing hymns. 'It's just not Christmas without "Oh Come All Ye Faithful".' We strolled home with Teresa, Silvano and Mario, all wishing one another a *Buon Natale* as we went into our homes.

Christmas Day was quiet as were, mercifully, the hunters. Teresa had spent it cooking for Carol for the past thirty years, so she must have been relieved that our life was a great deal less sophisticated. Finally able to enjoy a Christmas with her family, we assured her that Lawrence was very happy to cook our meal. In all honesty we were grateful to escape an Italian Christmas dinner, an eating fest of five to six hours. I'm not sure we would have been able to cope. Italians start their dinner with all the usual antipasti and then move on to *primi*, a special lasagne made only at this time. Then main courses of meat and poultry: turkey is not especially popular so duck, pheasant or pork are common, followed by *dolci* – different types of tarts and cakes plus the ubiquitous *panettone*, with wine, grappa and sweet biscuits. We encountered an exhausted-looking Maurizio on Boxing Day, who turned pale at the mere mention of food.

Our meal was much less ambitious: turkey, fresh vegetables from the *orto* and an Italian version of chipolatas, wrapped in pancetta. Todo was in scraps heaven and the three of us lingered over the meal for several lovely hours, before setting out to walk it off in the hills.

By Boxing Day, amazingly, Cyd had started to pull through and was able to come home with us, though with her restored strength, her wariness also returned. Sadly the diagnosis confirmed what our vet in London had suspected some years before: that Cyd had feline lymphoma. Viviana explained that the symptoms would return but for now she was, against all odds, recovering, and Woody and Bob welcomed her back, rubbing up against her and chirruping.

Italians say that Christmas is for family and New Year is for friends, and in keeping with this a good friend of ours, Ania, came to stay for a week. While pleased to see us, she was even more thrilled to see Todo and had brought him a very special present – a large red bandana. Modelled on those worn by cowboys from the days of the Wild West, it leant him a gentler air – Todo the seasoned traveller, perhaps. He couldn't have been more delighted, skipping around the sitting-room as if he'd worn one all his life. His bandana would become very special; putting it on him for a trip into Lucca would bring an extra spring to his step as he drew admiring looks, comments and strokes from countless people.

It also adorned his sweet face on longer trips out, known forever more as Bandana Days. From the moment I reached into the cupboard where it was stored, he became wildly excited, knowing a special day lay ahead. Our photo albums are filled with pictures: Todo and bandana on the Ponte Vecchio; Todo and bandana propping up Pisa's Leaning Tower; a bandana-clad Todo grinning outside his favourite restaurant in Parma.

For New Year's Eve we had booked a table at one of our favourite restaurants in Lucca. The three of us arrived at eight and, incredibly, managed to sit and eat for the next four hours as the staff brought us no less than eight courses. Or at least we tried to. In spite of Lawrence's best Italian, the first plate to arrive contained freshly hand-cut pink prosciutto and salami.

'Did you mention I'm vegetarian?' said Ania, staring down at the offending fare.

'I phoned ahead, but let me check again,' said Lawrence, gesturing to the waiter.

'Our friend doesn't eat meat . . .'

'Perhaps some vegetable soup?'

'That sounds lovely,' we chorused.

'That's just with meat stock,' he replied, smiling.

By the final course, a traditional *cotechino* – a blood sausage with lentils – untouched by Ania - we were ready to forswear food for the next week.

With midnight approaching, we staggered off to Piazza Napoleone for the fireworks. The piazza is used for celebrations and events throughout the year – the annual festival of chocolate, a summer pop festival, a skating rink in the winter and the huge Festival of Comics and Games which attracts nearly 100,000 visitors each year. We'd expected an organised display, like those held all over Britain, but the true anarchy of the Italian spirit was clearly evident in the free-for-all taking place before us. With the emergency services standing by in their bright orange uniforms, chatting happily with friends and watching proceedings as if it were a children's tea party, the citizens of Lucca went mad with large, lethal fireworks; setting them off with no concern for safety, lobbing firecrackers at each other and sending hand-held rockets into the happy crowd.

We had toyed with the idea of taking Todo but were mightily relieved we'd decided not to. On our return he was duly rewarded with an assortment of leftovers from our meal, including steak and almost all of the *cotechino*. It would have been wrong for him not to share in the final meal of our first year with him in Italy.

Early in the New Year we set out on our very first Bandana Day, to see the famous Ponte del Diavolo, the Devil's Bridge. Its true name is Ponte della Maddalena and we'd been intrigued each time we passed it on our way to the Notaio's office. The bridge emerges from the still waters of the River Serchio like a giant brontosaurus, an extraordinary shape, arching high into the air and so narrow that it can only be crossed on foot.

The bandana came out and soon we were speeding along

the Abetone road, taking us past Ponte a Moriano before rounding a large turn between two open-cast quarries and heading over the Serchio, with the Garfagnana in full view.

As I parked the car, Lawrence leapt out, striding purposefully to the bridge. Too impatient for guide books, he ignored me as I pulled mine out and started to read. 'It was built almost a thousand years ago, on the orders of the Countess Matilda; a classic donkey-back bridge with four asymmetric arches . . .' I trailed off; Lawrence and Todo were now at the foot of the bridge, Lawrence bending down, talking to him and tugging gently at his lead. But Todo had his back turned, his gaze locked firmly on the pizzeria on the other side of the road.

'C'mon Todo, even for you it's too early for lunch. Let's walk the bridge first then we'll see.'

But Todo was resolute. Normally happy to go anywhere with us, he stood stock-still and refused to place a paw on the bridge.

'Let me try,' I said to Lawrence. 'Let's go and explore, Todo. See those people all the way up there?'

No joy.

Lawrence went ahead, bounding his way irritatingly cheerfully up the very steep rise to the top. Finally, very begrudgingly, Todo set off alongside me, the two of us making our way up slowly, Todo trudging a few steps behind.

'Hurry up, slowcoach; the view's wonderful up here!'

I couldn't be sure if Lawrence was calling to me or Todo, so I cursed him on behalf of us both. But reaching the top I understood his enthusiasm. The breathtaking view, from the snow-covered Apennine mountains up-river to the gentler blue pine-covered hills towards Pisa, was more than worth the steep and dog-encumbered ascent.

We walked down the bridge on the other side and then

re-crossed, Todo still slinking miserably, his tail down. When the end was in sight he broke into a trot before bounding off the bridge and pulling me towards the car.

'What was that all about?' Lawrence asked him as I drove home. 'You didn't like that, did you? But why not?'

Later that evening, as Lawrence put on that favourite Schumann symphony again, I settled down with a book of Lucca legends. The doorbell interrupted us. 'Your turn,' he said.

I sighed. It felt as if we'd been up and down all evening. Whenever we sat on the sofa, Todo contrived to be on the wrong side of the French windows, breathing heavily on the glass and rubbing saliva and snot into it as he waited for one of us to open it, and he'd been even busier than usual that evening.

'*Buon giorno*, Teresa. Will you come in?' It was unusual to see her at the front gates but this was a social call. She had come to give us a leaflet advertising a concert on the coming weekend at San Martino. Following her towards the living-room, I could hear the music. Todo, just as he had the previous time we played Schumann, dashed past us, running up the steps to the garage before turning round and haring into the sitting-room again.

'Ah, La Signora's music,' Teresa smiled.

Lawrence asked what she meant. 'It was La Signora's favourite; she played it all the time. He must remember it. You know it, don't you Totino?' she said, bending to stroke him and calling him by his pet name.

We looked at one another. That explained his extraordinary, restless and excited behaviour. The music must have been a powerful connection with his past.

After Teresa left, with Lawrence and Todo settling down together to listen and enjoy, I went back to my book. I wanted to find out how the bridge got its nickname. Moments later I found the story and could hardly believe what I read.

'*That's* why he didn't like it.'

'What do you mean?'

'It's the legend of the Devil's Bridge!' The story handed down for centuries concerned the architect of the original bridge and his struggle to complete what he hoped would be a structure everyone would admire, recognising him as the greatest designer of his time. Standing on the half-completed bridge, searching hard to find inspiration, suddenly the devil appeared, offering to show him a way to finish it that would bring the fame and fortune he craved. But there was a catch; in return for his help, the devil demanded the soul of the first person to cross it.

The deal was struck and the bridge completed. Magnificent, it was opened with grand ceremony, but lurking beneath one of the four arches lay the devil, awaiting his payment. Desperate to find a way out of his predicament, the architect enticed a stray dog onto the bridge. Climbing to the top, the devil recognised the deceit and, outraged, picked up the dog, hurling him with such force that he crashed through the bridge into the waters of the Serchio and to Hell beneath.

Lawrence read the page out loud and we both looked at Todo, lying with his snout pressed against the floor; perfectly still except for one opened eye, looking knowingly at us.

'You were right, Todo,' Lawrence said solemnly. 'It's not a place for dogs! Well don't you worry, that bridge is strictly off-limits from now on. You're safe with us.'

18

Farewell to Cyd

Our first spring in Tuscany will stay in our memory for the saddest of reasons. Our lovely, wild and beautiful Cyd died.

She had recovered well from her Christmas illness, and with the warm weather approaching she was back basking in the sunshine, until one morning we found her hunched and still in the corner of the garden. We took her straight to the vets, but as soon as Viviana saw her and took her temperature she shook her head, telling us quietly, 'There's nothing we can do. The lymphoma is too advanced, she has only a few days left.'

Those last two days of her life were extraordinary but also heartbreaking. Vicky Halls, the animal behaviourist who had first helped us with Cyd and Woody, had told us that the stress hormones which seriously frightened animals produce, especially in their early days, can weaken their immune systems making them more susceptible to disease. With the lymphoma now attacking Cyd so virulently, it was as if the part of her that triggered fear had gone and in that cruelly brief time she became the perfect lap-cat, refusing to move from our sides.

It was a bittersweet experience: at last we could stroke her as much as we wanted and she could give us the love she so clearly had within her. Over the years she had come close to jumping up beside us on the sofa but something always held her back. Seeing her now, we realised how she must really have wanted to be near, but could never conquer her own fear.

With Cyd fading fast and beginning to have fits, we took her back to Viviana, who was warm and sympathetic, giving her a deep sedative before touching my arm, 'I'll be back in a few minutes.' She left us alone to say a final farewell, Cyd lying still and peaceful in my arms.

'Goodbye darling girl,' I whispered, 'no more fear now.'

Cats are such tiny creatures really and the final dose takes no time at all. One last check of her heart and Viviana told us, 'She's gone.' She kissed and hugged us both as we tearfully placed Cyd back in her basket.

Back home, Lawrence set about digging a grave while I put Cyd on the warm terrace, hoping the other animals would come to say goodbye. Todo came first. He loved the company of friends in the house, even if Cyd hadn't always appreciated his attentions! He sniffed gently at her and then wandered to the pergola a few yards away and lay down.

Bob and Woody came together, and Bob stayed for a few minutes before sloping off to a nearby olive tree. Woody sat next to his sister and remained there for a full half hour. We were happy to wait until he moved away, then Lawrence picked her up and we took her to the bottom of the garden. Once the earth had been replaced, I laid a small collection of the prettiest camellias on top. We went back to the office, but I noticed later that Woody had returned to her grave; he would stay there until nightfall.

When Teresa came the following morning she was both sympathetic and pragmatic; she adores animals as much as anyone I've known but recognises that their time with us is short and life moves on, and for her moving on meant only one thing: a new cat. By a lucky coincidence one of her females was pregnant and the kittens were due soon. 'You will have the first girl born,' she told us and I knew it wasn't a matter for negotiation.

Some weeks later Todo showed great interest in the contents of a small cardboard box I held carefully in my hands as we walked together down the hill from Teresa's house. 'No, it's not a chicken for you,' I scolded as we arrived home, taking out the tiny bundle of fur which became the newest addition to our family.

Following in a tradition established with the cats we had during the early years of our marriage, Lawrence wracked his brain to decide which famous footballer should have the honour of bestowing his name on our new kitten. Previously the exclusive preserve of Liverpool players, now he was ready to embrace our new home and culture. 'She's an Italian cat . . . she will be Totti after Francesco who plays for Roma!' *Poor thing*, I thought.

Quite the ugliest little kitten I had ever seen, with mud grey fur and a pointy little face, what Totti lacked in looks she made up for in personality. The other cats looked on disdainfully as she skittered through the house, eyes bulging and head whirling, and kept a polite distance. But she was not a cat to be ignored. When Teresa had proudly shown me the young litter, Totti – already larger than her brothers and sisters – pushed her paw into the face of another kitten, holding him back from the food bowl. *That's my girl!* So while the other cats resisted her overtures there was still Todo, who was at least tolerant of her advances. She soon decided it was a lot more fun being a dog than a cat and he gained another pal. Her line of thought was evident: *What point is that lovely feathery tail? The perfect material for a kitten to cling to. No dog should sleep alone in his basket; he needs a cat in there! Why should only humans accompany a dog on his walks? Cats can come too.* And indeed she did, even braving the attentions of Rex and Varco to become one of the gang, charging through the olive groves every morning.

Todo largely ignored her attentions: their relationship often seemed like that of a friendly cow swatting away a fly with a flick of the tail, but over time he came to enjoy her company. And of course there was the bonus of another food bowl around the house. Finding her food snuvered, Totti would exact her revenge, stealing from his bowl before beating a hasty retreat.

Teresa was delighted that Totti had settled in so well and laughed the first time she saw her get into Todo's basket with him, settling down for a nap.

One spring morning she came over to tell us she had arranged for Don Mauro, the priest of San Martino, to come and bless the house for Easter. Rejecting my argument that we weren't Catholics, she insisted. 'La Signora had it every year.' A couple of weeks later he arrived, and knowing him to be a great music lover Lawrence put on a CD of Bach's *St Matthew Passion*. Many years of singing in choirs at his local church and Cambridge gave him the spiritual advantage over me; he knew how to get into the Church's good books!

'Ah, the St Matthew,' the priest announced on entering, 'surely no music more profound for this time of the year.'

A slight man with neat dark hair and spectacles perched in the middle of his kindly face, he wore a traditional black cassock but over the top sported a padded puffa jacket. He spoke good Tuscan Italian and I was delighted that I could understand so much as we chatted about music, his desire to hold more concerts at the church and his memories of the valley, of Carol and of Poggiolino.

Finally losing my way in the conversation, I continued to nod and 'mmm' in what I thought were the appropriate places before glancing at Lawrence and noticing, to my embarrassment, that he had bowed his head. I hadn't realised that the prayers had started.

As Don Mauro recited several Easter verses, I quickly lowered my head too, though the reverent atmosphere was marred somewhat by the ringing of the Don's mobile phone halfway through.

As for Todo, he behaved himself impeccably throughout, only starting to sniff at the priest's shoes once we'd recited our last *Amen*.

Given that the trip to the Devil's Bridge had been something of a damp squib, we decided it was time for a real treat. On the Saturday of the Easter weekend, with Todo bouncing up and down excitedly, we produced the red bandana again. 'Today we're going to La Foce, near Siena. It's a long drive,' I told him.

One of the many writers whose lives have fed my hunger for things Italian is the Anglo-American author Iris Origo who settled in Italy in the early part of the twentieth century. After marrying an Italian, Antonio, she moved into La Foce, a large estate near Chianciano Terme. It was in a bad state of disrepair, and the restoration of the villa and garden became her life's passion. I'd wanted to visit ever since we moved, so I was nearly as excited as Todo.

He was his usual absorbed self in the car, rarely responding when either of us spoke to him, happy simply to stare out of the window as the rolling countryside flashed by, even foregoing his normal mid-morning nap so that he wouldn't miss a moment of the fun.

We knew this area of southern Tuscany well, having regularly visited the extraordinary medieval cities of San Gimignano and Siena, where we'd been lucky enough to see the Palio, the famous horse-race in which the splendour and passion of the spectacle leave modern sport in the shade.

We stopped for lunch at Montepulciano and walked up the main street from the city gate to the town square; the very same path along which Kristen Stewart, as Bella Swan, ran in the second of the *Twilight* films, heading to the square in an effort to save her darling Edward. I was quite excited, but Todo seemed strangely unimpressed.

He behaved himself beautifully as we walked through the magnificent gardens of La Foce. On the wall outside, with Iris and Antonio's famous man-made serpent road in the background, Lawrence took a photo of me with Todo and it became one of our favourites; he has a wistful look, leaning into me but staring into the distance, lost in his own thoughts.

Albertina told us Carol had visited La Foce regularly. I don't know if she ever took Todo but there was something about his look and manner that afternoon that suggested an uncanny awareness of his surroundings. After the incidents with the Devil's Bridge and the Schumann symphony, we had begun to wonder just how much lay locked away behind that endearing face. The drive home was long, but Todo stayed awake the entire way, still eager to look out of the windows, even as the light began to fade.

★ ★ ★

A few weeks later we decided to try Sunday lunch at a restaurant we'd heard about – Le Colonne at Matraia up in the hills. 'Order the grilled *gallino*,' a friend recommended.

When we arrived we found the restaurant bursting at the seams. We'd picked a day when many of the local children were celebrating their *cresima* or confirmation, and one party alone occupied forty-five places. The obliging owner set up a table for us in the front courtyard, overlooking the valley, with the bell tower of Montecarlo, some fifteen kilometres away, visible through the hazy sunshine.

The *gallino*, a small capon very popular in the area, came accompanied by a beautifully fresh salad. With a carafe of sparkling white wine it was perfection. Todo, well used to a regular supply of morsels, was sorely disappointed that we wouldn't feed him, concerned the meat might contain small bones. Ever hopeful, his face popped up expectantly every few minutes.

'Is the dog hungry?' asked the owner.

'This dog is never hungry,' replied Lawrence, 'he just loves food.'

'Would he like some steak?'

I laughed. 'I'd say that would be a yes.'

Minutes later the owner returned with a large piece of silver foil, unwrapping it to reveal a huge sirloin cut into bite-size chunks. I reached for my handbag, thinking he would give it to us to take home, but to my amazement he placed the foil on the ground in front of Todo's excited snout. '*Buon cane*, try this,' he said.

Whoosh! Seconds later the enormous steak was gone.

'Wow! That was impressive, even for Todo,' Lawrence exclaimed.

The look of pleasure on the owner's face was only slightly outdone by the one on our dog's.

From then on Le Colonne kept the undisputed top spot as Todo's favourite restaurant. We returned regularly, and every time he began salivating the moment the car door opened. Not that he was picky; Todo loved dining out, and became an old hand at the restaurant business.

Another favourite was La Cantina, a pizzeria in the Compitese hills. Tired and slightly hungover after dancing our way through that first Sagra, we had decided to head there for the first time on the recommendation of Umberto and Daniele for a restorative cure of pizza and beer. We had also been keen to take Todo out and about with us more and were beginning to realise that the Italians have a far more relaxed view than us Brits towards dogs – funny, given that we are so much more pet-obsessed. In fact they frequently allow dogs into restaurants, but at that stage we were still not certain that Todo would be welcome.

A tall dark-haired woman met us at the door of La Cantina and Lawrence asked her if it was okay to bring our dog in.

'*Sì, sì*, of course; he looks a good dog.'

And indeed he was. The restaurant resembled a very large cafeteria, with space for more than two hundred people upstairs and down, as well as another terrace full of tables and chairs around the corner from ours. I looped his lead around a table leg as we sat on the terrace under a brightly coloured parasol and, patting his head, told him he had to behave.

Lawrence started chatting with our waitress and discovered that the woman who'd greeted us was Federica, daughter of Alfredo who'd founded the restaurant back in 1965. We love these family-run places, where the welcome is warm, the produce grown locally and the resulting menu delicious and well priced. And this one didn't disappoint. After years of chain-restaurant pizzas, it was a delight to sample its wood-fired slices of heaven, steam still rising as they arrived on our plates. (Lawrence's devotion to La Cantina was cemented another Sunday a few months later, when Federica switched the big-screen TV over to English football, enabling him to watch Liverpool beat Bolton Wanderers 3–1. Pizza, beer, Todo and Steven Gerrard: what more could a man want?)

Todo managed to remain remarkably restrained on the first of our many subsequent trips; even when the dishes began to arrive, laden with focaccia, prosciutto and *pasta fritta* – a kind of small savoury doughnut sprinkled liberally with salt. His eyes fixed on me, pleading for a treat. Then, while I still hesitated, a large prawn landed beside Todo's grateful nose and was snuvered in a millisecond.

'*Ciao*, who's a good boy?'

I looked up to see the young man at the next table picking up another prawn from his plate for Todo, who was now hovering in a state of joyful anticipation.

The look of pleasure on both culprits' faces was hard to resist. At that point any remnant of the rule book went out of the window. Todo loved treats, we loved treating him and, as we said to one another if we ever entertained a momentary pang of guilt about it, 'Well, after what he went through, who could begrudge him?'

19

The New MacAndrews

The longer we spent with Todo, the more we realised that his greatest happiness was in having regained his life at Poggiolino. Although he loved being with us, following us constantly around the house and garden, he also determinedly did his own thing, a pattern established in the days when Carol would let him out of the garden each morning and evening so he could roam around the fields by himself.

Teresa loved to tell the story about the time he disappeared for two days. 'La Signora, she was very worried, calling the Carabinieri. I told her he would find someone to bring him home, and he did.' Maurizio confirmed that he'd been a devil to keep restrained when younger. All those blocks and bricks at the bottom of the garden fence failed to keep him in.

'He wanted to get out and have fun, so he did; he would always find a way. And he always came back – a good dog.'

While he might still enjoy exploring on his own – his

escapade with one of Teresa's chickens was testament to that – we discovered early on that he was slow to appreciate new places. During our first few weeks we would drive into Lucca on Sundays to promenade the ancient walls, along with many of the city's residents. Todo's tail and ears went down, he clearly wasn't pleased, and his erratic way of walking, criss-crossing in front of us and into the path of cyclists, made these Sunday excursions something of an obstacle course. There is always a whole little world taking place on the walls: walkers, joggers, the local archery club, one man taking his cat out in the basket of his bicycle, everyone chatting and greeting each other. It's a truly wonderful way to spend a Sunday morning.

On one visit we came upon an assault course erected by local police-dog handlers. Their perfectly trained animals were performing a variety of challenging tasks and sitting impres-sively still for minutes on end while diversions went on around them. After the display they offered the chance of a short train-ing session with your dog, under their expert guidance. Todo stood for a few moments staring at the other dogs jumping over hurdles, crawling through tunnels and fetching sticks thrown by the handlers, before looking up at Lawrence as if to say *I hope you're not expecting me to do any of that!* We assured him we weren't, and headed to the nearest bar, much more to his liking. Anyway, I thought, he has many talents those other dogs don't . . . I just couldn't think of any right then.

No, Lucca and the walls were for city dogs and at heart Todo remained a country boy, so back to our fields we went; it was always there, with space to roam and all the familiar sights and smells, that he was at his happiest.

After almost a year in Poggiolino, and with our Italian much improved, chats with the neighbours when we were out walking Todo were becoming much more interesting. Without language you become one-dimensional, unable to communicate anything complex, which I found incredibly frustrating. But all the studying, watching the news and listening to the radio were slowly but surely paying off. Lawrence had even started rowing in Italian, usually with courier companies claiming they couldn't find us. As we delighted in flexing our linguistic muscles, walks became increasingly social. While Todo meandered in every direction but forward, we would stop and chat to people busying themselves with their gardens and all-important *orti*.

Just beyond Teresa's house lived Frediano, who had been horrified to see Lawrence wearing a short-sleeved shirt one autumn day. 'You'll catch a cold, winter's coming,' he warned.

'It's 22°!' Lawrence whispered to me. Balmy to us, but as we were discovering, to the country people around us there was always trouble – and bad weather – just around the corner.

We thought Frediano had lived on the hillside the longest of any of the residents until we chatted more with our neighbour Lorenzo. His wife, Giuliana, gave us constant encouragement about the progress of our Italian and they both delighted in seeing Todo trotting past their house once more.

'We were so worried about him after La Signora died. We wondered what might become of him if somebody kind didn't buy Poggiolino,' they told us.

Renzo, as he was known locally, had been a favourite of Carol's. He'd worked for her for years and still helped Mario with the harvesting of both grapes and olives on the land she had owned around the villa. Lawrence asked him how long he had lived on the hill, and he replied, 'Well, my family has been here since 1741.'

One morning we met a red-haired woman in her sixties outside her beautiful farmhouse, a classic rustic Tuscan construction with thick stone walls and terracotta roof tiles. '*Salve*,' she greeted us but Lawrence recognised her accent as American and replied in English, telling her that we were new to the area.

'Welcome to the Colle,' she smiled. 'Where have you bought?'

'Poggiolino, just before the fork in the road,' he replied.

'Ah, the Signora's house.'

'Yes. Did you know her?'

'Not very well. I don't think we fell into her circle. I'm a New Yorker and I suspect she thought we were brash and not her sort. Once or twice she'd totter up here in her high heels and suit struggling with her little dog and we'd say hello, but we didn't socialise.'

As if on cue, Todo appeared from behind the tree where he'd been snuvering some corn that had been left on the ground.

'Don't tell me that's him!' exclaimed our newly discovered neighbour. 'It's been such a long time . . . I assumed he'd died too.'

As if to emphasise the misconception, Todo padded towards her and nuzzled her hand, though it might have had more to do with the chicken feed she was carrying than genuine friendliness.

She laughed and gave him a stroke. 'I'm Amy; it's nice to meet you. Next time come and have some coffee.' We thanked her, and promised we would.

★ ★ ★

Late in May we reached the anniversary of our move, and our first year as *Luisa e Lorenzo*. Despite the trials of adjusting to a new language and culture, the stresses of living in a building site, the tense weeks when we'd feared we might have to give up everything we'd worked so hard for and our sadness at losing Cyd, it had been a magical year.

'Any regrets about the move?' Lawrence asked me, over a celebratory glass of prosecco, and I could honestly say, 'None at all.'

The following Sunday, the first of June, sitting on the terrace eating my marmite and toast – one English indulgence I can't do without – I called to Lawrence to join me as Todo sang along to the bells. But as the 9.30 a.m. peal rang out and we looked towards Todo, he appeared oblivious and continued chasing after a chewy stick I'd given him the previous evening.

'Has he gone deaf?' Lawrence joked. 'Todo, Todo, it's the bells!'

Todo looked over at us then wandered back into the house.

It was exactly a year since we'd first heard his sweet song and he had sung faithfully every Sunday morning since, but after that day he would never again sing to the bells. I wondered, was it his way of letting us know that his sadness at Carol's death had passed and, even if we had missed those early years, we were now his beloved companions?

While we missed Todo's song each Sunday morning, there seemed little else on the horizon to spoil the summer that stretched ahead. With work going reasonably smoothly, we were able to enjoy occasional days off. We loved driving with Todo into the mountains of the Garfagnana to explore the dazzlingly beautiful scenery, take long walks and stop for a coffee in little hilltop villages. We also enjoyed time on the beach at Viareggio, just twenty minutes away. This art nouveau resort grew up in the 1920s and is wonderfully evocative of its bygone age, rows of brightly coloured umbrellas and parasols in long, neat lines on different sections of the private bathing area, many owned by some of the grand hotels set back from the seafront, their titles – Imperiale, Principe di Piemonte, Astor – betraying their aristocratic origins. In the sea you can stand facing the beach and see the dramatic backdrop of the bleached-white mountains of Massa and Carrara, from where was hewn the marble for Michelangelo's David.

It was here, on a holiday in 2006, that Lawrence had turned to me and said, 'We really should buy a house around here.' With his new wi-fi laptop, he had sat sipping coffee in the shaded area of our section of the beach, children playing noisily in the pool behind us, while checking and sending emails to and from the UK.

'The thing is, Lou, nobody knows I'm not at the office. With even better landline connections we can make this work easily.'

A month earlier we'd visited Bologna, celebrating Italy's dramatic victory in the World Cup final, marvelling at the clash of cultures and epochs as we watched on a huge hi-definition screen erected in the grand medieval Piazza Maggiore with the fourteenth-century church of San Petronio to one side. As the crowd erupted with Fabio Grosso's winning penalty, Lawrence had said determinedly, 'I want to be a part of this.' Or maybe, I mused, he just wanted to support a team in with a chance of winning the World Cup. But at that moment, and the second a month later in Viareggio, we knew, with sudden and defining certainty, that we wanted to move to Italy.

And at the house we had bought just four months later we were now – to our delight – being called the *new* MacAndrews, in semi-jest but with real affection. We continued to meet regularly with Herbert and Laura and had been to see him conduct a performance of *Tosca* at the Teatro Rassicurati in Montecarlo, a quintessential Italian theatre but on the tiniest scale, seating just 120 people. From the outside it appears like any of the houses in the street that runs from the town square to the Florentine gate, but inside, its gold-brocaded and ornately decorated boxes and stalls wouldn't be out of place in Rome or Milan.

'We'd like to take you kids to Carol's favourite restaurant, Erasmo,' Laura told us one day, making me laugh at the thought of two forty-seven-year-olds being referred to as kids! Arriving at the restaurant before them we were amused still further to discover Herbert had made the booking in the name MacAndrew.

It was easy to understand why Carol had liked it so much. Besides the exceptional food, created with traditional Tuscan ingredients and recipes, the place itself is full of history, having been in existence since 1760 when the Marcucci family opened it to cater for merchants coming from the Garfagnana to Lucca or travellers heading to Modena further north.

'What became of the family?' I asked the owner after he finished reciting a list of specials for the *Maestro* and the *Signora*.

'I am Lorenzo Marcucci; it is *my* family! I'm very pleased to meet you. Signora MacAndrew was one of our most welcome guests. And I hear you also have her little dog? I remember she would bring him here; a very well-behaved fellow.'

We assured him that Todo remained well-behaved, and were delighted when he replied, 'Then please bring him next time.'

Laura had previously been quite reticent about her career, but over lunch she told us how, while living in Rome, her reputation reached England and she received a call from the office of the great Anglo-American sculptor Jacob Epstein. He wanted to meet her and see her work, could she come to London? *Of course*, she replied, though she was a little taken aback when he suggested doing so in two days' time.

Packing as many of her sculptures as she could in the back seat and boot of Herbert's aged VW Beetle, she set off up Italy's main artery, the Via Aurelia. 'The Romans built a road on that route in 241 BC and it hadn't greatly improved since then,' she said. After two days of high-speed driving she found herself navigating her way around the streets of London, searching for the very smart restaurant Epstein had suggested.

Arriving, hot, tired and rather flustered, she was met by the great man himself as well as a coterie of other luminaries from the art world. Introduced as the exciting new discovery, she was amazed and not a little intimidated to find herself the star attraction of the dinner. With rationing only just finished in post-war Britain, Epstein had spared no expense and the centre-piece of the meal was a whole sea bass, then almost impossible to obtain.

Unfortunately, the effects of the long drive began to catch up with Laura and she started to feel faint and queasy. Trying her best to sparkle in the face of this lavish hospitality and the praise being heaped upon her, she attempted some of the fish, but within minutes her condition worsened until finally she had to excuse herself and rush to the ladies' bathroom. There she remained for the rest of the evening, much to the chagrin of Epstein.

'Do you know, I never heard from him again and left a couple of days later with my work unwrapped!'

As we laughed, Lawrence said, 'There's a famous statue of his outside Lewis's store in Liverpool, called "Liverpool Resurgent", and at school I stripped naked to read a poem while imitating it.' Thankfully omitting the costume change, he recited as much as he could remember, to Laura's amusement.

'Carol met some pretty famous people here,' said Herbert. 'One night we were all due to have dinner somewhere else, but she called me at the last minute to cancel, she had another engagement. I was a bit put out so next time I saw her I asked who with and she said, "Oh . . . Marcello and Gina."'

Not recognising the names, he'd wondered if they were people from the music business or perhaps some of the many financiers she courted, raising funds for the Society.

Still peeved, he'd quizzed her further, and she'd told him that dining in Erasmo a few days earlier she'd sat at an adjacent table to one where four very beautiful people were seated. She soon recognised two of them as the great Italian actors Marcello Mastroianni – star of *La Dolce Vita* – and Gina Lollobrigida. Mastroianni was well known in the Lucca area – he had a splendid house with an extensive vineyard and olive groves near San Martino in Freddana.

'Carol got on with everyone,' continued Herbert. 'Soon the two tables were pushed together and a joint booking made for a few days later. So I was passed over for a couple of film stars.'

As we were leaving the restaurant, Herbert took us to another of the dining-rooms, pointing at a spot on the bare brick walls. Clearly visible among other names were two signatures: *Marcello Mastroianni*; *Gina Lollobrigida*.

Excluded from the restaurant trip and unable to accompany us to the beach – one of the few places in Italy where dogs are banned – we felt Todo deserved another bandana day. He bounced around in anticipation as the scarf came out and soon we were heading south again, this time to the beautifully preserved medieval hilltop village of San Gimignano. We'd spent many days there on previous holidays, walking the tiny streets of this remarkable place – the New York of the thirteenth century, when a small number of ruling families built seventy-six great towers, competing with each other to create the highest. Fourteen still remain and, on past visits, we'd climbed most of them, usually in the afternoon heat with just German or Scandinavian tourists for company.

In the middle of the main square, just in front of the ancient *cisterna* – a deep well which for centuries was the city's only water supply – we met up with our old London neighbours, Mark and Sam, and their children, Tom and Molly. We'd last seen them at our farewell party in London two years before, so we were thrilled to catch up again. They were travelling with another couple we also knew, Mark and Tracy, and their two children, Ben and Annie. The four youngsters – who'd been promised a dog to look after for the afternoon – took an immediate shine to Todo.

With the exception of Diego, he'd known no other children so we were unsure how he'd be around them, but we needn't have worried – he was immaculately behaved. Tom, the eldest, took his lead from Lawrence and marched off down one of the side streets, Todo trotting beside him and the other three kids following behind.

I watched as Todo's little figure disappeared into the distance, and I sensed some of the pride parents must feel, seeing him behave so well and so confidently in the company of people he'd never met before.

As we strolled through the winding streets, stopping for lunch and *gelati*, each of the children took it in turns to have charge of Todo and he revelled in the attention, waiting patiently as the lead was swapped from one child to the next. Happily snuvering the tasty morsels that fell constantly to the floor during lunch, he showed no signs of flagging as the temperatures soared.

We adults sat in the shade over a cool drink as the Famous Five worked their way through a second *gelato* each while walking a patient Todo up and down the piazza. When we started towards the main gate of the city, I overheard Ben grumbling: '*You've* all had him twice, I've only had one go!' Todo had become the object of a tug-of-love dispute, one that was happily resolved without tears, and Ben had the honour of walking Todo as we all headed towards the car park.

A few weeks later more friends – Kate, who had worked with me many years earlier at the BBC, and her husband John, a fellow undergraduate with Lawrence at Cambridge – arrived with their three children, Esme, Fred and Dora, the youngest, who bounced into the hallway and hugged Todo, both of them behaving as if they'd known each other for years.

We went for drives, walked the streets of Lucca and ate pizza in celebration of Kate's birthday, Todo taking it all in his stride. The visit coincided with the Beijing Olympics and each morning we'd sit and enjoy the latest British success, every medal greeted with shouts of joy from the children and accompanying barks from the dog.

One evening we staged our own gymnastics competition, the kids bounding off our footstool in a thirty-second display. As each ran to accept the applause of the assembled masses (all seven of us) Todo would run alongside, head bashing against them as they shrieked. And at the end of their three-day visit he was declared the undisputed winner of the Gold Medal for Snuvering and we sang the national anthem for him, though only after some debate as to his nationality, given that he was Italian-born and his first owner American. In the end we claimed him as a naturalised Brit!

Kate and John's departure seemed almost to signal the end of summer, and as the last day of August drew closer the realisation dawned that with September would come the return of the dreaded hunters.

20

What Did He Just Call Me?

Sitting in our favourite coffee bar in Montebello, we picked up a copy of the local newspaper, *Il Terreno*. I was thrilled to find, leafing through it, that I could actually understand several of the articles. I came across one in which key phrases leaped out at me: *new laws*; *reduced time limit*; *nothing within a distance of 100m*.

'Look at this,' I told Lawrence – he was giving Todo the last piece of croissant – 'doesn't it say they've made things tougher for the hunters?' I handed him the paper.

'Yes, looks like it. The hundred-metre rule is being extended to olive groves and vineyards.'

We exchanged excited grins. The report gave us real hope that the rogue hunter who had plagued us the previous winter would no longer be able to. The hide he'd created in the long reeds by the stream at the bottom of our valley was immediately next to our olive grove. Now that would be illegal.

'I'm not surprised they've brought this law in,' I remarked.

'They're shooting at one of the busiest times in the fields. I wouldn't be surprised if a few farm workers are accidentally shot every year.'

Full of optimism, I told friends, both Italian and English, that this awful practice that had caused us, and Todo, so much stress for four months last year was at an end and we could enjoy the autumn in peace.

The first day of the hunting season arrived in mid-September and although we could hear shooting, most of it was distant, high up in the woods. We breathed a huge sigh of relief. As for Todo, although he would still head home if a shot came too close, usually he was fine and we could continue with our usual walks.

It was October, a month into the season, when we were woken suddenly at ten past six. BANG, BANG. It was horribly close.

Lawrence looked furious. He was up and out of the door within seconds, letting it slam behind him.

He returned with bad news. 'It's the same guy as last year with all the same equipment.'

This time, emboldened by what we had read of the new laws and with a greatly improved command of the language, Lawrence decided to confront him. Walking towards the hide the hunter had again made in the thick reeds on the banks of the stream, he called to him. After some minutes the man appeared, approaching with a rifle slung over his shoulder. In his best Italian, Lawrence told him politely that it was not right for him to be shooting there because of the new laws.

'The new laws don't apply here. I have permission from the owner of the land.'

'But it's not about permission, it's the law,' argued Lawrence.

'My family, the Merdinis, have been shooting here for forty years; it is my right.'

Lawrence's Italian started to run out shortly after this exchange and though he stuck to his guns the penny soon dropped with Signor Merdini that his opponent could be dismissed: he was English.

As Lawrence's words deserted him and his temper frayed he resorted to a few age-old Anglo-Saxon expletives. And the hunter gave as good as he got. The Italian word for fig is *fico*. There is also a rude word for a particular part of the female anatomy, *fica*. Lawrence's Italian may have failed him as tempers rose but he was a hundred percent sure that Merdini didn't call him a stupid English fig at that point.

Lawrence can hold his own in any argument but a diminishing vocabulary, a growing sense this was getting him nowhere and the fact that a loaded rifle was just feet away made him turn and walk away, though he did exit with the warning, 'I will call the police.'

'Call them,' came the reply followed swiftly by a shot, some way over Lawrence's head but in his direction and sufficiently close to scare him.

We didn't call the police because, as foreigners, we were afraid we wouldn't be taken seriously, and were also worried that we would be seen as troublemakers.

We were sure our neighbours would take issue with him, not least because we thought (wrongly, it turned out) that this man, with flagrant disregard, flouted the laws while they were now having to drive considerable distances to hunt legally. Unlike Lawrence they had a great deal more language to use and guns of their own and we could see that it was annoying them almost as much as us. But not a word was said, only a shrug of the shoulders and upturned hands. 'This is Italy, after all,' they would say when we asked why no one called the police. So we tried to resign ourselves to another autumn of disruption and, before long, Todo was back under our bed.

Feeling increasingly desperate we sought advice from everyone, but nobody could offer words of encouragement. Chatting with Mario was usually a delight, but when I talked to him about the hunter one morning, his reply left me stunned. 'Of course, La Signora tried her hardest to do something about it but even she failed.' He shrugged his shoulders.

Walking home, I felt devastated. *If the indomitable Carol MacAndrew couldn't solve this in all those years, what hope did we have?*

I went upstairs to our bedroom where Lawrence was chatting soothingly to Todo as he pottered around, tidying up. I sat on the floor beside Todo. 'Don't worry, we won't give up,' I promised him. 'There's got to be something we can do.' I thought for a moment and then turned to Lawrence. 'Maybe I should give it a go?

'What?' Lawrence replied.

'Talking to the hunters; a little less macho, perhaps?'

'Macho?! I don't know *what* you mean, Lou!'

The noise had continued unabated since Lawrence's failed attempt at arbitration and poor Todo was so miserable it had even begun to affect his appetite. He was suffering dreadfully, as his cough had returned and I think he dreaded the prospect of me stabbing him with hypodermic needles again even more than I did.

On the days when the hunter and his friends weren't there we'd still take pleasure in the wonderful sight of the flocking starlings swooping over the fields and groves in their hundreds, forming perfect swirling shapes which flowed in one direction and then suddenly switched. But five days a week, these poor birds were shot down, dozens at a time, by the hunters, who fired relentlessly and without mercy.

One afternoon a loud crack rang out as I clumped through the long grass of our field and, to my horror, a shattered bird landed only a few yards in front of me. Almost instantly a dog appeared from beyond the stream between the fields, racing in my direction. Behind it tramped Signor Merdini, his moustachioed face as grubby as the mud-covered camouflage gear he was wearing.

I had planned a calm, reasoned approach.

'I suppose you think you're clever; get off our land!' I screamed in English. Er, not quite the start I'd intended. He couldn't understand my words, but the tone I used would have left him in no doubt as to their meaning.

When he shouted back, 'That's my bird, I can collect it on anybody's land,' I let rip. All the fury of the weeks spent putting up with his terrible racket, watching Todo trembling in terror, and seeing dead and injured birds raining from the skies, poured out in a torrent of furious abuse. But of course it did no good. He marched back to his hide, looking at me as though I was a madwoman, and, shaking and scarlet, I stomped back to the house.

'How did the less macho approach go?' Lawrence enquired.

After that we spent many hours fantasising about smashing the bizarre decoy, cutting down the reeds, playing very loud music to scare the birds or simply sitting in the field each day, but finally it was heavy rain that drove him away. We experienced an incredibly wet autumn, and the long days of non-stop rain proved too much for the hunter, who left his soggy hide and headed, presumably, for the hills.

We could only pray for more rain in the new year, but in the meantime Lawrence had been doing further research into the law, and he discovered that the state-run Corpo Forestale had jurisdiction over matters relating to the preservation of the, mainly agricultural, land in the immediate area and beyond. Signor Andrea from their office in Lucca told him, 'Now they've gone we can't investigate but, should they return, please come and see us.'

'Oh, we will,' replied Lawrence.

Autumn turned into winter and the rain showed no signs of abating. 'I think it's your fault,' scolded Mario. 'This is *English* weather; you must have brought it with you!'

But the weather delighted Frediano as it meant his hunting was especially fruitful, not least because the loathsome Merdini continued to stay away. He was in pursuit of something rather more ambitious (and to our food lovers' minds, far more justifiable) than countless starling and one morning, after we had heard isolated shots very early, he sidled up to us as we passed his house on our walk, the ubiquitous cigarette secreted behind his back.

'Do you like wild boar?'

'Yes, of course; delicious,' replied Lawrence.

Frediano leaned in even closer. 'Tomorrow. When you pass with the dog . . .' His forefinger tapped at his nose.

The package was duly handed over the following day, not without several darting looks around to check that no one else was watching. Lawrence joined in the intrigue, the two men like co-conspirators in some American prohibition B-movie. Though not illegal, hunting boar at this time was frowned upon by many of the local farmers. Two days later the wild boar stew with white wine, tomatoes and black olives put paid to any lingering feelings of guilt.

* * *

On the communications front, things had been going well. Too well to last, as we might have known.

One morning Lawrence switched on the Internet radio for Radio 4's *Today* programme, a daily favourite, as a way of keeping in touch with events in the UK and bringing a little bit of England into the Italian countryside. But not today; no warm rumblings of British voices, no sports report or details of the congestion at Junction 19 of the M25.

Lawrence went downstairs to investigate. 'Internet's off,' I heard him cry. Followed a few minutes later by, 'It's the telephone line. I'll have to call Telecom Italia.'

Now downstairs and preparing breakfast for Todo, I heard Lawrence dial and, impressively, navigate the dreaded automated system in Italian . . .

Welcome to Telecom Italia, please listen to the following options. Press 1 for Sales; Press 2 for Billing; Press 3 for Faults.

'It's ringing.' He sounded pleased with himself.

'*Buon giorno, Signora MacAndrew.*'

'Ah, well, actually this is not in fact her . . .'

Without any further words the receiver went down with a thwack at the other end. Lawrence repeated the procedure.

'*Buon giorno, Signora MacAndrew.*'

'I'm sorry, this isn't her, but . . .'

'*We can only speak to the name on the telephone bill, goodbye.*'

Ever since they'd reconnected Carol's old phone line, a year earlier, we'd been paying her phone bill, hoping that the day wouldn't come when precisely this scenario would transpire.

'Why have they cut it off now?' I asked, already feeling anxious about the impact this could have on our business.

'Who knows; she'd be ninety-nine by now, maybe they've finally realised she's dead?' Unusually, this crisis didn't seem to have upset Lawrence greatly. No shouting, no kicking of doors, nothing had been flung at the wall. Was the laid-back Italian attitude to life really rubbing off at last? Months earlier an entire day had been ruined by an Internet blackout, which coincided with one of Teresa's visits. From her many stories, and especially those of Silvano and Albertina, I knew that she would have been accustomed to a fiery temperament at Poggiolino but when Lawrence's cursing grew in volume and intensity she shot me a look of great sympathy, and ushered me into the dining-room. 'Perhaps it'd be best if I came another day?' She was an expert at gauging the mood and, smiling, I could only concur.

'I'll switch everything over to the backup.' We had a second line, the one we'd ordered in the first place had finally been installed, and via that we had Telecom Italia's own Internet service as a fail-safe. But it wasn't a fast enough service to support all our business needs, so it was vital we got a new line, and restored the full Internet connections, as soon as possible.

'This means I'll have to go and see the lovely Manuela again . . .'

Aha. Perhaps here we had the real reason for Lawrence's even-tempered response. '*We'll* go.' I smiled sweetly.

21

Signor Garibaldi

Two days later we were sitting in the waiting-room at the vet's and Todo was catching up with his friend Giro, the cheeky cocker spaniel owned by our neighbour Lorenzo.

'Is Todo OK?' Lorenzo asked us.

'Oh yes, he's fine; just this cough he gets. We usually give him antibiotics and it clears up,' I replied.

'How old is he now, about thirteen?

'Around twelve, we think.'

'Mmm,' he answered, sounding surprised and taking another look at Todo, who was now sniffing around the small packets of complimentary food Viviana and Tiziana left out.

'They obviously realise people might have to wait a long time,' joked Lawrence.

Viviana was delighted to see us, giving Todo a hug as we placed him on the treatment table. 'I think it's the same thing back again, but why don't we run some other tests just to make sure?' Seeing the concern on my face she reassured us, 'It's nothing to worry about, I just want to see if there's something we can do to prevent it coming back.'

Over the coming days I was heartened by two things. The rain continued to fall steadily and heavily – not normally a cause for celebration as Lawrence hates bad weather, but it meant our nemesis Merdini stayed away – and Todo's cough responded well to the cortisone Viviana gave him, this time mercifully in tablet form so we were all spared any further ham-fisted attempts at injections.

In Italy it is perfectly normal to buy your own flu jabs over the pharmacist's counter and administer them yourself, just as you do with animals' medication. Lawrence had initially thought it might be a good idea to inoculate ourselves, given that we were likely to be in flu-ridden wintery London before too long, but his opinion had changed rather dramatically after seeing my experiments with Todo.

Viviana arranged for a specialist vet, Dottoressa Negri, to visit from the clinic at nearby Monsummano Terme, and we duly reported with Todo for a series of X-rays, scans and tests. He impressed everyone as he sat patiently hooked up to a variety of machines and the diagnosis, when it came, was our third piece of good news. They discovered an enlarged lymph node very close to his trachea, putting pressure, and in all probability, causing the discomfort which made him cough. The condition almost certainly arose from his prolonged time outside after Carol's death, but while saddened by this, we knew it could have been much worse and the full report from Dott. Negri was very positive. 'He is a very healthy dog, everything is in excellent order. He has a big and good heart.'

You didn't need to run tests in order to tell us that.

Delighted, we thanked both vets and rewarded Todo with a fresh bone; we treated ourselves to a celebratory meal rounded off with lemon sorbet and grappa.

Christmas came and Todo and all three cats feasted on the vast amounts of turkey we couldn't manage as we watched the orange and red glow of the winter sun just dipping behind the hazy hills in the distance.

The shrill of Lawrence's mobile broke the spell. 'Hello, I am at the airport but Maestro is not here,' squeaked a distant voice on the end of a very bad line.

'Sorry, who is this? Is this Cherry?'

'Yes, I am waiting for Maestro; his plane has landed but he is not on it.'

'Hang on,' Lawrence ran to the office to turn on the computer. 'Why are these damned things always slow *just* when you need them to be fast.

'Hello, Cherry . . . Maestro arrives for the rehearsals tomorrow. British Airways, London to Beijing 26 December. Call me when he arrives. Happy Christmas!'

The joys of running your own business.

A week later, with the fireworks exploding all around Lucca visible from our garden, we welcomed in 2009 at home, deciding against the eight-course meal and death-defying obstacle course that is Lucca's New Year celebration. Lawrence had cooked English sausage rolls – a new treat Todo took to with the appreciation of a canine connoisseur – and we spent the evening comparing the festive fare on offer from both English and Italian TV, where the scantily clad girls on RAI made it, in Lawrence's opinion, a close contest. We celebrated midnight twice – any excuse for another glass of champagne – and toasted our first full Italian year with Todo, who wisely opted for another sausage roll rather than the champagne.

Festivities duly recovered from, and full of New Year's zeal, we set about tackling a bureaucratic task that had taken on almost epic proportions. Friends and colleagues had told us about the *carta d'identità*, which would be confirmation that we had a home in Italy and therefore useful for all kinds of official dealings. In Lawrence's eyes the card began to assume almost mythical status, even if, to his chagrin, it would confer nothing that would make us in any way 'Italian'.

We'd been told to return to the same office from which we'd acquired Carol's death certificate, where we found ourselves sitting on the same uncomfortable chairs watching the same stout receptionist in her leopard-print outfit – her hair now a fetching, if alarming, shade of red – walk along the queue demanding to know everyone's business. This time, sadly, it wasn't window number five for us but a firmly closed door, through which no one had ventured in forty minutes.

Finally it opened and, like a headmistress surveying naughty schoolboys, a stern-faced woman looked around, beckoning us in. As Lawrence explained what we were after, she started to scribble on a small yellow Post-it, then pushed it across the desk. 'Come back with these and we'll see.'

Pleasantly surprised to discover that we were already in possession of all five requested documents, we returned a few days later. The same procedure, though our friend in the waiting-room was now in white leather, and half an hour later the headmistress was looking at the neat pile of papers we handed over. More scribbling on a fresh Post-it. 'You'll need these also. Come back when you have them.'

My heart sank when I saw that four more documents were

needed, including an Italian translation of our wedding certificate. *Why hadn't she told us that in the first place?*

I wondered if we should bother to continue with the quest,
but there was no stopping Lawrence. Though he might never
use it, he wanted a formal document with his photo beside some
florid Italian lettering. 'And stamps, I want Italian stamps!'

Finally we had everything together, in a blue plastic folder.
'Let's hope she doesn't come up with another list of documents. Perhaps she'd like our O-level certificates in Italian,' I
said gloomily.

Lawrence reached for Todo's lead and the bandana. 'This
time we're going to crack it; I'm taking our secret weapon.'

Todo bounded up the steps and made a beeline for the
receptionist who reciprocated his warm greeting. But it was a
different, though equally stern, woman who beckoned us into
the office. Did this mean we'd have to start all over again? I
handed over our folder and she began scrutinising closely the
documents.

Todo sat patiently at my feet for a few minutes and then
sneaked around the side of the desk towards her. Before I
could pull him away, she let out a loud cry. '*Amore*. Ahh, what
a dear boy. He is yours? Here, in Italy?'

We nodded enthusiastically as she petted and stroked him.
Taking just one more perfunctory look at our papers she
announced, 'Let me get the form for you and we can complete
it today!'

If dogs could wink . . .

Almost, but not quite, there. The form required answers to
more than fifty questions. When she reached 'Profession?' and
we told her what we did, she looked up excitedly. 'Classical
music? But I am the secretary of the local polyphony choir
here in Lucca. Would you like to come to our concert this

Saturday?' Rummaging in her bag, she handed us several leaf-lets. 'Bring your friends too.'

Minutes later we were back outside, clutching two suitably official-looking, stamped cards.

'Result, Todo.' Lawrence was delighted. 'How about *gelato* for three?'

By early March the temperatures were already in the mid-20s. The Tuscan spring is a joy, the fields a carpet of soft white daisies and wild hellebores, iris and purple-pink anemones bloom in the woods and beneath the olive trees, whose branches are covered in the fresh green shoots that will become silver leaves.

From our terrace the sun rises from shrouds of swirling mist, through which the familiar landmarks, cypresses and church towers, gradually emerge. It's an enchanting time of year, and one of the highlights for us is the Camellia Festival at San Andrea di Compito. It is an opportunity for all of the local growers to bring their most treasured specimens and there are lectures, symposia and competitions all devoted to this most noble of plants, which has been a feature of Lucchese gardens for centuries.

We visited first in 2007, after signing our *compromesso*, but missed it in 2008 because of London commitments, so this year we were looking forward to going as 'locals' and taking Todo, who leaped into the car, his bandana at a jaunty angle.

Visitors to the festival have to park by the village hall, a mile or so away, and then take a small bus. Stepping onto it I was struck by the sense of excitement from all the passengers. Nudging me, Lawrence whispered, 'Look at that!' Two girls, barely into their teens, were videoing each other on mobile phones, then one called a friend, shrieking, 'We're on the bus to the Camellia Festival.' It's a simple, gentle day out, the air rich with the scent of a thousand camellias and food cooking alfresco; sausages, panini, vegetable soup.

We wandered through the stunning variety of camellias on display, before reaching the stalls selling plants. Lawrence took hold of Todo's lead before turning to me; 'Off you go! You couldn't buy any last year so knock yourself out.' I didn't disappoint, emerging minutes later, my arms full. He laughed, 'Remind me how many camellias we brought from London; nine was it?' About to reply, 'And how many football DVDs have you bought recently?' I was interrupted by a cry.

'Ah, Signor Garibaldi!'

An elderly man, standing among his prized plants, beckoned to Todo. 'It's your dog. That neckerchief is like our great Garibaldi!'

After a compliment like that, I felt I *had* to buy another camellia from him.

As we left he shouted, '*Arrivederci, Signor Giuseppe.*'

'There you are, Todo; that man thought you looked like the great Italian liberator. What do you think of that?' Lawrence laughed.

Todo seemed underwhelmed; I think he was disappointed that the old man hadn't given him some of the delicious-looking prosciutto he had for lunch.

Along with camellias, my other passion is roses. And in the garden of Poggiolino, they grew spectacularly and easily. We watched solemnly as Teresa showed us how Carol would prune them; from years of growing them in England, we already knew the technique, but didn't want to stand guilty of ruining La Signora's flowers.

Teresa clearly enjoyed showing us other Tuscan ways of doing things, maybe a reaction to thirty years looking after somebody who knew everything! How, and exactly when, to cut the succulent purple heads from our carciofi, the art of part-cooking then freezing the fresh – and abundant – beans which were one of her regular gifts. She also delighted in letting us into Silvano's secret to successful planting, which revolved around the phases of the moon; 'Not everyone knows this,' she whispered conspiratorially. Any scepticism would vanish when the next crop of zucchini appeared better than ever.

But she also knew how to praise, and commented regularly on our restoring of La Signora's garden, which had begun to take shape gradually after the builders had finally handed it back to us. Its parched brown hue had given way to verdant green with laurels and a new bay hedge providing the perfect frame for splashes of bold colours dotted in between the many olive trees. Having seen her vision still thriving at Villa Carola, we felt no need to make radical changes but, as a passionate gardener of many years, I wanted to adapt it with some of my ideas, embellishing Carol's original designs.

First and foremost, the rose-beds still had space for some new additions, so one spring day we set off in the direction of Pistoia, both Teresa and Albertina having informed us that the *only* place to buy roses was Rose Barni.

Driving through the gate we were met by a glorious sea of colour. If the most beautiful, elegant, perfumed roses of the world had decided unanimously to take a holiday then it would be to here they'd come: every shade, every hue, every shape and size. A Pink Mermaid – 'We're having one of those!' (a phrase I would utter several times before the afternoon was out) – covered the fence at the end of the display area twenty-feet high with an abundance of candyfloss flowers.

Inside, the framed certificates that adorned the walls told the story of a family-run business which had been entering – and winning – competitions in Europe for more than seventy years.

As we scoured the catalogue I gave Lawrence convincing arguments for at least twenty roses; where they'd go, how they'd complement existing ones, how this one would provide a contrast, how that one would hide a little dull spot. Poor man: it was hot, lunch was more than two hours ago and he was tired. Experience had taught me it was a strategic moment to strike – when his defences were low!

Little more than an hour later, Paolo Barni's credit-card machine ran hot.

In other societies, Paolo would have been a footballer, a male model or perhaps even a gigolo. Deeply tanned, with jet-black hair and a smile which could have persuaded me to spend twice as much, he told me he was the great-grandson of the original Barni. Sensing this could become a meaningful relationship and not just a casual one-off, he whispered words that took my breath away. 'Would you like to go on our mailing list?'

Having given him our email address, I swallowed my disappointment that he didn't ask for my phone number too, and headed for the car with a large barrow full of plants.

Todo looked affronted at his personal space being invaded by these newcomers, edging into a corner of the back seat as we piled the thorny plants in, as if to say, *What are they for? I can't eat them!* It was an opinion I suspected Umberto would have shared. Finally we ran out of room, so Todo was forced to share the front seat with Lawrence for the journey home. They both looked distinctly put out, but I didn't care: I'd been a woman on a mission and had accomplished it. I couldn't wait to get going in the garden.

We arrived home at the same time as the postwoman, who handed me a large bunch of mail, most of it re-directed from

London. With Todo scrabbling under my feet and Lawrence blocking the hallway, I flipped through the post and spotted a glossy magazine; a Rose Barni catalogue with a discount voucher! 'Blimey, that *was* quick,' I said.

Lawrence took it and turned it over. 'Have a look at the address label.'

I had to laugh.

Signora Carol MacAndrew.

In April we made an extended trip to London for, among other things, a couple of opening nights at the opera. We had a surprise for Todo; this time he wouldn't be left with only Totti for company. Friends from England were coming to dog- and house-sit. We'd made the same arrangement a couple of times before. Todo loved the company, especially as guests – and soppy English ones in particular – could be relied upon for a better supply of treats than the more frugal Teresa. And all our visitors adored him. After they left, calls and emails would start with, 'How's Todo? Is he doing well?' CDs would arrive some days later, with photos of their stay, almost all of Todo. If he wasn't central to the picture, he'd managed to sneak in somewhere.

One set of friends, Jane and her mother Sylvia, who'd visited during our first year, even sent us a recording of Todo in full voice, singing to San Martino's bells. We treasure it. Sylvia also gave us a hilarious account of a lunchtime stroll with Todo and Totti, Todo on the long lead and Totti swinging from it every few yards as Todo did his best to ignore her. When Jane let him off the lead he suddenly bolted back the way they'd come, Totti in hot pursuit. Jane followed, but couldn't see them anywhere, until she heard laughter coming from the field nearby. There was a family enjoying a picnic, and Todo, helping himself – *a sandwich here, a slice of chicken there, and mmm a nice sausage too, thanks* – while Totti looked on from an adjacent tree. The family of German tourists were, thankfully, enchanted by Todo and happy to share their feast with him. After that, every day for the rest of their stay Todo managed to escape from the garden and head back to the same spot, hoping, no doubt, to find a stray sausage that had been overlooked.

We were always glad when we could leave him with friends at Poggiolino. They all told us the same story: how Todo would spend the first day or so after we left sitting in the hallway staring at the front door. From time to time he'd pad upstairs, poking open the bedroom door to see if we were there. And every time he heard a car, he dashed to the front gate, eager to see if we were home.

22

If Only Dogs Could Talk

A month later I was off again, leaving Todo and Lawrence to their own devices. Australia-bound, I would miss the anniversary of our second year at Poggiolino to celebrate my sister's fiftieth birthday.

Lawrence was used to my trips down under, and I suspected he rather enjoyed the solitude. In London he used to complain that friends and colleagues would call continuously, worried he might be lonely when all he wanted was to finish work then veg out with his favourite films, music or the sport on TV. This time he spent a few days in London, working, then flew back to Pisa to catch the train to Lucca, taking a taxi home to a waiting Todo. Lucca is a small city with only a handful of taxi drivers, most of whom knew Lawrence, but this time, an older man he'd not seen before was behind the wheel.

'Where to?'

'San Francesco di Compito.'

'Ah, it's been a while since I've been there; many years.

Usually my son drives, but his wife is in hospital today so I'm stepping in for him. I retired more than ten years ago.' As they approached the house, the driver exclaimed, 'Signor Jim's house! I used to bring him here all the time when his wife was away. A wonderful man, very generous, devoted to La Signora.' Chuckling to himself he went on, 'All us drivers knew him in those days; often he'd have been out in the city for an evening and couldn't always remember his address, but we'd bring him home. He liked a drink or two! I'd help him down the steps and into the house and tell him, *pay me next time, Signor Jim*, if he couldn't find his money.'

'Did you know Signora MacAndrew?'

'A little,' he answered. 'I drove her once or twice. She'd always talk about Signor Jim. Tell me, what happened to her lovely dog after she died? What is it, three years ago?'

'Four,' said Lawrence, 'and there's the little dog in question!' Todo had woken from a nap and stood at the gate, tail wagging, waiting to welcome Lawrence home.

The two men shook hands and the driver patted Todo's head as he said goodbye. 'A charming house. I hope you are happy here.'

And he was. Life at Poggiolino agreed with Lawrence so well that he even abandoned his usual hermit-like existence in the week or so before I returned. Lunch with Teresa and family was followed by a night at the opera in Montecarlo, hearing Puccini's *La Bohème*. On the telephone later he told me all about the evening, though the music barely rated a mention. 'I thought I was going to die before Mimi!' Albertina had very kindly offered to drive him, and he soon discovered that her driving skills owed everything to her Italian heritage. Her blue Fiat sped down the narrow road, navigating the sharp, blind bends with no thought of oncoming traffic. Completely focused on the story she was telling, she paid no attention to the car haring towards them while she made a sharp left turn, right across the oncoming lane. Lawrence closed his eyes, hoping for the best, opening them in time to see the face of the other driver, just inches from the side of the car. The usual Italian beeping and hand gestures followed, but Albertina was unmoved. 'Oh you silly man, it's not as if you hit us!'

A few days before my return, Todo and Lawrence went out on a longer than usual walk to take advantage of the glorious weather. Lawrence told me afterwards that as they turned onto our driveway, he noticed a bicycle propped up against the wire fence and the gate open. He assumed someone had dropped in. *Another visitor wanting to ease the pain of my absence?*

Funny, he thought, *no one at the front door. It must be Teresa*; he entered the garden and saw one of the French windows open. *Maybe they'd like me to go round for another meal.* Walking into the sitting-room he called out, 'Hello.'

'Hello,' came a muffled reply. *Odd, it was a man's voice; and why did he answer in English?* Still puzzled, he turned around, looking at the French window. Some wooden splinters lay on the tiles and then he saw the plate prised from its lock. A man he didn't recognise came out of the office.

'Who are you?'

'Nobody.'

'What are you doing here?'

'I'm here to see the lady of the house.'

The man's American accent threw him. *Was this someone who knew Carol?*

Todo appeared, having found the bone he'd gone in search of. Dropping it, he began to growl. *It's like he knows him . . .*

Lulled by the warm day, the pleasant walk and the friendly

ambience of the area, Lawrence had been slow on the uptake.
But the penny finally dropped. We were being burgled.

'What the hell are you doing?'

The man burst past him, running through the summer
house with Lawrence and Todo in pursuit. A spurt of pace
and he reached the bicycle, pushing it in front of him while
trying to climb on. Turning onto the road he had one foot
on a pedal. Lawrence reached out his hand . . . *almost* grabbing the burglar's shoulder but he slipped away and within
seconds was halfway down the road. Lawrence hurled a
stream of expletives after him and turned to trudge back up
the hill.

Tucked up in bed in the guest room of my mother's house
in Sydney, it was approaching midnight when my mobile rang.
Any irritation at the late hour disappeared when I heard the
news.

'I can't talk too long, we've been burgled.'

'Tell me what happened. Are you alright?'

'I can't, I need to get the Carabinieri. They're not far; maybe
they'll be quick enough to catch him. But I can't remember
the number . . .'

'Go to Teresa's, she'll know. Call me later.'

Lawrence told Todo to wait and went up the hill. Teresa was
shocked to hear what had happened and offered him a coffee
as Barbara called the Carabinieri.

There is a whole tradition of jokes about Italy's local police
force. Our desire not to have them influence our opinion of
the Carabinieri's performance took a jolt when Barbara's
opening words were met with, 'Can you pop round to the
office and tell us what happened?'

Silvano arrived home and offered to take Lawrence to the
station, just a few minutes away. When they got there, a notice

informed them; *Opening hours: 09.30–12.30 and 2.30–6.30, Saturday 09.30–12.30, Sunday closed.*

'Sunday's a good day to be a criminal,' joked Lawrence.

The station was a display of Carabineri pride, its walls replete with photos of officers, many on horseback, all in heroic poses.

A sympathetic young officer, who insisted on being called Alessandro, invited Lawrence to sit down. As he told the story in detail, Alessandro stopped him, 'You say he wasn't Italian?'

'Well his accent was American.'

'That's very odd.'

Trying to list what had been taken he began to stumble on certain words. *What is bracelet in Italian? How do I say iPod?*

'I haven't been through everything properly yet and I won't know until my wife gets back from Australia exactly what jewellery's been taken.'

'Definitely American . . . ?' Alessandro looked puzzled. 'We will come to the house later, will you be home?'

Lawrence replied that he would and they left the room, to be met by a short man in immaculate uniform, complete with white sash and gun holster. 'I am Captain Agnelli. I am sorry to hear of your intruder. You say he was American?'

Alessandro and another officer arrived at the house after lunch. Keen to help, Silvano appeared and the officers directed most of their questions towards him while Lawrence and Todo stood and listened. The American accent clearly remained a salient point for the Carabinieri and they were further intrigued when Silvano told them about Carol and the regular flow of visitors to Poggiolino.

Lawrence was becoming resigned to the fact that this looked like the end of the story. Not too much had been taken, no one was hurt, it would remain a curiosity on their records and the third burglary in the four homes we'd owned. They'd taken only a cursory look at the door where the burglar had forced entry, then walked through the house and gone upstairs, where he'd found my jewellery box and taken some things, though Lawrence still couldn't think exactly what.

'He tried this door. What's in here?' Alessandro asked.

'It's just a loft space, olive oil jars, spare floor tiles and the old alarm.'

'It doesn't work?'

'Not anymore. Is it important?'

'Mmm, interesting that he seemed to know there was an alarm here.' Downstairs again he talked once more with Silvano. 'Do you remember anyone suspicious Mrs MacAndrew knew? She had good security.'

'You should ask Signora Albertina, she knows more about it,' he suggested and the two officers exchanged handshakes and left.

'You've had quite an adventure today!' It was Albertina on the phone, in typically irrepressible mood. 'I've had your Carabinieri here this afternoon and we think we've figured it out.'

She told Lawrence the story. One of Carol's carers had a son believed by many to have problems with drugs and petty crime. 'He was *known* to the police,' said Albertina, 'and sometimes would just turn up at Poggiolino looking for his mother, to beg some money from her. Teresa never trusted him and after a while Carol asked her to turn him away.

'The thing is: he knew Carol was American and that people called her *the lady*; he had been in the house many times so knew where things were, in particular the alarm. The police think he went upstairs to disable it.'

The problem was that Albertina couldn't remember his

name, or indeed his mother's. 'I called Teresa and even she can't.'

'You say little Todo growled at him? Teresa told me he never took to this man, growled at him whenever he appeared but his mother would shoo Todo away. Oh well, good luck my dear.'

Lawrence put down the phone. *Great*, he thought, *so now we've inherited Carol's burglar as well!*

Todo was sitting at his feet. *If only dogs could talk.* 'Would you recognise him in a line-up, old boy?'

He slept fitfully that night; for once Poggiolino's isolation felt forbidding. The silence is something we normally treasure, unbroken except for the occasional owl or the rustling of a fox or wild boar in the fields, but that night it seemed unnerving and Lawrence was happy to allow Todo the indulgence of sleeping on the bed. I ignored his comments when he called the following morning that my snoring is worse than the dog's.

Teresa arrived, full of sympathy, and with more stories of our prime suspect. She showed him the marks on the shutter door of Carol's bathroom where, years ago, someone had tried to force an entry. 'La Signora was sure it was him. She'd told him to leave the house earlier that day.' She also gave him the telephone number of the company that had fitted the original alarm some thirty years ago. 'Paolo still works for them; make sure you ask for him and say that I sent you.'

Beckoning him over to the large Tuscan cupboard in the hallway, her voice dropped to a whisper, 'This is what La Signora did when she was away.' Opening the left door she bent down, pushing hard at the bottom. The thick piece of wood comprising the floor of the cupboard came up with a jolt and she pulled it to one side. It was a false bottom and now revealed a secret compartment about six inches deep. 'Here she would put jewellery and valuables; she didn't like to rely on alarms and she wouldn't let other people have her possessions.'

Lawrence spotted a long-forgotten, white silk evening glove. Picking it up gently, he remarked to Teresa, 'She had tiny hands!'

'Yes, La Signora was very petite . . . but very strong!'

Todo appeared, sniffing curiously at the opened drawer and the elegant glove.

'Is it just this half of the cupboard?' Lawrence asked Teresa. 'There isn't one on the right?' She shook her head no and he handed her the glove; it seemed right that she should place it back in its hiding place before closing up the whole thing, which she did with great care.

'Do I need a ticket for the dog?'

Some days later Lawrence was joking with the cashier at Lucca train station, as Todo paced up and down impatiently on the marble floor of the entrance hall. The two were heading to Pisa Airport to meet me.

'How old is he?' the cashier replied, getting out of her chair and peering down at Todo's smiling face.

'In human years; over sixty,' came the reply.

'Then he's a senior citizen and travels for free!'

Todo behaved impeccably on the train. Clearly disappointed not to be allowed on the comfy seats, he contented himself with lying on the floor at Lawrence's feet. Pulling into San Rossore station, Lawrence looked out of the window at Pisa's famous Leaning Tower. 'Look, Todo, do you remember we came here with Ania two years ago?' Todo didn't respond; his attention was fixed on the small group of children who had just got on the train and were now sitting opposite, eating *gelato*.

As I stepped through the sliding doors of the arrival hall, an excited bundle of chestnut and golden fur bounded towards me, soft fuzzy tail wagging furiously. Kisses and embraces were exchanged, after which I stood up and hugged Lawrence. 'I know my place,' he laughed.

Arriving at Poggiolino half an hour later, I was thrilled to be home. After unpacking and giving Lawrence and Todo their much anticipated treats, I was anxious to check the contents of my jewellery box. But first I wanted to see this secret compartment in the Tuscan cupboard. Lawrence opened it and Todo once again showed the keenest interest as I held the evening glove in my hands. 'Do you remember this?' I asked him, but by now he was sniffing madly at the wood, which exuded that lavender and mothball scent so reminiscent of maiden aunts. He stopped in turn at the neat piles of papers, ornaments, bric-a-brac, postcards and linens in the cupboard. I thought he might be searching for a favourite toy he'd left some years ago. We hadn't been able to bring ourselves to throw out these precious mementos of Carol

'Do you know this?' I asked, showing him an embroidered table napkin. 'Did La Signora make this?' I waved a small, hand-knitted scarf in front of him.

'Do you realise you just called her La Signora?'

I hadn't noticed, but Lawrence's comment gave me goose bumps.

'I dare say he saw these things every day when she was alive.'

By this time Todo was sniffing frantically at the other side of the cupboard.

'Teresa said there was just one hidden compartment, right?'

Lawrence nodded. I was curious at Todo's insistence and

bent down to investigate. A hard shove later and, with a creak, the shelf lifted.

We stared at each other. 'My God, when do you think this was last open, if even Teresa doesn't know about it?'

'Is there anything in it?'

I reached my hand in and pulled out an oval silver serving dish and then another; both monogrammed *JKM*. 'James MacAndrew,' Lawrence said as we gazed on these intricately finished treasures. Next was a heavy wooden box, bound in deep crimson leather. Opening the brass lock I lifted its lid and found a set of delicate silver cutlery with white bone handles, bearing the engraved name of its London maker. As I took out each of the knives, forks and spoons, Lawrence reached in under the shelf and produced a third large silver serving platter, its edges bevelled with a traditional egg and dart pattern and in the centre the same *JKM* monogram.

We sat back in wonder at Carol and Jim's silver. It wasn't just that the pieces themselves were of such beauty – they gave us an insight into the splendour of the lives they'd led.

'Do you think they were used for her friends from the White House?' asked Lawrence, after a long pause.

Carol kept notes of all the menus from her dinners in the diaries we had found when we moved in and now I found myself picturing the whole salt-baked sea bass arranged on the large platter with the dauphinoise potato either side; steamed beans fresh from her *orto* in one of the oval dishes, covered with her own olive oil and lemon wedges from the many trees she grew and stored in the *limonaia*.

Fetching my trusty tin of Silvo and a pile of dusting cloths, I set about polishing the tarnished silver with the same vigour I'd used to bath Todo for the first time almost two years earlier. We could decide what to do with the dishes later, but it didn't seem right that they should lie at the bottom of a drawer, neglected, forgotten and unloved. Two hours later our dining table was filled with gleaming silver. 'As good as new,' I exclaimed proudly.

'Just like Todo,' Lawrence joked.

Still with no clear idea of how we should use them, I placed each piece of cutlery back in its allotted groove in the box and returned it, together with the platter and dishes, to their secret drawer. The knowledge that they would always be there, waiting perhaps for the right occasion, was good enough for us.

Todo was curled up asleep in his basket. Perhaps he was just over-tired at the end of a long day but the thought flashed through my mind that some things weren't so permanent and I kissed him extra tenderly before heading for bed.

23

But *Every* Dog Likes Swimming

Summer exceeded all expectations with soaring temperatures and endless blue skies. Most Italians headed for the beach but, confirming our reputation as the slightly unhinged foreigners, we decided to undertake the laborious task of painting all the door and window shutters. It was one of the jobs we hadn't got round to – they were still a grubby, faded brown, and as we couldn't afford to pay anyone to paint them, we thought we'd take advantage of a quiet work period and get stuck in.

'You mustn't do it now,' argued Lorenzo and Silvano when they passed the house. 'It's far too hot; we always paint in spring or early autumn when it's cooler.'

Lawrence explained that summer was quieter for us in the office and spring and autumn our two busiest periods, but I don't think it altered their view that we were certifiably mad.

Teresa took particular interest in our work. 'La Signora

would have it all painted every two years; I would supervise the workmen,' she told me.

'And La Signora?' I asked, scrubbing at my brush, my hands smelling of white spirit and oil, my overalls filthy and hair damp with sweat.

'Oh, she would take herself off to America for two weeks, or perhaps stay with friends in Rome.'

Naturally.

We persevered, however, and in due course the smart green shutters were met with nods of approval as our neighbours passed by.

Meanwhile several heavy trucks had arrived in the fields on either side of the stream. After two very dry summers, one of the measures being taken by the Comune was to cut down the huge reeds that ran along its full length – the very same ugly reeds that provided shelter for the rogue hunter every autumn. We dared to hope that it might even force him to try elsewhere.

In celebration of this, and the application of the last coat of paint to the freshly gleaming shutters, we decided to take a trip to spend a few days in northern Italy on the shores of Lake Maggiore. On our first Italian holiday in 1998, the one that sent Lawrence into his spin of wanderlust, we spent the first few nights there and loved everything about it. We'd stayed at a bed and breakfast, Monterosso, high up a steep hill in the middle of a pine forest. Lawrence had never got over the thrill of dropping off the luggage in our room, after the long drive from Milan Airport, then feasting on home-cooked dishes of salami, pasta, risotto, meat and grilled vegetables. We spent a joyful final evening with another English couple, eating fresh pink grapefruit sorbet while watching France win the World Cup. Italy had previously suffered penalty shoot-out heartbreak at their hands so we favoured Brazil, but as the grappa flowed we no longer cared – or indeed were entirely sure – who won.

On the morning of our departure for Lake Maggiore, Teresa dropped by to wish us *buon viaggio*. Seeing our luggage, including basket and blanket for Todo, she smiled.

'Ah, La Signora would take even more cases. She would watch every few days for her dollar and our lire and I remember she'd call me. "Teresa, I'm much richer than I was last week, Todo and I are going for a holiday!" I had to pack and a bag for Todo too. We'd spend most of the time choosing which cases to take; do you know she had twenty-two, each for different occasions or places?'

Teresa told us that with everything in the car – Carol herself carried nothing but the lightest bag, usually Ferragamo – she'd call to Todo, who'd jump into his place on the back seat and seconds later Teresa would be waving at her, speeding her way down the hill, off to somewhere glamorous and exciting. The destination and duration were hardly ever thought out in advance and perhaps a couple of days later Teresa would receive a call, 'We're in Orvieto, it's just lovely. I think we'll be back next Tuesday.'

As we busied ourselves with final arrangements, Lawrence ensuring all the technology was packed and working, I couldn't help but laugh to myself. After more than two years here every little thing we did would still prompt a reminiscence of La Signora from Teresa.

The drive from Lucca to Lake Maggiore is long but our spirits were high and the change from the parched brown countryside of Tuscany as we headed north through Liguria then Emilia-Romagna and into Lombardia was breathtaking. Once you get past the industrialised area around Milan, vast expanses of lush green stretch out on all sides, the terrain of the great lakes, with the Alps in full view and the Swiss border just a few miles away.

Todo skipped his usual mid-morning nap, preferring to stay bolt upright throughout the five-hour drive, zigzagging between the back windows to catch the best view. At refreshment stops all three of us enjoyed the delights of the Autogrill, with its freshly produced food, a world away from the UK motorway services.

To get to the b&b meant navigating forty-two hairpin bends up from Verbania to Monterosso, around five kilometres above. Eleven years earlier, Lawrence set me a challenge: how quickly and with how few stops could I make it? 'Same rules still apply,' he remarked cheerily as we approached the first bend.

Many Italian hotels welcome dogs and Todo had stayed with us in several. On a visit to Milan he had behaved as if he were manor born, trotting alongside Lawrence in the well-appointed hotel lobby before disappearing into the lift as if he'd done it a thousand times before. While that hotel might have been grander, Monterosso was undoubtedly his favourite. For a dog with such a finely honed sense of smell, the surroundings must have seemed like paradise, an abundance of forest full of animal and food scents. On the first day he made friends with two pigs and a sheep before rushing back to our room and collapsing into his basket.

When we walked over to the main house for dinner, we were greeted by the owner Iside, 'It's so nice to see you again . . . and now you have a dog! Does he like beef?' It could have been just months since our last visit, rather than eleven years.

As it turned out, we all enjoyed the beef, after a succession of antipasti and two types of pasta. Tucking into a rice and tomato salad, I spotted a little girl at an adjacent table smiling at Todo and tugging at her mother's sleeve.

'What's your dog's name?'

'Todo,' I replied.

'Toto; like *The Wizard of Oz*?'

The exact origins of Todo's name, indeed its exact spelling, had long since become shrouded in the mists of time. We'd understood his name was Todo with a d, but Teresa seemed to pronounce it Toto, with a t. Neither she nor Albertina could recall if Carol had intended naming him after Dorothy's little dog, or perhaps the great Italian actor known for his wide, tragic clown's grin.

I chose the simplest option. 'Yes, like *The Wizard of Oz*.'

'He's funny; can I take him for a walk?'

I looked at Lawrence, who did a quick recce of the dining area to make sure it was safe and nodded. Before her parents could object, the girl was at our table. 'I'm Ilaria and I don't have a dog at home.'

'Well, Ilaria, Todo's a very friendly dog and I'm sure he'll like being your friend for the evening.'

The rest of dinner was spent with Todo happily following her around, stopping for treats from our table then Ilaria's. Along the way, two children from another table came to join in and Todo obliged with wags of his tail and licks of their hands, to squeals of delight.

As the moon grew brighter and the lights in the valleys far below gleamed like fireflies, Lawrence whispered, 'Who would have thought we'd be back like this; almost Italian, and with the most popular dog in the country?'

When bedtime arrived, Ilaria came slowly back to our table with Todo and hugged him before saying a tearful goodbye. 'Goodnight, Todo, we leave tomorrow morning. I won't see you again.'

'Don't worry,' Lawrence told her, 'we'll make sure to see you at breakfast.'

After another emotional farewell from Ilaria the next morning, we set off for the lake. With the temperatures still high and the water warm, I was determined to find a secluded place to swim, and after a morning of sightseeing we arrived at the little town of Lesa on the shore and headed to the pebbled beach.

Lawrence is not a swimmer, so for him Lesa's chief delight was the delicious cinnamon gelato he devoured while watching me approach the water. 'It's bracing,' I shouted to him.

'Is that your way of saying it's freezing?' came the reply.

I revelled in a glorious swim. A few yards away a yellow Labrador was paddling, retrieving a plastic ring his owner was throwing into the water for him.

'I bet Todo would love a swim,' I told Lawrence. 'C'mon old boy, look at the other dog. Why not come into the water?' Todo looked in the direction of the Labrador with what didn't appear to be great enthusiasm. As I coaxed and cajoled he followed me tentatively into the water until it came halfway up his legs, before turning and heading hurriedly back to the beach and sitting beside Lawrence in a show of solidarity.

'But *every* dog likes swimming,' I shouted.

'He's not every dog.'

'C'mon Todo,' I yelled, walking him back in until the water brushed his chest. He lifted one paw as if he might start paddling at any moment, and hesitated.

'Go on, Todo; you can do it,' came from a few yards away. Two women, watching from the beach, were transfixed. 'That's it!' we all cried as he lurched forward and took off. But within seconds he executed a quick turn and was on dry land again. The vigour with which he threw himself around suggested he wanted to rid himself of this horrid wet stuff as quickly as possible. He eyed me with suspicion for the rest of day.

That evening we arrived at dinner to find a sign on the dining-room door: *Due to popular demand – Gourmet Night – Porcini Mushrooms – Four courses.*

'They'll have their usual menu as well,' I suggested hopefully.

They didn't.

Mushroom hors d'oeuvres and canapés were followed by mushroom soup; then a choice of risotto or pasta with mushrooms and finally steak with . . . mushroom sauce. Images of Lawrence lying on the cold, tiled floor of various Italian hotel bathrooms flashed through my mind. He hadn't even eaten any and he was beginning to look queasy; the air in the dining-room was filled with the pungent smell of the fresh wild forest.

He tried explaining the problem to the waitress, but all they were able to bring him was one small mushroom-free omelette.

'What do you suppose is for dessert – mushroom sorbet?' he moaned.

I tried hard to disguise my enjoyment of the delicious meal, but it was with a heavy tread that Lawrence plodded back to our room once I'd finished.

I attribute the strange culinary exploits of the next day directly to the evening's deprivation.

It was our last full day and we took a boat to the extraordinary Borromeo Islands on the lake. 'Dogs aren't allowed on Isola Madre,' we were told. We couldn't think why. The largest and most splendid of the three islands, it's noted for its wonderful botanical gardens. We settled for visiting Isola dei Pescatori (Island of the Fishermen) and Isola Bella, named after Isabella the first Countess of Borromeo.

He may not have enjoyed his dip in the water, but Todo appeared to love being on it. Sitting at the prow of the boat, he stared out over the water like a ship's captain searching for land, his ears ruffled by the breeze, tail thumping happily on the deck.

On our return, Lawrence announced, 'I'm sick of Italian food. I saw a sign for a doner kebab shop in Bavena; let's go there for lunch.' After the previous evening I didn't feel I could refuse him, so we got in the car and drove off in the direction of fast food.

The road running along the lake is not easy to navigate and there are few natural turning points, so when he shouted, 'You've just missed the sign, it was back there,' it took a significant amount of willpower to contain my potential replies. A couple of miles on I was able to turn round. Lawrence headed in the direction of the sign, as I gave Todo some water.

Minutes later, his scowling face reappeared. 'It's closed.'

And things had been going so well, I thought.

We retreated to a small bar which served a disappointing cheese and ham panini, Todo devouring his share with rather more relish than Lawrence. Fearing the worst for the rest of the day and tomorrow's return home, I resorted to emergency tactics. 'There's a McDonald's on the way back to Monterosso.'

His face bore the same transparent delight as Todo's when the words *lamb bone* were uttered. The cloud lifted immediately. His mood hadn't been helped by the message on his mobile, informing him that Bolton Wanderers had just scored against Liverpool. I said a silent prayer for a hamburger and chips and a Liverpool equaliser and, to my amazement, both appeared at the same time.

'Torres, 2–2; two burgers, two fries and two cokes please.'

We sat in the car devouring the food as if our last meal had been days before. It wasn't Lawrence's intention to give Todo a chip but, with one in his hand as he held forth about something to which I wasn't paying attention, a long snout appeared from the back of the car and it was snuvered in an instant! Another found its way to the same destination, followed by a chunk of burger. I hated to think what Carol would have said.

We headed back to Monterosso and I might have broken my record for fastest ascent had Lawrence not put me right off my stride by yelling, at bend number seventeen, 'Gerrard; 3–2!'

Things were back on track.

The trip had been a wonderful break for all three of us, but we agreed it would be good to get back to Poggiolino. A dull morning gave way to a warm afternoon and by the time we exited the A11 for Lucca, we both felt quite soporific after five hours in the car. Todo had finally given up his battle against sleep and was stretched across both back seats, issuing little grunts of contentment every so often. We passed the sign for McDonald's just after the motorway exit, 'Do you think he's dreaming of more chips?' joked Lawrence.

Nearing the roundabout after Fontanella, Todo woke up and began to pace in the back of the car excitedly as we drew closer, finally letting out joyful little yelps as we passed the cemetery and made our way up the hill to Poggiolino. As soon as I stopped the car he dashed down the steps towards his water bowl. Totti came running to meet him and they sloped off together; I wondered if he was telling her about his adventures and how I'd tried to drown him.

Two days later, Lawrence was loading photos of the trip onto his computer. There were the pigs; Todo on the boat; the cinnamon gelato. As the photos of our aborted swimming expedition came on screen I looked at them and then at Todo lying in his basket, one eye open, watching us.

'Do you think Todo's coat's growing back as quickly as usual? It seems to be taking a long time.'

I looked a little closer but Lawrence seemed unconcerned, 'I don't suppose it's the same every year.'

I tried to dismiss the thought, but as the days passed I was certain that last year his fur had grown back much faster after his summer haircut. And I knew, deep down, that it meant something wasn't right.

24

Bad News Comes in Threes

A week before our third hunting season was due to start, we could see Signor Merdini stalking around the fields once more, surveying the area where the reeds had given him shelter, kicking out every now and again at the grass and swearing. As he stomped away to his car, I let out a cheer; it seemed a combination of the new laws and the loss of his natural habitat might have solved our problem.

Two days later we watched in dismay as he erected a simple hide of poles and tarpaulin in the middle of the field. At 6.30 a.m. on the third Sunday of the month, the day on which the season starts, our hopes were dashed and peace shattered as the familiar volley of shots rang out.

Lawrence was on the phone to the Corpo Forestale early on Monday morning. Explaining the situation in his much-improved Italian, I heard him conclude, '*Grazie*, we will see you tomorrow.'

The following day we headed to their office at Piazzale Verdi in Lucca where Andrea welcomed us in, beckoning us to sit. We were encouraged to hear that others had complained before us and that Andrea had visited and talked with the shooter, explaining the objections. But there was bad news to come. We sat in front of his computer as he showed us the map of our land and the immediate area, explaining, 'I'm sorry, but you're wrong about the new laws; the hundred-metre rule is only for houses and streets.'

'We understood it also applied to olive groves and vineyards . . .'

He shook his head. 'They are proposals, but nothing has so far been passed. Look, here's the problem.' He set his desktop ruler on the image. 'Signor Merdini is clever; he has a telemeter, so . . .'

The spot where he'd placed his hide was carefully positioned: 140m from Poggiolino; 130m from the house further down the hill; 160m from San Martino Church; 120m from the road. He was perfectly within the law.

'But surely it's wrong that he can terrorise us and our neighbours in this way? All the other hunters have gone to the woods.'

'I couldn't agree more with you, Signor Lorenzo, but we have tried everything and there is no more we can do within the current regulations. I can think of only one thing that would make a difference.'

He went on to say that if a new dwelling were to be built in our field, close to the stream then the hundred-metre law would come into effect and Signor Merdini could be stopped. Without pausing to think where we might find the money for this new dwelling, Lawrence leaned forward. 'We could really solve it this way?'

'Yes, certainly, though you would need to obtain planning permission for the structure.'

'Who would we get permission from?'

'Ah; that would be us,' replied Andrea, 'but the land is zoned only for agricultural use so we'd turn you down.' He smiled. He was clearly trying to cheer us up.

Neither of us saw the funny side. We shook hands, he commiserated again and we left. The drive home was silent; we'd never come across a situation where someone was so clearly in the wrong, yet nothing could be done. I knew Lawrence felt it particularly badly and I worried that it might seriously affect his enjoyment of our Italian adventure. He'd joked before that if things got too much then we could always return to London. Lawrence had been the prime mover behind our decision to come, he had settled in faster than me and I knew he loved Poggiolino, so I'd tended to dismiss these jokes as being nothing more than reassurances for me, when I was occasionally feeling overwhelmed by the stresses of adapting. But he'd also kept a keen eye on the fall in the value of the pound that meant Poggiolino's value had risen quite considerably. Now his reaction to the shooting problem, and his strong sense of the injustice of it, made me concerned that he might be seriously considering a return.

I couldn't even contemplate such an idea, not least because I knew that it would be wrong for Todo; he wasn't a city dog. Back home he lay dozing in the sitting-room and I went to sit with him. I couldn't bear the thought of what he'd have to put up with in the coming months. I felt we'd failed him.

Lawrence joined us. 'We're not giving up yet, Todo.' He seemed brighter and I had a feeling he was hatching a plan.

The following day he was on the phone to our good friend and Suffolk resident, Bruce. Bird-scarers were the answer!

'They're going off all the bloody time around here. No birds, nothing to shoot at; problem solved.'

A frenzied day of Internet surfing ensued as Lawrence explored the different means available to us. Armed with sheets of printed material he sat me down to discuss our options: too big; too expensive; too difficult to work. Nothing seemed to fit the bill, so we consulted the Suffolk sage once more.

'CDs. Simple, really. The light reflects off them which scares the birds and they stay away. It must be worth a try.'

It most definitely was. I raided Lawrence's copious store of blank CDs and with a dexterity of which *Blue Peter* presenters would be proud, fixed several of them onto the bamboo poles we had cut down in the garden (Carol's second great horticultural mistake, after the tree). With Lawrence looking on, somewhat bemused and not a little doubtful, I marched in my green wellies down the garden, through the gate and into our field.

The laughter from the two men in the hide was audible before I got within twenty metres of them but I ploughed on until I came to the very last patch of our land.

So what now? I thought.

I started shaking the poles, causing the CDs to sway gently and rather elegantly in the breeze. 'Good God, Louise, what are you doing?' I muttered to myself.

But the laughter in the hide soon stopped and a head appeared slowly. I also realised that for the last few minutes there had been no shots and, more importantly, no birds! 'Well, bugger me, Bruce . . . it works!'

Standing in the cool, late September air, images ran through my head of the wonderful Italian holidays we'd enjoyed: the Piazza del Campo in Siena; the fields of sunflowers; the

Palazzo Ducale in Urbino; Rigoletto's house in Mantova; sunny drives along poppy-lined roads with the hills and lakes seeming to go on forever. Then I thought of Frances Mayes' *Under the Tuscan Sun* and laughed. Look where we'd ended up. 'So this is *our* Italian dream!'

Lawrence appeared with two more poles and, more importantly, a cup of his delicious latte. I wrapped one hand around the warm mug. 'Told you it would work; no need for fancy bird-scarers.'

He held his pole aloft with military zeal and we waved together. Emboldened and triumphant, after half an hour I asked him, 'How do you say *you missed* in Italian?' Smiling he replied, '*Non l'hai preso.*' I had to wait just minutes before an errant shot came from the hide.

'*NON L'HAI PRESO!*' I yelled at the top of my voice.

Dark mutterings were heard from the hide; the shooters' anger was rising. They were on the phone and at one point we heard one of them say to the other, 'There are lots of other places.' They began dismantling their gear and we kept waving. It took them an hour to take the hide down and pack everything into the car.

In the three hours that I had stood there (Lawrence had been a little less resolute than I, but he did make and bring a beautiful tomato and mozzarella panini for lunch) we had seen one bird and none had been a casualty of the shooters. Flushed with success and convinced that we had found the solution, we made our way home, but not before I called out one final retort, '*Vittoria per gli inglesi!*' Victory for the English. Not exactly mature but it felt good.

Walking back up to the house I told Lawrence we must make more CD poles, perhaps put some in the ground permanently. I rushed to tell Todo of the great battle we'd fought for him! Opening the front door I heard a familiar sound and my heart sank; it was Todo coughing, and this particular bout went on longer than previously. 'It's the vet for you tomorrow, old boy; let's hope Viviana doesn't make me inject you!'

It seemed to trouble him less the following morning and he was very happy to see Viviana when we walked into the treatment room. 'So, it's back,' she said, patting him affectionately. 'Well, let's try the same medication and see if we can get rid of it quickly again.'

A week later we had to return with the worrying news that the treatment had made little impact; if anything, the cough was increasing both in frequency and severity.

Viviana looked concerned, 'How old is he now; thirteen?' We nodded. 'Has your aim got better? I think you'll need to give him shots again, something stronger. It might be worse with all this rain we've been having.'

It had been unusually wet again for early autumn, leading a number of our neighbours to joke once more that it was all the fault of us English. But today it had stopped and the sun was out, making everything seem brighter, though my mood was dampened by the news that we'd have to make poor Todo suffer again through our inaccuracy with a needle.

The next morning, a Saturday, dawned bright and sunny and Lawrence enjoyed a rare first-time success with the injection, eliciting just a small yelp from a long-suffering Todo. 'I'm much better with darts; maybe we should draw a target on him and I can throw from three yards away?' he joked.

After lunch, Lawrence settled down to watch English football on our Italian TV service, 'Six games, all live; this is more than I can get in England!' and, taking advantage of continuing good weather, I was up to my elbows in horse manure, mulching every plant in the garden. Totti was my constant companion, helpfully digging out some of the muck I had just put in.

'Lou!' came the yell from inside the house. Lawrence has an endearing habit of shouting to me every time Liverpool score, so I assumed that a red shirt had been successful again and ignored him.

'LOU!' he repeated, louder, 'PHONE!'

Cursing him and whoever might be calling me, I trudged up the slope of the garden, tugging off my boots and went in. Lawrence didn't look up from the TV, just pointed to the office where I'd left my mobile. *Damn, it'll be work. Who's forgotten what this time?*

The first message was long and interrupted, the second briefer. I had to listen to both again to fully comprehend what had happened. There was something horribly incongruous about standing in the middle of a beautiful Tuscan landscape flushed with the joys of a free weekend and hearing that a huge scandal was about to engulf one of my clients, and that his name would be splashed all over tomorrow's front pages. With a sense of déjà vu, I got on the phone to his PR company to see what they might be able to do. Almost exactly a year on from the Great Video Legal Drama, I was once again embroiled in a serious case of damage limitation, and this time it would be played out in public.

All our previous dealings with the media had been positive, our clients sought for interviews or to lend support to campaigns, but from the first call it was clear that this would be a different ball game altogether. My client, a lovely man with a wholesome family image, had been accused of making a remark considered deeply offensive. This was merely the beginning of the storm, the kind we'd observed many times before and which spread like wildfire. But it was horribly and immediately apparent that this time we were right in the thick of it, not just faintly interested bystanders.

As the afternoon wore on I became conscious of two things: first, this was going to take up all my energy for the next few days; second, with the afternoon sun fading and temperatures cooling, Todo was still coughing. I could hear him spluttering in the background while I was on the phone to one of the tabloids involved. The conversation wasn't going well. They were going to print and there was nothing to be done, even with the intervention of PR people and lawyers. The evening was spent in dreadful anticipation and, thanks to the wonders of the Internet, around 10.30 p.m. we could see what would appear in the Sunday papers the next morning. It didn't make for pleasant reading.

Monday morning saw TV and radio take up the story with full weight and the phone-ins had their subject for that day. It was to continue for weeks. Previously grateful to Lawrence for enabling us to keep us in touch with UK radio and TV, now I cursed him; I wished I wasn't able to see or hear any of it and this was especially true some days later on our way back to the vet. By now the numbers ringing my mobile were getting all too familiar and, pulling into the car park at Fontanella, one appeared that I knew meant further bad news. Sure enough, while Lawrence was speaking with Viviana about why Todo wasn't improving, I sat in my car trying not to break down in tears during a call from a national newspaper.

When he returned it was with uncertain news. 'Viviana thinks he should be getting better by now; she wants to give it another week then do some more tests and another X-ray. It might be that trachea problem again.'

All I wanted to do was sit with Todo and try to make him better but the following day we had to leave for London. As his body jerked with each, more strenuous, cough, I felt he was worsening almost by the hour. He tried his best and when the coughing subsided you could almost believe nothing was wrong as he trotted around the house, chasing Totti and sniffing at any food bowl in sight.

Leaving him felt awful and I longed for the days in London to pass as quickly as possible. We called Teresa every day and she would tell us all was fine, things as normal but I wasn't reassured. One evening, just before the curtain went up on an opening night at Glyndebourne, my mobile rang. Fearing it might be her with some terrible news I answered in a panic, with Lawrence looking at me anxiously. He didn't understand why I started laughing until I told him that it was one of the tabloids asking whether I could confirm the story that my client was missing a toe on his right foot. 'I can honestly say I've never seen him with his socks off . . . and you can quote me on that!' I retorted.

On our return Todo seemed brighter so we set off the following day for the vets feeling more confident, though our mood wasn't helped by the shooting which had started in the field early that morning.

Viviana was quiet as she examined Todo, listening very carefully to his breathing. 'We'll do the X-ray first then, if necessary, the other tests, but I'll want to send those away for more examination.' I wondered what she meant by *if necessary*. After helping her to take the X-ray – Todo lying perfectly still on the cold metal table – I joined Lawrence in the waiting-room.

After what seemed an age – but was, in fact, just fifteen minutes – the door opened and Viviana appeared. She beckoned us in but even before she spoke, her face told us everything.

'*Mi dispiace, ho cattive notizie.*' I'm very sorry I have bad news.

The tests wouldn't be necessary; the diagnosis was very clear. The X-ray showed a large mass on Todo's right lung – cancer.

'I'm so sorry,' Viviana looked stricken. 'I don't think there's anything more we can do.'

The news felt completely out of place; Todo had seemed better. It was almost as if we'd strayed into the wrong appointment and Viviana was giving us another patient's diagnosis. Stunned by the finality of her words, I couldn't say anything.

Finally Lawrence spoke. 'There must be something. He's a strong dog, Dottoressa Negri said so last year. Is there chemotherapy; can we operate? Tumours can be removed.'

Viviana hesitated. 'He is an old dog,' she told us. It wasn't possible to tell if he could be treated or even if he would survive such an operation. And the costs would be very high. 'It might be time to think about putting him to sleep.'

My heart virtually stopped; 'No, no, it's too soon.'

Lawrence was defiant. 'We will do anything that is possible; I don't care if it's difficult, or how much it costs.'

Viviana explained that the clinic where Dott. Negri worked, Valdinievole, was a highly regarded specialist one run by another very eminent vet, Dottore Lotti. At her suggestion that she call him, we both nodded vigorously and I looked at Todo, still sitting happily by my feet unaware of the drama unfolding around him.

The call was made and an appointment fixed for the following day. As she had done when Cyd died, Viviana hugged us before we left.

That evening was a strange one. Todo was very excitable, accepting all the treats we gave him and not coughing once. It seemed surreal that he showed such strength and vitality on the day when we'd had such dreadful news. But I kept looking at the X-ray and the large mass on his lung that couldn't be ignored. Sometimes appearances are deceptive. Our beloved Todo was very ill indeed.

25

He Deserves the Best

Dottore Lotti was a middle-aged man, his greying hair and strong features lending him an air of authority, so that as he greeted us I felt a surge of confidence. The clinic appeared impressive and high-tech. I looked at the walls, full of photos showing happy dogs and owners, many with handwritten thank-you notes to the vets. We passed dogs hooked up to drips and three with obvious post-op dressings. I looked at Todo sitting bolt upright, snout in the air, the ever-present smile on his bright face; it seemed difficult to believe that he couldn't be helped.

Examining the X-rays, Dott. Lotti was blunt. 'Your vet at Fontanella has given us her prognosis and I think she is right. This is a very large tumour and he is a small dog. And, he's . . .' – looking at the file – '. . . thirteen years or so old? I think surgery would be too much for him.'

For once even Lawrence was lost for words and I touched his arm, wondering if it was emotion or just the struggle to think how to express himself in Italian.

'You can speak English, if you like,' Dott. Lotti said, smiling. 'The way I see it; we can cure the cough but not cure the dog. It might be kindest to put him to sleep now.'

'We would like to look at the surgery,' Lawrence said finally. 'He is a strong dog; a very special dog.' He began to explain the history of how we'd come to have Todo but Dott. Lotti interrupted with a wave of his hand.

'Excuse me, but everyone thinks their dog is special and that we should operate; it's very rarely successful.'

'Whatever is possible,' said Lawrence firmly.

'OK, if you are sure. The first thing we must do is a CAT scan and biopsy. That will determine the nature of the tumour and will give us a better idea of whether surgery might work and is even possible on such an old dog.'

'Todo,' interjected Lawrence, clearly annoyed at this dispassionate refusal to call him by his name.

'The clinic is at Sasso Marconi, near Bologna.' We nodded, we knew where that was. 'Let me call them and fix an appointment; you do realise it will cost around €1,000?'

'Please make the call,' replied Lawrence.

Back in the waiting-room, Todo wagged his tail at a cocker spaniel he'd befriended earlier. Half an hour later Dott. Lotti appeared, handing us a letter of appointment, his immediate report and the envelope containing the X-rays. 'Next week, is that good for you? I understand from Dottoressa Viviana that you go to London a lot.'

We assured him it was fine, thanked him and shook hands. 'Good luck,' he said.

On the half-hour drive back home, Todo was his usual self, switching from one window to another in the back of the car, catching glimpses of the villages that we passed on the A11 to Lucca and Poggiolino.

The week passed and, with the medication the clinic had given us, Todo was more comfortable, though at times he looked his age. Each morning when we opened the door to the *cucina di cane* to wake him, he took longer to get out of his basket and his first steps were less certain.

My tabloid troubles continued to rumble on and nearly every day I had to tear myself away from work and Todo to deal with yet another scurrilous accusation. More than once I had to stop myself from yelling at a reporter to sod off; all I wanted to concentrate on was Todo, as the day of our appointment drew closer and he grew noticeably weaker.

Bologna is a city we know well and love, having visited many times. That morning we took the familiar drive from Lucca to Florence then the A1 north – the road running down the spine of Italy, connecting Milan to Rome. Every time we'd passed the exit for Sasso Marconi before Lawrence would point it out as the place where the great Italian inventor was buried. Now the irony loomed large – that a radiographer would today use Signor Marconi's invention to conduct a test to determine whether Todo's life could be prolonged or if these were to be the final weeks we would spend with him.

Lawrence had to help him into the car, and he lay in the back without stirring; no excited scampering from one side to another, no face pressed against the window, no pushing towards the front seats at the merest suggestion there was a treat to be had. A chill hung in the air and the dark grey clouds didn't lift once during the two-hour drive; it felt prophetic.

Todo cheered up a little as we arrived and we walked him briefly around the grass outside the clinic. The welcome we received was a relief; a smart young vet who spoke English took us into a treatment room to prepare Todo for the procedures. His humour was infectious, and he was warm to Todo, who appeared suddenly brighter. He stood patiently while the fur on his paws were clipped, blood taken and a thorough examination carried out. We stroked him throughout, encouraged by the vet's assertion that he appeared healthy.

He replaced Todo's collar with a simple rope lead and, lifting him gently to the floor, we all left the room to be met outside by another vet, Dottoressa Rossi, who would conduct the CAT scan and biopsy. A petite and pretty blonde, she managed to be both pragmatic and encouraging. Another English speaker, she explained that Todo would be sedated for both examinations and we should return in two hours.

A clock started ticking in my head. What if the news was bad? In just two hours' time, might we really have to accept the fact that Todo's life was almost over?

We had no idea what to do with ourselves. Just after one o'clock, and with everything closed for lunch, we wandered through the deserted town centre. 'I suppose we should eat something,' said Lawrence and we got in the car to drive to the closest pizzeria. It was a simple place and, when we explained why we were there, the jolly waitress refused to allow us to wallow. We toasted Todo and wished him good luck, and the pizzas were so good that Lawrence insisted we would come back another day, 'when Todo is better; he'll love it here!'

Returning to the clinic, Dott. Rossi met us and told us all had gone well. Inserting a CD into her computer she showed us the images of the scan, explaining the size and position of the tumour. Every now and then she'd lose her English and slip into Italian which meant I didn't follow everything but Lawrence did and I saw by the look on his face that it might be good news.

Taking out the CD and putting it into a file she gave us her conclusion. 'In all other respects he is a healthy dog, and the best news is that there are no signs of the cancer spreading to any other parts of the body or even the bloodstream. It is contained entirely in the lung and is clean.'

'So an operation is possible?'

'Dottore Baroni at the Valdinievole clinic is a very fine surgeon. I am confident that he can perform a successful operation and the dog can make a recovery.'

I smiled and thanked her, wanting to shout at the top of my voice. I could see Lawrence was struggling to hold things together, his face strained and eyes red.

'We'll bring him through in a few minutes.' She showed us back to the waiting-room and we hugged each other. Shortly after, the door opened and a long snout appeared, followed by those familiar shaggy ears and smiling face.

Lawrence rushed off to the loo. A soppy bugger at the best of times, he'll cry at *E.T.* and *The Railway Children* in front of me, but I knew at this moment he needed to be alone with his tears. When he returned a few minutes later, Todo rushed over and Lawrence kissed him. 'I was right all along, I never doubted you'd come through it. What a special boy.'

There was one more hurdle to cross. We still had to wait for the results of the biopsy to confirm that Dott. Rossi was right. She suggested we call in at Monsummano Terme on the way home to give Dott. Lotti the file and on arriving it was clear the news had preceded us, as the receptionist, Renza, told us how pleased she was. Dott. Lotti greeted us, a little more reserved, though his smile was broad as he explained that the results would be with him in a few days and that he also wanted to know the outcome of more detailed blood tests which would confirm that there were no infected cells elsewhere. After that the operation would go ahead as soon as possible.

'You may be right about the dog,' he laughed.

'Todo,' we both corrected.

The drive back was a more joyous one with Todo, fully recovered from the effects of sedation, as bouncy as usual. Skipping down the steps to the house he executed his usual athletic leap off the final three, as if he had recovered already.

The following morning, later than usual, I heard a shot ring out from the valley. We were already in the office, but downed tools and twenty minutes later were at our posts once more, CD poles in hand.

Signor Merdini cursed, and his friend came out from the hide, shouting at us. One of the silly joys of learning a new language is discovering swear words but they uttered none that we knew, even if the tone left us in no doubt as to their meaning.

In need of my morning coffee, I sent Lawrence to the house and just a few moments after he left I spotted the flashing blue light of a police car coming slowly up the road before stopping at the entrance to our field. Two Carabinieri got out of the car, picking their way through the damp, muddy grass, anxious not to spoil their resplendent red and blue uniforms.

'Signora, what are you doing?' the older officer barked.

I have never been good with authority, often joking that, faced with a uniform, I would confess to anything. And this gun-toting officer was definitely intimidating. But I held my ground. 'This is *our* land, we can do what we like on our land.' I have learnt since this is not the wisest approach with the Carabinieri, particularly the more senior ones.

The officer yelled at me, his face red. I didn't understand a word but his younger colleague came over, asking me more calmly what was happening and I tried to explain, more politely, that this was our land and I could see nothing wrong in what I was doing. Even with his softer tone I knew this was *an incident.* When he demanded my documentation I told him I would go to the house to get it and headed off, while the senior officer went to talk with the shooters.

Lawrence sat checking emails and preparing to bring me my latte.

'I need my passport.'

'Why?'

'Because the Carabinieri are here.'

To my surprise (Lawrence would be the first to admit that he doesn't always take bad news well) he seemed slightly amused until I explained what had just happened. That grim expression which I had come to know and love so well spread across his darkening face and, grabbing his passport too, we returned to the field.

'Ah, Signor Kershaw,' came the greeting from the senior officer. 'How are you?'

'Fine, thank you Captain Agnelli; but I think we have a problem.'

This, it seemed, was the officer who had dealt with Lawrence after the burglary and relief oozed from me at the cordiality of the exchange. I noted the look of sympathy Agnelli gave my husband, accompanied by a subtle roll of the eyes in my direction and a similar one from Lawrence, accompanied by his best authentic Italian shrug. So the male conspiracy would resolve the situation and the silly English woman would be put in her place. Well, on this occasion (I'd already begun mentally preparing a press statement to accompany my deportation) I was relieved to be the wife who hadn't quite understood.

While Lawrence spoke with both officers, I did my best to look contrite, nodding at what seemed appropriate moments in the conversation. I followed his expressions, which ranged from incomprehension, solicitude and pleading to exasperation. I could tell that it wasn't going our way. They explained to us that we were perceived as the guilty parties here and we must *desist forthwith* or run the risk of being charged with *molesting* a hunter. The connotations of that word seemed horribly out of place, but there could be no doubt that this was to be their final word.

Captain Agnelli walked off, leaving his junior colleague to play out the role of good cop, at which point two loud shots rang out from the hide, causing both officers to wince. Agnelli returned, telling us that he had spoken with the shooters and wasn't in disagreement with our case, but could not approve the methods. Lawrence told him again we had visited the Corpo Forestale and this met with a nod of approval. 'That is the right thing to do, not this . . . this terrorism!'

Back at home, relief that we wouldn't have to pack a bag and get out of town that evening was tempered by the realisation that we had almost certainly lost this battle and would have to resign ourselves to the hunters' intrusion.

To our dismay, our next trip to London coincided with our appointment to see Dott. Lotti for final confirmation of the decision to proceed with Todo's operation. He had improved significantly in the past week, even if the cough remained a problem, but it was distressing to leave him. Lawrence refused to consider that something dreadful might happen while we were away but I knew he was worried too.

As usual, Teresa would come to see Todo in our absence, as well as giving him his injections, a prospect which caused her no concern whatsoever, 'I did it with Maurizio when he was a boy.' She and Silvano had also offered to take Todo to Dott. Lotti. The appointment had been made for late afternoon, by which time we would be at a rehearsal in London's Cadogan Hall, before a concert there that evening.

Late November in London was cold. We stood in the corridor outside the concert hall and even Rachmaninov's beautiful Second Symphony, my favourite piece, couldn't distract me.

I pestered Lawrence to call.

'Look; they're always late at the clinic and then it'll take Silvano at least forty minutes to drive home. Just wait.'

I wondered if he was having trouble with the idea of making the call. We'd come so far and yet everything still hinged on the vets being sure that the operation would be possible. Even if they said yes, it still held no guarantee of success, but we wanted so badly to give our blessed boy every chance. After everything he'd given us we owed it to him, and to the memory of Carol. She'd been a fighter and had battled through to the very end, seizing as much of life as she possibly could. Her dog – our dog – deserved the opportunity to do the same.

It was an hour past the appointment time then a further thirty minutes went by as we tried to force down a drink and some crisps in the foyer bar. Lawrence looked at me. 'The reception's lousy in here, let's go outside.'

He dialled Teresa's number and a few seconds later said good evening to Silvano.

'*Sì, sì*; I understand. *Grazie mille*, Silvano and best wishes to Teresa.'

No words, just thumbs up followed by a long hug. While London busied itself around us, our thoughts were 950 miles south, with Todo.

26

Our Turn to Wait

With just days before Todo would have to enter the clinic for his operation, we decided to enjoy him and spoil him as much as possible.

Just in case . . .

We began with lunch at our favourite Lucca trattoria, Rusticanella Due. We went so often that we were greeted as family, and our favourite waitress, Viviana, knew all about Todo's condition and was delighted to hear the positive news. A tiny bundle of energy and humour, we always enjoyed her performance and today's, as she brought out dozens of dishes, greeted customers and came back every few minutes to stroke Todo, was a real *tour de force* – full of theatrical calls, whispers and grand gestures.

On the way back to Poggiolino, Lawrence received a call.

'Ah, yes; I understand. In fact we're just a short way from home. We'll be there in five minutes.'

It was the Carabinieri and they were at the house, waiting for us. 'I think he said they've got the Corpo Forestale with them.'

Pulling into the drive we saw two Carabinieri cars, four officers including Captain Agnelli, and a Corpo jeep from which emerged Andrea from the Lucca office and another officer; a veritable buffet of uniforms and firearms. 'I think it's a sit-down,' said Lawrence, in *Sopranos* mode. 'Whaddaya gonna do?'

Greetings were exchanged before Captain Agnelli and Andrea got down to business. They reiterated that, while sympathising with our position and acknowledging how terrible it must be for us, *the law was not being broken by the shooters*. In fact we were in violation of regulations and *must stop this molestation*; the poles with CDs we had positioned permanently in the field must be removed immediately and we had to agree not to take any more down there.

Lawrence's hackles rose. 'So you're telling us we can do nothing and this *bastardo* can do whatever he likes within feet of our land?'

As Lawrence squared up to the two officials, tension running high, proceedings were interrupted by the famous Ennio Morricone theme from *The Good, the Bad and the Ugly*. It turned out to be Captain Agnelli's mobile – at least he had a sense of humour. The tension of the moment was broken, everyone laughed and the Captain stepped aside to take his call. All for backing down and slinking off, I had been impressed by Lawrence's stand and wondered whether I could set him loose on the tabloid reporters who were still hounding me. The story about my client had long since run out of steam, but they just wouldn't let it go.

Andrea told us that they would try to do what they could and would speak with the hunters once more, Agnelli – having finished his call – nodded in agreement. They added that any time that we felt it was becoming too much we should call them and they would come out to have more words.

Well that was something at least, and we were thrilled when they assured us that the shooting would finish earlier this year, around mid-December. We didn't understand why and asked if it was something to do with the new regulations. Agnelli's reply was accompanied by knowing looks which passed between all the Carabinieri and Corpo officers.

I don't think Lawrence understood what they were saying, but he joined in with the nodding and shrugging and there seemed a very masculine accord between all of them. Handshakes and backslaps followed. Lawrence's broadest grin came when the Captain's finger wagged firmly in my direction. 'Signora, CDs are for listening to music, not molesting hunters.' He followed this up with a comical shaking of his arms, mimicking our actions with the poles.

We didn't have to wait until mid-December. We never discovered what had been said or done but, to our relief and delight, there wasn't a single shot fired from the field after that day. As we toasted the end of the shooting – for that year anyway – we liked to believe that a bit of British pluck had helped conclude the problem.

Todo was due to go to Valdinievole on Tuesday 1 December. His operation would not take place until Friday, but the vets needed him in three days before, for pre-op treatments and tests.

The day before, 30 November, we padded together out of the gate to Poggiolino and down the hill to the cemetery of San Martino. Carol MacAndrew had been born exactly one hundred years ago, and nothing could be more appropriate than to visit her grave.

The cemetery is small but beautiful, surrounded by a high

stone wall, topped with terracotta tiles, the iron gates to its entrance flanked by small statues of religious figures and of two children in prayer. A place of peace, as we slipped through the gates it was at its best, filled with flowers left from the festival of All Souls at the beginning of November.

Everywhere there were expensive lilies and great bouquets of brightly coloured, scented roses and chrysanthemums. All Souls is a celebration of the lives of those resting there and, with the enamelled pictures of the deceased adorning most headstones, it is easy to understand the feeling of closeness it brings for its visitors.

We made our way to the newer section where Carol and Jim lay. Beside their headstones stood a simple vase filled with some of the wild flowers which covered the fields and hills of the area. 'Teresa,' I said to Lawrence, and we placed the flowers we had brought from our garden next to it. We stood for a few minutes and, though we'd let him off the lead, Todo stayed close to us and to the headstone, which read simply: JAMES K. MACANDREW 1908–1983, CAROL COFER MACANDREW 1909–2005.

The following morning I had to fly to London for meetings arranged some time before. To catch my 6.40 a.m. flight I was up before 4 a.m. With what lay ahead of him today I didn't want to disturb Todo's sleep, so had said goodbye to him the night before. He'd had a bad coughing fit in the evening and was obviously unsettled, but I refused to allow myself any doubts. 'I'm back in two days and I'll see you at the weekend.' I knew I was reassuring both of us. Driving to Pisa Airport in the dark I remembered Dott. Lotti's words; *he's a strong dog*.

Lawrence had fallen asleep after I left, but woke at six to hear Todo coughing. Silvano had offered to drive them to the clinic and they'd arranged to leave at seven, so he got up and went down to see Todo. He appeared very low, and not just because he couldn't eat the night before, or have any breakfast; he didn't attempt to follow Lawrence back upstairs, as he often did.

Right on time, Silvano's jeep appeared. Although he's an animal-lover, like many of his countrymen his attitude is not at all sentimental – there is no equivalent of the word *pet* in Italian. Fully aware of the implications of the operation and how it must be affecting Lawrence, he chatted cheerfully about any and all subjects during the hour-long drive. It proved a useful diversion for Lawrence and he was happy to see Todo sitting up all the way, gazing out of the windows.

Their arrival at the clinic pretty much coincided with mine at Stansted. Checking my watch I resisted the urge to call. *Better to wait. He's got more important things to do.*

'Shall I stay?' asked Silvano. 'That's very kind, but you should be getting back now. We don't know how long it might be.' Although grateful for his kindness, in truth Lawrence wanted to be by himself.

He checked in with the receptionist and stood waiting, Todo's face pressed against the glass door, greeting other dogs as they arrived. Finally Dott. Lotti's colleague, Dottoressa Ratto, appeared. They went through the checklist: no food for the previous twelve hours; last medication this morning; weight 15 kilos – two less than his normal size. After that there remained just the matter of Lawrence's signature granting permission for the operation and exempting the clinic from liability in the case of failure.

Reading the form it hit him hard just how dangerous this could be. Four boxes indicated the *Level of Risk*: None; Low; Medium; High. Dott. Ratto had ticked the last option. He signed and she took off Todo's brown leather collar, replacing it with a rope, and handing it to Lawrence. He asked if she might leave them a moment and she told him she'd be back shortly.

Bending down he held Todo tightly, kissing him. 'You're a brave boy, this'll work out just fine. We'll be in to see you at the weekend and I promise to bring your favourite biscuits.'

After one last goodbye, Dott. Ratto led Todo into the clinical rooms. Lawrence stared after them for a few seconds then headed back to reception where he had to pay. Half now; the rest afterwards. Normally he'd have made a joke about discounts or money-back guarantee but his mood was solemn. He handed over his credit card and signed the slip given to him, realising he still had Todo's collar in his hand.

It was a long journey home. Monsummano Terme is a charming old spa town, though not as elegant as its close neighbour Montecatini. Charming also meant difficult to get to and from. The only way to reach Lucca was to get a bus to Montecatini and pick up a train from there, but buses aren't too frequent in this car-dependent part of Tuscany and Lawrence waited for thirty minutes. Still tired from the early morning and drained emotionally, he finally arrived at the elegant art-nouveau station in Montecatini to find that the Lucca train due in ten minutes had been cancelled and the next, a slow one, wouldn't be for more than another hour. He bought a bus ticket instead and was boarding the Lucca-bound bus as I arrived in central London and called him. He reassured me that everything had gone well, explaining how good Todo had been in the car and that he'd trotted off happily with Dott. Ratto. Then we both fell silent. We were in the hands of Dott. Baroni, the vet who would perform the surgery, and we'd hear nothing more until after it was over, on Friday morning.

Poggiolino was a different house on my return the following day. No excited face greeted me at the gate, no scurrying legs under my feet heading to the food bowls, no clicking of paws as Todo padded around after us. It was so quiet without him and we were quieter too, with none of the constant chatting to him as he wandered in and out of the office, wanting to be let out into the garden or trying to coax another treat from us. I even missed his noisy slurping from the water bowl.

In the afternoon the doorbell rang but was unaccompanied by the barking and rushing to the front door we'd grown to love. It was Umberto, who'd brought our olive oil. The harvest had been earlier than usual and more than twenty litres of fresh cloudy green nectar now sat in two large flagons on the table in Todo's room.

'How is he?' asked Umberto and we explained that he'd been fine but tomorrow was the big day.

'He's a strong dog, he'll come through. Why would he want to leave you two? The life he has here!' We thanked him and assured him we'd let everyone know the outcome as soon as possible.

An hour later Mario and Lorenzo dropped in, taking a break from olive harvesting. Lorenzo looked at the jars. 'I see Umberto's brought you this year's oil; have you tasted it yet?' Ignoring Lawrence's reply, he went on, 'How is little Todo?' We repeated what we had told Umberto and they nodded in agreement that he was a good dog and would surely pull through. I was touched by their concern, these two men not given to displays of sentimentality.

We began to realise just how much Todo meant to everyone in the area. 'Look how much he means to us,' said Lawrence. He was right. It was only two and half years since we'd come to Poggiolino and yet almost impossible to remember a time when he wasn't part of our lives.

At supper there was no expectant face sitting below the table. Lawrence insisted we keep some roast pork in a bag – 'We'll give it to him next week.' I wanted desperately to share his confidence but the stillness in the house made it very difficult. I wondered if things could ever be the same without him; if he hadn't been at Poggiolino we would never have given the house a second viewing. We'd never have discovered its magic, or known of Carol MacAndrew, met Herbert, Laura and Albertina; never have experienced the kindness shown to us by Teresa and her family. Todo had given us so much. Surely he couldn't leave us yet?

27

Borrowed Time

Waking early the following morning, I opened the door to Todo's room and stared at his empty basket. More than I had ever wished for anything before, I longed for him to be back there in a few days. I was grateful for the distraction of our weekly Italian lesson.

At ten o'clock, just before we were due to leave, Teresa came to clean as usual though she was clearly subdued. 'What time will the operation be?'

Lawrence answered, 'They've probably started by now. We can call them around one.'

'We're all thinking of him, and I know La Signora will be too.'

Our lovely Italian teacher, Anna, had previously given us lessons at home before the birth of her first daughter. Now we went to her house in Toringo, just south of the city. She'd met Todo on many occasions and knew all about his operation, giving us long hugs, or *abbracci*, as we arrived. A ball of energy,

Anna had lived in South London for a number of years, just a mile or so from our house in Vauxhall, and we loved hearing her speak English with a London accent. She is the perfect teacher, encouraging and informative, and her classes are always fun, though that day Lawrence seemed ill at ease and I saw him checking his watch regularly. As we left, all our classmates wished us good luck and Anna told us, 'He's such a wonderful dog, I have no doubt he'll come through it.'

'It's only 12.30, but I'm calling them,' Lawrence said as we set off for home. I barely had time to think but I felt my stomach twist with anxiety. After a few seconds he was through to Renza. 'His name is Todo, he was having an operation this morning . . . thank you.' They were putting him through to Dott. Baroni, so the surgery had clearly ended. When the vet came on the line, Lawrence's responses sounded positive.

'*Grazie mille*, I will call later. Thank you for everything.'

I stopped the car and looked at him.

'It's gone fine. They're happy they've removed the whole tumour, it was a clean surgery and they didn't see any sign of it spreading elsewhere. They had to take part of the lung.'

'So it's good news?'

'Yes, but too early to tell and he's not come round from the anaesthetic. I need to call again later but it sounds good.'

Neither of us ate lunch, though we tried to attend to work. Thankfully it was quiet and later that afternoon Lawrence called the clinic again. Renza said she would fetch Dott. Lotti. What did this mean? He was the head of the practice and spoke good English. Did this mean bad news? The wait dragged on and Renza apologised constantly, saying she was still trying to locate him. In those moments I began to believe that we'd lost Todo.

'Hello Signor Kershaw, Dott. Lotti here. Well; the dog has

come out of his sleep and we have him under constant monitoring.'

'Dott. Baroni told me he was pleased with the surgery.'

'Yes, things went well but now we have to wait. As I told you, he is an old dog; we don't know yet how he will react to something so big.'

'But you're confident?'

'We will know more as time goes on. The next forty-eight hours will be crucial. Call again tomorrow and we'll update you.'

Shortly before dinner, Teresa came with Maurizio and Diego. We invited them in and told them of Dott. Lotti's call. Teresa was more steadfast than us; in her mind Todo was well again. 'What a fighter, just like La Signora. You will have him home next week!'

Going to bed that night her words were a comfort. *No one knows him better than Teresa. I'll bet she's right.*

Saturday morning dawned sunny and bright. Turning on the mobile, Lawrence found a missed call from Dott. Lotti. Did this mean something had gone wrong?

Renza recognised his voice; 'Ah, *buon giorno.* I'll put you through.'

'She sounds very upbeat,' he whispered to me.

This time Dott. Lotti came on the line immediately.

'Well, it seems the dog is doing fine, he's had a little to eat and we've taken away some of the drips.'

'Do you think it might be possible to come and see him?'

'Mmm, I think it's a little early for that. We still need to get him through the next twenty-four hours before we will know for sure. Call this afternoon and we'll see how he is.'

We had to go to the supermarket but decided to call in on the vets at Fontanella to give them the news. Sitting in the waiting-room it felt such a long time since we'd first brought Todo in with his cough. As the door opened Viviana's delighted face appeared, 'I already heard from Dott. Lotti; congratulations!'

At the Esselunga we bumped into Albertina. 'How is the dear one?' she asked, and we were able to tell her that things seemed positive. 'Didn't I tell you he'd be fine? What a splendid little fellow.'

Arriving home, we found messages from Anna then Laura and I called them both, and then Ania phoned from London.

By three o'clock we were getting restless.

'Should we call?'

'No. Sod this, let's just go. You never know.'

We jumped in the car and forty minutes later pulled up outside Valdinievole. Renza was excited and delighted to see us, disappearing behind the doors marked *No Entry*, then reappearing shortly afterwards; 'Someone will come to see you.'

We sat at the far end of the waiting-room for several minutes. The clinic door opened and, walking very slowly, a small chestnut and brown dog appeared, followed closely by a vet. Stopping uncertainly, he turned. Instantly that plumed tail shot bolt upright and he came trotting towards us. I thought my heart would burst as we knelt to hug him.

A large bandage and a draining dressing covered much of his left side, but otherwise Todo looked just as he'd done when Lawrence had said goodbye four days earlier. The young vet told us, 'Only five minutes; he's still very weak,' and sure enough his legs began to slip and he was soon lying on the ground, but by then we knew this wasn't to be the end of our story.

I asked if we should come again tomorrow, and she agreed.

I can't recall anything we did for the rest of the day; Lawrence didn't even bother to watch the football that evening. Still a little cautious, we didn't crack open a bottle of champagne but he put it in the fridge, 'to have when he's back'. I phoned family and friends in Italy, Sydney and London, telling them the good news.

After Sunday lunch we were about to set off for the clinic when Lawrence dashed back into the house, emerging again with treats. 'I doubt they'll let us give them to him, but you never know.'

When we arrived, Renza smiled and went to fetch the vet. This time, when the doors opened, Todo saw us immediately and he almost ran to us. 'Would you like to take him outside?' she asked.

'Really?' I replied.

'Yes, it'll be good for him to have some fresh air.'

We went out to the clinic's lawn and then, with Todo clearly eager, crossed the road to the field opposite. We were delighted yet incredulous. 'He had major surgery two days ago!' Lawrence was to repeat this several times before we went back in. As we waited for the vet to appear, he took out one of the chewy sticks and broke it into pieces. Todo grabbed the first, chomping happily. I gave him another, and then one more; each time it was swallowed in seconds and followed by that expectant look we had come to know and love so well.

When the vet returned, she said she'd take the remaining pieces and let him have them during the evening.

'When do you think he can leave? Dott. Lotti thought maybe a week here.'

'Come tomorrow afternoon and they can decide.'

It wasn't exactly a welcoming committee but both Dott. Lotti and Dott. Ratto were standing at the entrance when we arrived that Monday afternoon. Taking us into the treatment room, Dott. Lotti explained exactly how the procedure had gone and what they now expected. 'Todo is a remarkable dog. He has such strength. None of us can believe his recovery, this quickly.'

It was the first time he'd called Todo by his name.

Dott. Ratto went to collect him and when they appeared she bent down to stroke him, 'Good boy, Todo. Good boy.' Our dog had worked his magic once more!

'When do you think he might be well enough to come home?'

'I see no reason why he shouldn't go with you today. We're all happy here; there's nothing more we need to do with him. I think he'd be better off with you now.'

Saying a final goodbye, and thanking everyone for all they'd done, we left, Todo trotting beside us. The minor detail of making the second payment for the treatment was forgotten. There would be time for that another day. As Lawrence said, getting in the car, 'What are they going to do? Make us give him back?' We were bringing him home – to *his* home, where he'd given such joy to his first companion and would continue to give joy to us.

When Lawrence pointed out the date on the discharge form, 7 December, we realised it was exactly three years to the day since we first viewed Poggiolino and met Todo. At that first meeting we could never have imagined just what a change he would make to our lives and how quickly we would grow to love him. Or how much.

We marvelled at his recovery; within days he was trotting around the house and garden, managing a run every now and again and keeping up a good pace when we took him for short walks. His appetite remained unaffected and I'm not ashamed to say we indulged him more than ever. If this was borrowed time then it was going to be the best we could give him.

What a Christmas we enjoyed, even with (so Teresa told us) Compito's heaviest snowfall in more than forty years. We didn't mind and nor did Todo; to keep him warm where his fur had been shaved for the operation, we bought him a rather snazzy black polo neck jumper which he took to immediately.

Many Christmas cards from friends contained messages for him and he was greeted like a hero when he managed the walk up the hill, bumping first into Lorenzo and Giuliana, then Mario, who complained that the snow had held up the last of his olive harvesting on the 700 trees which had once belonged to Carol.

There remained one issue regarding Todo's recovery: Dott. Ratto, an expert in cancer of dogs, advised us that he should have a course of chemotherapy. She told us to forget any preconceptions about what we'd seen and knew of the treatment in humans. For animals it was much gentler and she didn't foresee any terrible side effects. Still, we were unsure, until we had lunch with two Dutch friends, Saskia and Ernest, who live at nearby Segromino and had their daughter, son-in-law and grandchildren staying with them. It was a happy occasion and Todo once more delighted the toddlers, as well as Ernest with whom he'd bonded – under the dinner table – many times before. An eminent oncologist, we asked Ernest to take a look at the report from Todo's operation and his verdict was immediate: it had been an aggressive tumour, we *must* do the chemo.

'Of course, it is all preordained anyway,' he smiled, going on to explain that a body of opinion held that the heart is programmed with a set number of beats. 'Once you've reached that number, it's the end,' he continued, rather too cheerily, I thought.

Another New Year, another toast; this one reserved almost

exclusively for Todo. As January continued, cold but sunny, we established a new, slower routine with him: gentle walks three times a day, his usual time in the office and trips with us in the car wherever we went, even if just to the supermarket or post office.

Todo's chemo began in early January and he was the perfect patient on our weekly trips to Dott. Ratto for the treatment. Each time one of us would help her during the twenty minutes or so it took to administer the chemicals and he was as brave as ever. Typically, for such a strong dog, he suffered no serious side effects, not even the loss of any his beautiful black *baffi*, or whiskers, and we hoped that he saw the time there as just a small interlude in his blissful life at Poggiolino.

For my birthday in February we took our first big trip in several months, up to the alpine ski-resort of Abetone, high in the Garfagnana, to a restaurant we'd enjoyed many times before with him. When a waitress recognised him and we explained the reason behind the black jumper, which looked even more dashing topped with the red bandana – he was treated like a VIP. With eight-feet-high snowdrifts outside, the three of us sat next to a log fire enjoying plate after plate of the most delicious local specialities.

Looking out at the snow-covered mountains glistening in the bright winter sun it felt like a perfect moment in time. But as we sipped on a glass of sweet moscato grappa, Todo let out a couple of coughs. Nothing serious, in seconds he was fine, but it broke my daydream. While Lawrence paid, I went to the bathroom. Forty-nine today, I suddenly knew that we wouldn't celebrate my fiftieth with Todo and I wept.

Lawrence saw my distress and kissed me, squeezing my arm as we stepped out into the deep snow.

Soon afterwards we invited Albertina, Herbert and Laura for

lunch and the afternoon turned into a celebration of Todo and reminiscence of Carol. Knowing he was the centre of attention, his energy never flagged during the hours we sat talking, eating and drinking. More than once the parallel was drawn between dog and first owner; brave fighters both of them, though our octogenarian guests agreed wholeheartedly that the four-legged half of the two possessed the greater charm!

As spring progressed, so did he. Walks became longer and at times he'd shoot off in the opposite direction, then rejoin us, ears flapping and mouth open in that familiar grin. Totti came every day, and once or twice even Bob tagged along.

Todo had always loved his Joki Dent – rectangles of dried cow hide. They were supposedly good for his teeth, but Todo preferred to bury them – no place was safe enough for the precious Joki Dent. He would pad to and fro in the garden for hours, burying one, only to dig it up seconds later and move it to another prized spot. At night after being let out for the final time before bed, he would find the Joki Dent and attempt to bring it into the house. We could only prise it from his jaws by tricking him into dropping it, rubbing a piece of ham against his mouth. Todo would try to get the meat while maintaining his grip on the Joki Dent, but after the fourth or fifth time he would drop it and we'd give him the ham as his reward.

One day in early spring I gave him a Joki Dent and this time he didn't bury it. He took it everywhere with him and for the first time, he began playing with us, getting us to grab it and then grabbing it back, over and over again, with evident delight. After the trials and tribulations of the past five years perhaps this was his celebration of a rebirth, or at least a second puppyhood.

It was a frantically busy time for us at work, so there were trips to and from London throughout March and April. Each time we went it was with heavy hearts, but Teresa would come to the house before we left, sometimes bringing Diego, and she and the family spent more time with him, often taking him back to their house to be with their dog, Lulu, and the growing number of cats.

Our homecoming welcome was always the same: the face pressed against the gate, a sniff of us and our bags – checking what we'd brought him – before a rush down the steps. He would still launch himself off the last three in one leap; *who's calling me old?*

In the first week of May we had the second of two short trips. We knew from friends who had stayed at the house that Todo now accepted them easily, as necessary interludes in his fun, knowing our return was never too far away. Even with an early start he was bright and attentive as we busied ourselves with bags and breakfast.

He came up the steps to the car with us and we kissed him goodbye. As he ran back down I shouted to him, 'Don't jump!' but to no avail, as he essayed one of his most impressive arcing descents from three steps up. He turned to look up at us, the broadest of smiles on his sweet face.

28

His Number of Beats

Lawrence always took the Italian mobile to London in case friends or neighbours needed to call us – particularly Teresa with any news of the house or, of course, Todo – and since the operation he switched it on each day when we were away with a sense of trepidation.

Leaving it on for half an hour or so a few times each day, he would turn it off again with a sigh of relief, though in truth neither of us believed anything terrible would ever happen while we were away. We trusted that Todo would be there to greet us when we returned to Poggiolino.

This trip was full of meetings and concerts, as well as a surprise eightieth birthday party for Lawrence's mother in Liverpool. Edna had visited Poggiolino a few times since our move and though she was not a renowned animal-lover she too had fallen under Todo's spell, always asking after him when Lawrence called.

The party was a great success. Lawrence turned back the

clock with a rendition of 'Smoke Gets in Your Eyes' and impressed all the guests by carrying on a long conversation with a young Italian girl at the party who spoke almost no English. In truth I wondered if he spent just a little too long with her, but obviously he was concerned that she shouldn't feel left out.

Returning to London the next day, we read about the re-emergence of the Icelandic volcanic ash cloud which had blighted so many travellers' plans the previous month. Concerned about getting back to Todo, we were relieved to hear it had passed, and our flight the following morning would not be disrupted.

After our arrival in Pisa we called into the Esselunga on our way home to stock up for the first part of the week. We finally pulled up to Poggiolino in the late afternoon, longing to see Todo. He wasn't waiting at the gate, but as soon as we opened the front door there was the familiar tap of paws on tiles and he emerged, tail in overdrive, to greet us. A little slower perhaps, certainly less frenetic than he used to be, but looking well. I dropped my bag on the floor, bending to cuddle him and he buried his head under my arm.

An hour later we were walking in the fields with Todo and Totti. The day had turned warm and it was a joy to be back on our beautiful hillside. As always, we called on Teresa to let her know we were back and thank her for looking after the house and all the animals.

Todo had been unwell one day, she told us, listless and tired. 'But,' she clapped her hands, 'all fine the next day, catching up on what he hadn't eaten the day before!'

Lawrence prepared a simple supper, chicken and salad, and Todo found himself the recipient of gifts from both our plates. 'Well, there's a first,' I said as he toyed with a piece of chicken before eating it. 'Is it possible he's not hungry?'

'Mmm, Teresa did say he'd been unwell; perhaps there's still something up?' Lawrence reached down to stroke him.

We settled down to catch up with the Italian news. Even native Italians find their *Tele Giornale* hard to follow and this evening it seemed particularly difficult; in just a few days away our language skills felt rusty.

Todo seemed to be having difficulty settling.

'Let's see how he is tomorrow, we can always mention it to Dott. Ratto,' Lawrence said. We had an appointment the following day at Valdinievole for the last of Todo's monthly checks following his chemotherapy.

As the evening wore on, Todo still wouldn't settle in either his basket or on the rug at our feet. We both stroked and hugged him and he lapped up the affection, but as soon as we stopped he seemed agitated and uncomfortable. I tried putting him into his basket and closing the door to his room for a few minutes but he came out again in the same state.

I noticed he was lifting his head all the time, as if trying to make his breathing a little easier. We'd seen this before, especially since the operation, after a particularly vigorous run, or heading up the steep incline to the gate. I wondered about taking him to Valdinievole now as they had a twenty-four-hour service but Lawrence was unsure. He tried to encourage Todo to rest but the head-lifting grew more frequent.

As he sat with him, Totti came in. Emerging from behind a sofa she looked at Todo and stopped dead in her tracks. Her eyes grew huge; she arched her back and slowly backed away from him. Now I was really scared. She adored him and they usually spent evenings together in his basket. I knew he was in serious trouble.

'C'mon Todo, let's get you a treat.' Lawrence encouraged him into his room. Usually the rattle of the cookie box alone would bring Todo scurrying from whichever part of the house or garden he was in. Now he sniffed, then turned his head away. I saw the expression on Lawrence's face change and he reached immediately for the phone.

Explaining that Todo was already a patient he told the duty vet that he was experiencing discomfort in his breathing. Given the lateness of the hour and our uncertainty about Todo's symptoms, he expected a suggestion that they look at it the following day. But the response was 'Bring him now!' and we knew we had an emergency on our hands.

Grabbing my car keys I headed out, leaving Lawrence to lock up the house and bring Todo. Just before the front door, Todo turned, as if to head upstairs, but the effort was too much and he stopped, even before Lawrence encouraged him outside.

I started the car, watching Lawrence pick up Todo gently, carrying him up the steps and placing him carefully in the back seat.

'Should I sit in the back with him?'

I was unsure. I hadn't fully grasped what might be happening but I think Lawrence knew and he wanted one of us to be with Todo.

'I'll sit with him, just to make sure.' His voice was very quiet. He climbed in beside Todo who was circling gently, finding a comfortable position.

I drove the well-travelled route through Fontanella, past the local vet's onto the main road and to the Autostrada sign for the A11 and Montecatini Terme. Lawrence kept talking to Todo all the time, stroking him. We passed the industrial park, sped through the Telepass toll and were on the A11, just twenty minutes from the clinic.

'He's a little calmer,' Lawrence told me, and I felt reassured.

Let's just get him to the vet; they'll know what to do. Please don't let this be the end, not today when we've only just got home. If his time is up, give us a few more days so we can say goodbye.

Glancing back, I saw that Lawrence had his arm around Todo. 'I think his breathing might be a little easier.'

A few minutes later, Todo lifted his head again and let out two quiet sighs, before his head dropped on to his paws.

'Lou . . . I think he's gone.'

His voice was strangely calm, and for a moment I didn't take in what he had said.

'What do you mean?'

'Todo's died.' This time his voice broke.

We were five minutes away from the clinic and, not knowing what else to do, I kept on driving, though my tears made it almost impossible to see the road.

When we arrived, Lawrence leapt out. I opened the rear door and there lay our beloved friend lying peacefully in his usual place. I'd seen him like that hundreds of times; it was as if nothing had changed.

I stroked his head, telling him over and over again he was the greatest dog ever; the best companion and friend anyone could wish for. 'You've given us so much, so much; we love you and we will never forget you.'

We carried him in his blanket, into the clinic. On the treatment table he lay as though in a deep sleep as the vet checked for a pulse.

'It was his heart; I'm so sorry. Everyone here knew how special he was and how much he meant to you. He was one of our greatest successes.' She touched Lawrence's arm as he stood next to her, stroking Todo.

'He'd just had his number of beats,' he whispered to me and I nodded.

Lawrence thanked the vet who had been so kind, asking through tears if she could let Dott. Ratto know we wouldn't make tomorrow's appointment.

Placing Todo back in the car we set off for Poggiolino and Lawrence managed a half-smile. 'At least he died in his favourite place.' I laughed but it sent me into sobs and I had to pull over. We sat holding each other close, both of us crying uncontrollably.

I asked Lawrence to tell me what had happened. He sighed. 'It was so peaceful, just like a clock winding down. He got slower and then just stopped. He won't have felt a thing . . .' He couldn't go on, and we finished the drive in silence, both lost in our thoughts.

What an extraordinary boy. Our greatest dread had been the prospect of having to take him to the vet to be put to sleep and, generous to the end, he'd spared us that.

Shortly after midnight on 11 May 2010, Todo arrived home for the last time. We carried him from the car and laid him in his basket in the *cucina di cane*, *his* room. Kissing him and wishing him goodnight one last time, we went to bed. We'd begun the day in our flat in London, excited about going home to Todo, now we were ending it with the stark realisation that our dearest friend had gone.

At 3 a.m. I was woken by Lawrence sobbing. Neither of us slept much, but in the morning we went downstairs and opened Todo's door. He looked as peaceful as he had always done.

A little later we went over to tell Teresa. Silvano was with her and I started to tell her that we had some bad news, but couldn't continue.

'Todo died last night,' Lawrence said quietly. 'There was no pain, no distress; it was very peaceful.'

The word stoic might have been invented for Teresa but

there were tears in her eyes. Taking me gently by the hand she told us that the day Todo had been unwell she knew something was wrong. He'd perked up a little but for the first time he refused food that morning and, though he walked up the steps with her to the gate, he managed only a few unsteady paces before stopping. She went back down to the house with him and settled him into his basket, where Totti joined him, squeezing her way in.

Teresa had bent down to stroke his muzzle and those shaggy ears. 'There's a good boy, are you not feeling so well today? Don't worry, Luisa and Lorenzo will be home soon. You'll want to see them again, just hang on. Only two days, just two more days.'

She had urged him to wait, and he had.

They took us inside and, while Teresa made strong coffee, we sat talking about Todo, La Signora and Poggiolino. When we'd visited on a cold November evening to tell them of the diagnosis they'd been sympathetic but Silvano had also said, 'Oh well; you must get another dog.' This time he spoke only of Todo: what a mischievous puppy and young dog he'd been; how he'd matured, always remaining a free spirit, but such a dear and devoted companion to the ageing Signora.

I had often felt sad that we never knew Todo as a puppy, or watched him grow. Carol had been lucky. But then so had we, he had given us three joyful, life-affirming years.

Teresa was pleased when we told her we would lay him to rest in the garden.

'Would you like to come and see him?' Lawrence asked.

'No; I'll remember him as full of life, but will say a prayer for you later.'

By lunchtime rain had begun to fall on the already sodden earth. We lifted Todo out of his basket and carried him to the terrace overlooking San Martino and the bells he'd sung to so blissfully. Lawrence went to fetch a spade and right in the middle of the garden, close to the mandarin tree, he dug Todo's grave.

When we returned to Todo, the cats had gathered beside him. Woody and Bob sniffed gently, and went to sit a few feet away. Totti walked slowly around him for almost a minute before lying down next to him. She stayed for a little while, then got up and padded gently down the garden.

It was time.

We found Totti waiting for us at the grave, then we lowered him into the ground; I placed his favourite chewy stick next to him before we covered him with the rich, moist soil.

We stood for several minutes, both of us drenched, each lost in memories of the dog with the clown's smile and the big heart, who had waited so faithfully, and changed our lives.

EPILOGUE

Todo's Legacy

It is mid-morning in late May 2011, the anniversary of our fourth year at Poggiolino, and just over a year since Todo died. In the office I switch on my mobile and staring back at me is the sweet photo we always joked would be perfect for his passport. In fact we did begin the process of applying for one, in order to take him to visit London, but in the end we didn't need it.

I turn on my computer and enter my password: OurdogTodo. Seconds later there he is again, this time with that beaming smile, sitting expectantly upright below our table in a restaurant just outside Siena, the day we visited the wonderful gardens of La Foce. Memories come flooding back of those happy times.

In the days after Todo's death we grieved, of course, but our sadness was lessened by the thanks we gave for the time we'd shared with him and by the knowledge that his passing had been so peaceful. After we'd buried him, Lawrence made a call to Dott. Ratto to explain what had happened. She knew already, he was so highly thought of and loved at Valdinievole that the news had spread and she offered heartfelt sympathies, 'He was such a special dog, very brave.'

Neighbours wished us well, many dropping by, having heard the news. Their smiles as they recalled his wonderful spirit cheered us, and on excursions to Fontanella, Montebello and Lucca when people asked us why he wasn't with us, sadness soon turned to laughter, as we remembered visits with him. Todo always brought out the best in people.

When we told Albertina she insisted again that she thought he was older than fourteen. It set Lawrence on a fresh search through Carol's papers and journals. This time he found her diary for 1995 and to his great shock there he was; it wasn't 1996 he came to Poggiolino but a year earlier. Fifteen – he really did have all his years. That big and good heart had taken all its beats!

My thoughts are cut short by the sound of eight paws hurtling in from the garden. Before me stand two excited young dogs, tails wagging furiously, insisting on their morning walk.

Weeks before Todo's death, Teresa had told us excitedly that her dog Lulu was pregnant and she wanted us to have one of the puppies. We'd wondered several times about getting a second dog, not least as company for Todo, and had even visited a couple of the rescue centres around Lucca. It was initially heartbreaking to see so many abandoned animals, until during the afternoons, when a group of warm-hearted women from Lucca descended upon the place. They carried treats with them, took the dogs for long walks in the surrounding fields and knew nearly all of them by name, assuring us that Nero would be a good dog for us, or perhaps Buffy, or Mickey.

We'd decided against it then, but within days of Todo's death we knew that the house, and our life, couldn't remain dogless.

We returned to the rescue centres, somehow feeling that we owed it to Todo to take in an unwanted dog. This time we extended our search to Montecatini Terme and Pistoia and it was at the Rifugio there that we saw a large black Belgian Shepherd puppy among all the older dogs.

He wasn't what we'd been looking for, but the following day neither of us could get him out of our minds and I called the Rifugio to enquire if he was still there.

'Yes, but his sister has already been taken. If you want him you must come quickly.' We jumped into the car and dashed back to Pistoia and minutes after seeing him again, he sat on my lap as Lawrence filled in the copious paperwork and handed over a donation. He turned to me, stroking the puppy who was well behaved and bright, and said, 'What a little cracker you are.' The name stuck, even if many of our Italian friends and neighbours had difficulty pronouncing it and some wondered why we'd called our dog after a Class A drug.

The receptionist told us he'd been found abandoned in the Piazza del Duomo and was about two months old. 'Do you know, that's where we called Roy from when we bought Poggiolino?' Lawrence said. The irony wasn't lost on me.

A few weeks later, Cracker acquired a little sister. Teresa had insisted we must take one of Lulu's puppies, and as with Totti, there was no refusing. Mimi was a name much easier for locals to pronounce and fitting given that we'd settled so close to the city of Puccini. She was connected to Todo, as Lulu had been a friend to him and, had he not chosen so determinedly to remain at Poggiolino, he would have been her adopted brother. Mimi's father – from a list of several possibilities – was probably Giro, Lorenzo's black cocker spaniel and one of Todo's regular companions on walks up the hill. An enchantingly pretty dog, within days of her arrival the two became the best of pals. The big dog shares the same sweetness of nature as Todo, perhaps a legacy of the gratitude of rescue; the smaller shares his healthy appetite!

It felt good to have dogs in the house and helped ease the pain we still felt over Todo's death. There was a huge hole in our lives but gradually they helped us fill it. We'd always wanted a dog but our life in London – and the irregularity of our working pattern – meant it was impossible. How odd that we had to move nearly a thousand miles to have one and how quickly it felt that a house and life without one was bereft. That was part of Todo's legacy to us.

But only a small part. In truth we'd never have given Poggiolino a second look had it not been for the excited bundle of brown fur that followed us as we strolled outside that chilly December morning. Yes, the location was beautiful, but – without the spirit of its extraordinary owner and after two years of neglect – it didn't leap out at us.

It wasn't the fifteenth-century Tuscan farmhouse of our dreams. It wasn't even one of the splendid Victorian homes we'd lived in for almost twenty years. For us, though, it was the perfect place to write a new and very different chapter in our story. It might have been Teresa who turned the key to the gate but in truth it was Todo who unlocked the door and welcomed us in.

Three years with him was too short but his life had been a long and happy one and we were thrilled that we'd been able to give him back the time that he'd lost after Carol died. From day one we told ourselves that getting back those two years would be something to aim for. We made it a year longer and

his time with us, even after his risky and complicated operation, was full of joy.

I am profoundly sorry we never met Carol MacAndrew
and, indeed, her devoted Jim. They sound like our kind of
people and their legacy is huge, in the life they created for
themselves, the house they built so lovingly and the spirited,
loving dog Carol passed on to us.

In the autumn after he died we paid a visit to Rose Barni,
seeking out a special rose to plant next to his grave, and in the
days leading up to the anniversary small buds began to appear.

With his usual impeccable timing, the first delicate pink
flower bloomed on 10 May, the exact date on which he'd left
us; a perfect rose, 'Complicato', which was at once beautiful,
full of life and thriving happily – in its place at Poggiolino.

We have countless photos of Todo; his image adorns computer screens, phones and calendars. But really we have no need
for them; his presence is here with us in Poggiolino. More
than that, he is in our hearts and our thoughts every single
day. We will never stop loving Todo or thanking him for what
he gave us.

Acknowledgements

This book would not have been written without the determination of Laura Zeigler and Herbert Handt who suggested we put our story down on paper and nagged us constantly until we did so. We would like to record our affection and admiration for them. We also owe a huge debt to Albertina Castoldi who befriended us as Carol and Jim's successors at Poggiolino. Many people helped us along our Italian way and we give our thanks to Tina Geraldi, Roy Santi from www.housesintuscany. com, Nicola Masini, Elizabeth Adcock, Miriam Keller from www.anticacasanaldi.it, Umberto and Daniela Marsili. We would like to pay special tribute to all our wonderful vets in Italy who have managed to decipher our queries and concerns and who have treated our animals so kindly. Dott. Tiziana Baccelli, Dott. Viviana Petri, Dott. Silvia Diodati and Dott. Ugo Lotti, Dott. Massimo Baroni and Dott. Marina Ratto and to Vicky Halls for her patience and wisdom. We still enjoy wonderful memories of our move and the help so generously given by our friends Bruce Jefferson and Hugh Raynor and to Ania Koscinska for giving Todo his bandana and lots of cuddles. Our thanks also to Jane and Sylvia Evans for their love of Todo and Poggiolino and for the priceless video footage of him singing to the bells. We would like to thank Annamaria Biagi for her excellent translation work and for putting up with us as students and to Carla Nolledi for the photographs she has given us of Todo as a puppy and of Carol and Jim. Thank you also to Woniya Fedoroff for all her patient assistance at the *San Francisco Examiner*.

Louise would like to particularly thank her mother Angela Badger for her unfailing encouragement, helpful advice and inspiration in every way and both she and Lawrence thank their families for their continued love and support. Lawrence would like to acknowledge gratitude to Miss Green, his English teacher in secondary school; 'you were right that grammar is important'. Many friends have kept faith with us along the way and we especially thank Rosalind and Simon Harrison and Cameron Duncan for their early enthusiasm and advice. We also thank Ernest Pauwels for his kindly medical advice for Todo and for the many treats dropped from the table.

This book would have remained just a nice idea one summer without the encouragement and kindness of Rupert Lancaster at Hodder & Stoughton who amongst many excellent suggestions introduced us to the brilliant and remarkable literary agent Sheila Ableman. And our book would not be what it is without the dedication and skilfulness of our wonderful editor Caro Handley and the watchful eyes and advice of editor Helen Coyle and copy editor Tara Gladden. We would also like to extend special thanks to Christine King for her early support and belief in our story. Finally but in no way least we would like to extend our gratitude and thanks to our inspirational publisher Lisa Highton at Hodder & Stoughton for having faith in us and Todo and for the work of her excellent team, Juliet Brightmore, Anneka Sandher, Kerry Hood and the marvellous Valerie Appleby in bringing this story to life. Todo would be very proud of you all!

Editorial credits:

San Francisco Examiner
Di Monaco, Bartolomeo. *Tales told in Lucca*. Lucca: Maria
   Pacini Fazzi, 2007.

Picture credits:

Most of the photographs are from the authors' collection. Additional photographs are courtesy of the following: Carla Nolledi, page 1 above, page 2 above right; Associazione Musicale Lucchese, page 2 above left; Signora Teresa, page 2 below right; from the private collection of Carol MacAndrew, page 2 below left.

An invitation from the publisher

Join us at www.hodder.co.uk, or follow us
on Twitter @hodderbooks to be a part of
our community of people who love the very
best in books and reading.

Whether you want to discover more about a book
or an author, watch trailers and interviews, have the
chance to win early limited editions, or simply browse
our expert readers' selection of the very best books,
we think you'll find what you're looking for.

And if you don't, that's the place to tell us what's missing.

We love what we do, and we'd love you to be a part of it.

www.hodder.co.uk

@hodderbooks

HodderBooks

HodderBooks